Islamic Microfinance

Praise for this book

'This collection of case studies of some of the leading Islamic microfinance institutions globally is long overdue. It is an excellent start to what should be an ongoing effort to study this niche industry which has demonstrable and considerable demand in highly populous regions. The cases depict the sheer diversity in practice and products of IMF delivery models, and concludes with important questions that merit further exploration.'

Nimrah Karim, Project Manager of WomenX, Enclude

'This is an idea whose time has come, given the vast number of youth all over the world, not just in the Islamic countries, who need to become self-employed for there are no jobs for them. Unlike micro-credit with its fixation on on-time repayments and high interest rates, the principle of profit (or loss) sharing in Islamic microfinance products makes these perfect for financing micro start-ups. This book demonstrates what is possible, and a lot is.'

Vijay Mahajan, Founder, BASIX Social Enterprise Group

'*Islamic Microfinance* makes a unique contribution to the large body of literature on microfinance not only because of the diversity of the 15 IMFIs described but also for the creativity each Shari'ah- compliant institutional and product model demonstrates in its responsiveness to client needs, which has been lacking at times, from non-compliant microfinance.'

Dr Bill Maddocks, Program Director, Sustainable Microfinance and Development,
Carsey School of Public Policy, University of New Hampshire

'Inspiring stories by accomplished people.'

Dr Muhammad Amjad Saqib, Founder and
Executive Director, Akhuwat, Pakistan

Islamic Microfinance: *Shari'ah* compliant and sustainable?

Edited by
Malcolm Harper
and Ajaz Ahmed Khan

PRACTICAL ACTION
Publishing

Practical Action Publishing Ltd
The Schumacher Centre, Bourton on Dunsmore, Rugby, Warwickshire, CV23 9QZ, UK
www.practicalactionpublishing.org

A catalogue record for this book is available from the British Library.

A catalogue record for this book has been requested from the Library of Congress.

ISBN 9781853399558 Hardback
ISBN 9781853399565 Paperback
ISBN 9781780449562 eBook
ISBN 9781780449555 Library PDF

Citation: Harper, M. and Khan, AA., (2017) *Islamic microfinance: Shari'ah compliant
and sustainable?*, Rugby, UK: Practical Action Publishing
<http://dx.doi.org/10.3362/9781780449555>

Since 1974, Practical Action Publishing has published and disseminated books
and information in support of international development work throughout the
world. Practical Action Publishing is a trading name of Practical Action Publishing
Ltd (Company Reg. No. 1159018), the wholly owned publishing company of Practical
Action. Practical Action Publishing trades only in support of its parent charity
objectives and any profits are covenanted back to Practical Action
(Charity Reg. No. 247257, Group VAT Registration No. 880 9924 76).

Cover design by Andrew Corbett
Typeset by vPrompt eServices, India
Indexed by Elizabeth Ball
Printed in the United Kingdom

Contents

List of figures, tables, and boxes

Figures

Tables

Boxes

Acknowledgements

A collection of this sort is the result of many people's efforts, and they all deserve as much credit as those whose names appear on the cover. Most important, of course, are the writers of the 15 case studies that are the core of the book. They are named at the head of each chapter, and very brief details about them are also included. They have done most of the work, without any remuneration, and they have also patiently tolerated our frequent requests for more data and other assistance; we are very grateful to them all. Their email addresses are also included at the end of each case study, and readers are encouraged to contact them if they want further information.

We hope that the institutions whose work is described in the book will benefit from the exposure the book will give them, as we are confident that others will benefit by reading about them. They are in business, often in competition with others, and have been willing to share a great deal of financial and other information with us; we are duly grateful.

The microfinance literature is full of information about individual clients; these case studies are no different, and we should like, through the writers, to express our gratitude to them all. Most of the cases contain information about people that few of 'us' would be willing to share with strangers, even if our identities were disguised; we hope that their time and willingness to share their personal stories will be repaid by the benefit it will bring to others like them.

It would not be possible to acknowledge all the friends and others who have helped by identifying appropriate institutions, writers, and other details, but we should like in particular to thank Dr Amjad Saqib, founder and CEO of Akhuwat; Justin Sykes, lately of Silatech and now with Innovest Advisory; Dr Badr el Din, President of the Microfinance Unit, Central Bank of Sudan; and Jamil Abbas of PNMBT Indonesia. And as ever, of course, Clare Tawney of Practical Action Publishing has been patient, understanding, and helpful.

About the editors

Malcolm Harper is Emeritus Professor at Cranfield University; he has researched and advised on microfinance widely and has advised Islamic microfinance institutions in Sudan, Somalia, Yemen, Pakistan and India. Ajaz Ahmed Khan is Senior Microfinance Adviser, CARE International. He has extensive experience working on microfinance in countries as diverse as Honduras, Nicaragua, Ecuador, Bosnia and Herzegovina, Kosovo, Pakistan and Sudan; and including helping to establish and develop Islamic microfinance institutions.

Preface

I first came across Islamic microfinance over 20 years ago in Omdurman, across the River Nile from Khartoum in Sudan. I was studying sources of finance for urban micro-enterprises, and I was not looking for Islamic approaches in particular; indeed, I had hardly even heard of Islamic finance at the time.

I wanted to find institutions that provided reasonably priced and accessible finance to low-income people, and I was introduced to the two 'Productive Families' branches of the Sudan Islamic Bank. The bank was providing what was essentially micro-venture capital, to men and in particular to women. If the businesses did well, the clients repaid their loans with a substantial premium, and if they failed, they repaid only the sum they had originally borrowed, or even that amount might be forgiven.

The branches were profitable for the bank and for the clients, and I was particularly impressed because this system appeared to overcome what I have characterized as the 'double whammy' of conventional fixed-interest microfinance.

To take a very simple example, if a woman takes out a traditional fixed-interest loan to buy a cow, which may be her only source of livelihood, and then the cow dies, she is left with no livelihood as well as a debt with increasing interest and no income to repay it. If her neighbour is more fortunate, and her cow has two calves, it is no problem for her to repay both the loan and the interest.

If these women had borrowed from the Sudan Islamic Bank, the more fortunate borrower would repay her loan with a share of her profit, and this would be sufficient to enable the bank to forgive the loan that had been taken out by her less fortunate neighbour.

I was told that this system was Islamic, or *Shari'ah* compliant, because Islam prohibits fixed-interest lending. It was known as a *musharaka* partnership investment, not a loan, because both parties invested in whatever assets were bought with the bank's assistance, and both shared in the results. Partnerships where the bank covered the full cost and the client (or more properly the 'partner') provided only her or his labour and management were called *mudaraba* investments. I was impressed not because this approach conformed to any particular religious rules, but because it was more equitable and fairer than traditional fixed-interest lending.

Not long after my visit, the emphasis on *musharaka* in the two 'Productive Families' branches was changed; the experiment had initially been championed by the then chair of the bank, who was appointed to be a minister in the national government, and by 2003 this form of financing amounted to less than a fifth of their business (Badr El Din, 2003).

Since that time, I have come across – and in some cases worked with – a number of other Islamic microfinance institutions (IMFIs) in Sudan and in Yemen, India, Pakistan, Morocco, and Somaliland, but it has not been easy to find many other examples of successful *musharaka* or *mudaraba* profit- and loss-sharing approaches. Most of the institutions are using *murabaha* or *ijara* methods, and one particularly notable example, which has recently reached the figure of over a million clients, is using *qard hasan*.

I recently decided to search more methodically for cases of successful IMFIs, from which it should be possible to draw more systematic conclusions than has been possible with a small number of incidental contacts. I was fortunate enough to be able to persuade Ajaz Ahmed Khan of CARE International to join me in this endeavour, and this collection is the result.

I should make my own position clear; I am not a Muslim, although I have family members who are and I have a great respect for Islam, as I do for the positive aspects of all religions. I am interested in identifying, learning from, and, if appropriate, disseminating information about effective methods whereby low-income and other marginalized people can access high-quality and equitable financial services.

It seemed to me many years ago in Omdurman – and still does – that the Islamic approach to microfinance has much to offer, and not only to Muslims. There are many practical problems that make it difficult to offer *Shari'ah*-compliant financial products, particularly those which share the profits and losses with the clients, but some of the institutions whose operations are covered in these case studies have managed to overcome these problems and are growing rapidly, and profitably. Others have the potential to grow, and lack only the financial resources that might enable them to reach the scale at which they can break even and become profitable.

I hope that this book and the collection of cases will help Islamic microfinance to become more widely recognized, not only within but beyond the Muslim world, and that microfinance institutions of all kinds everywhere will be able to learn something from it.

Malcolm Harper

Reference

Badr El Din, A.I. (2003) *Poverty Alleviation via Islamic Banking Finance to Micro-Enterprises (MEs) in Sudan: Some Lessons for Poor Countries*, Sudan Economy Research Group Discussion Paper No. 35, Bremen: Bremen University.

CHAPTER 1

Islamic financing principles and their application to microfinance

Ajaz Ahmed Khan, Bridget Kustin, and Khalid Khan

The need to conform to certain religious principles affects the structure and operations of Islamic microfinance institutions. We outline the basic principles of Islamic finance and provide an introduction to the different financing instruments commonly used by Islamic microfinance providers. While Islam advocates profit-sharing techniques such as mudaraba *and* musharaka, *most Islamic microfinance institutions consider these too risky and complex to implement and instead favour the simpler cost plus mark-up or* murabaha *technique. Islamic teachings propose that the poorest should be assisted through* qard hasan *or interest-free loans.*

Keywords: *riba, gharar, qard hasan, mudaraba, musharaka, murabaha, ijarah, bai salam, takaful*

This analysis outlines the basic principles of Islamic finance and provides an introduction to the main *Shari'ah*-compliant financing methodologies used in Islamic microfinance. The principles and practices upon which Islamic finance is based are drawn from teachings contained in the *Qur'an*, *Sunnah* (the word and living tradition of the Prophet Muhammad, peace be upon Him), *ijma* (the consensus of Islamic scholars), and *qiyas* (the process of analogical reasoning which is used to solve or provide a response to a new problem). While Islamic teachings often provide quite specific guidance – for example, the longest *ayah* or verse in the *Qur'an* (2:282) deals with financial transactions and contracts – in general they emphasize honesty, transparency, and above all fairness in economic activities and behaviour between all parties regardless of status.

The different Islamic financing methodologies are applicable according to the skills, capacity, and economic resources of the different parties as well as the nature of the business and the period for which the project is to be financed. Importantly, though, all methodologies are founded on the core belief that money is not an earning asset in and of itself. Ensuring that money is used as a medium of exchange rather than as an earning asset helps prevent exploitation and unfairness that would guarantee self-benefit at the direct expense of broader society.

http://dx.doi.org/10.3362/9781780449555.001

Principles of Islamic finance

There are some general principles that are of particular importance for Islamic finance. Firstly, *riba*, most commonly translated as interest or usury, is forbidden in that it is a predetermined, fixed sum owed to the lender irrespective of the outcome of the venture in which the funds are used. This does not imply in any way that capital is free of charge, that it should be made available without any cost, or that there should be absolutely no return on capital. Rather, a return on capital is allowed, provided that the supplier of capital participates in the productive process and is exposed to risk. Secondly, any transaction that involves excessive uncertainty and risk, deceit, or fraud (*gharar*) is prohibited. *Gharar* refers to any transaction of items whose existence or description is not certain due to lack of information or knowledge of the ultimate outcome. For example, it is not permitted to sell what one does not own; therefore, 'short-selling' – that is, selling something that one does not own in the hope that it can be bought cheaper at a later date – is impermissible. Thirdly, there should be no funding of *haram* or prohibited activities such as the production and sale of alcohol, pork, illegal drugs, pornography, or gambling since Islam considers these as morally and socially harmful. Instead, funds should only be used to support *halal* or permitted activities – preferably activities that are 'socially productive', although what exactly this term means remains open to interpretation by an Islamic microfinance institution (IMFI). Lastly, a financial transaction needs to have a 'material finality': that is, it should be directly or indirectly linked to a real, tangible economic activity or asset as opposed to financial speculation or debt, and the product or service that is bought or sold must be clear to all parties.

In addition to these general principles, Islamic teachings also emphasize the importance of honouring contracts and agreements.[1] In general terms, contracts should be clear, by mutual agreement, the responsibilities and benefits of all parties should be clearly detailed, and the agreement should be for a known period and price. In this regard, there are certain principles that need to be considered, particularly since some of the clients served by IMFIs may lack formal education and have poor literacy skills. Firstly, an offer (*ijab*) and acceptance (*qabul*) should be made before entering into a contract to reduce the possibility of disputes in the future. Secondly, the dates of repayment must be specified in the contract to avoid any ambiguity, and preferably there should be a written contract.[2] Lastly, there should be at least two witnesses present when the contract is signed.

To ensure that the activities of IMFIs adhere to Islamic finance principles and procedures, it is essential to seek approval from qualified Islamic scholars on the manner in which operations are structured and implemented. Some IMFIs have *Shari'ah* advisers for this purpose and also conduct regular *Shari'ah* audits to ensure that their operations remain 'authentic'.

As will become apparent from the following analysis, Islamic finance permits only one type of actual loan, namely *qard hasan*. Strictly speaking, the other techniques are not loans at all; they are investments or financing arrangements. Before describing the various financing techniques, we further discuss the issue of *riba*.

Riba

Riba is the Arabic word for the predetermined return on the use of money and it can be translated as 'increase', 'excess', or 'usury'. The consensus amongst Islamic scholars is that *riba* includes **all** forms of interest and it is a sin under Islamic law – even those hired to write the contract or who witness and thus confirm the contract are party to the sin.[3] This also means that, if the money of an IMFI is pooled with *riba*-bearing funds, the pool of profits is considered 'tainted' and should be disbursed to charity or otherwise removed. The motivation for the strong prohibition of interest is to prevent the ability of one party to receive unfair gain at the expense of another. Extrapolated beyond a single contract or transaction to broader society, it is believed that *riba* contributes to systemic oppression and exploitation, exacerbating conditions of poverty. This perspective is, of course, not something that is unique to Islam – Christianity and Judaism also maintained strong traditions against usury.[4]

Interest is considered an unjust instrument of financing. Thus, if a micro-entrepreneur's venture is unsuccessful through no fault of his or her own, it is unfair for the lender to receive a fixed rate of return or to demand repayment. Equally, if the micro-entrepreneur earns a very high rate of profit on the venture, it is unfair that the provider of finance should receive only a small proportion of that profit even though it supplied the majority of the funds for the enterprise. Prohibition of *riba* means that money can only be lent lawfully for either charitable purposes (without any expectation of return above the amount of the principal – that is, *qard hasan*) or for the purposes of doing lawful business (that is, investment on the basis of profit and risk sharing). Indeed, economic activity and prosperity are viewed as a religious virtue or even an obligation in Islam, provided the activity conforms to *Shari'ah*. The prohibition of interest is therefore a way to promote fairness between parties.

If a small business applies for finance to an IMFI, the organization should decide whether or not to support the project on the basis of a cost–benefit analysis of the project, not on the basis of collateral. Practically, however, this cost–benefit analysis commonly takes into account personal elements of the small business owner that an IMFI deems to have a bearing on the potential outcome of the project, or that suggest trustworthiness and the likelihood of repayment, or that place the client in a part of the population that the IMFI seeks to target. These elements can include age, marital status, a monthly income threshold, landownership, and so on.

Although the *Qur'an* prohibits the use of interest and encourages legitimate commerce, trade, and wealth creation, it does not specify any commitment to particular types of contract. In the remainder of this analysis we describe some of the principal Islamic financing techniques that have been developed in accordance with *Shari'ah* and are most commonly utilized by IMFIs, including those institutions examined in later chapters. Broadly speaking, we can distinguish between techniques that promote partnerships, such as *mudaraba* and *musharaka*, and arrangements that are essentially sales contracts, such as *murabaha, ijarah, bai salam*, and *bai muajjal*.

Mudaraba

Mudaraba is a form of partnership in which an IMFI provides the capital required to fund a project, while the micro-entrepreneur manages the investment using his or her expertise. For example, an IMFI might provide the necessary funds to both rent land and buy sheep, while a farmer uses his or her skills to raise the animals. In a *mudaraba* contract, when a profit is realized – for example when the sheep are sold – it is shared between the partners according to a predetermined ratio. The profit-sharing ratios must be determined only as a percentage of the profit and not as a lump sum payment. In the case of a loss, providing it is incurred in the normal process of business and not due to neglect or misconduct by the micro-entrepreneur, the IMFI loses its money, while the micro-entrepreneur loses his or her time and effort. In case of proven negligence or mismanagement by the micro-entrepreneur, however, he or she may be held responsible for financial losses. The micro-entrepreneur does not invest anything in the business, save his or her labour, and should not claim any fee or wage for conducting the business. In practice, most IMFIs lack the funding, staffing, or technical capacity for robust monitoring and evaluation of the micro-entrepreneur's activities, and, in any case, the small scale of such activities is likely to make the transaction uneconomic. For this reason, *mudaraba* contracts are considered to be risky and require a great deal of trust and confidence, and are unusual in Islamic microfinance.

There are many distinguished instances in Islamic history of partnerships and involvement in trade: for example, the first four Caliphs and the famous Islamic jurist Imam Abu Hanifa were traders. However, perhaps the most prominent example of a *mudaraba* partnership was between the Prophet Muhammad (peace be upon Him) and his wife Khadija (may *Allah* be pleased with her), who was a venture capitalist. Before their marriage, she offered him the opportunity to travel as part of a caravan heading to sell goods in present-day Syria, according to a profit-sharing arrangement. It is reported that the Prophet Muhammad (peace be upon Him) returned with goods which Khadija (may *Allah* be pleased with her) sold for nearly twice the price they had been bought, making a considerable profit.

Musharaka

Literally meaning 'partnership' in Arabic, *musharaka* involves two or more parties contributing towards financing a venture. At the end of the project, the costs of production are deducted from the revenue, and a certain percentage is earmarked for management fees. Any profits are shared exactly in proportion to the equity participation of each partner or according to another previously agreed ratio, but losses must be borne exactly according to the ratio of each partner's investment. All partners have a right to participate in the management of the project but they can also waive this right in favour of a specific partner. If a micro-entrepreneur wholly manages the project, the management fees go to him or her, in addition to his or her profit share. If the IMFI is involved in management, it receives part of these fees. Management fees usually range between 10 per cent and 30 per cent of the profit, depending on the micro-entrepreneur's bargaining power and the nature of the project (for example, if the activity requires special skills, the share of the micro-entrepreneur may be greater). The micro-entrepreneur does not have to contribute in cash to the proposed investment. Instead, his or her share might be in-kind inputs, labour, and the rent of machines or equipment.

The main difference between *musharaka* and *mudaraba* is that under the latter the micro-entrepreneur offers his or her labour and skills only, without any contribution in cash or in kind, and any losses are borne entirely by the IMFI. A *musharaka* can be continuous (to the end of a project's lifespan) or it can be a diminishing partnership, in which case one partner is allowed gradually to buy out the other partner's share.

Partnership financing for small enterprises has various advantages, the most obvious being that it avoids the necessity of demanding repayment from a micro-entrepreneur when a business does not succeed for reasons beyond his or her control. Since the IMFI is obliged to monitor the business closely, and sometimes take part in management as well, it broadens the organization's understanding of financed activities and the needs of its clients. Partnership finance also encourages innovation and entrepreneurship, since in relatively profitable ventures the return on investment can be much higher than in other modes of finance, and it also reduces the effects of inflation since debt financing is replaced by equity- and share-based financing.

However, IMFIs face several challenges in promoting successful partnership finance. Many micro-entrepreneurs lack the necessary bookkeeping skills to keep accurate accounts and as a result it may be difficult to calculate the exact level of profits. A grocery kiosk owner might take his own family's weekly staples out of his stock, provide groceries on credit to regular customers, and automatically roll cash towards purchases of next week's stock. Accounting processes for cash flow versus profit versus debts might be porous. How, then, should profits be calculated and distributed, and according to what time frame? Furthermore, small businesses may also try to conceal actual profits or report greater losses than they actually experience; the intent and personal ethics of each client will be as diverse as the individuals themselves – one cannot assume that all those using Islamic microfinancing are uniquely pious.

The lack of simplicity – relative to equal repayment instalments – makes partnership finance more difficult for both the IMFI's loan officers (especially when they may each have several hundred loans to monitor) and micro-entrepreneurs to understand. A further challenge facing IMFIs is the burden in terms of time and cost of monitoring and following up partnership trans-actions. Building a relationship and conducting business using profit and loss sharing techniques involves more time, effort, and resources because they are built on trust and confidence. Although *mudaraba* and *musharaka* can theoretically be used to extend microfinancing, they are not necessarily cost effective. In practice, this means that only a limited number of loans are given to established entrepreneurs with a proven track record and 'credit' history. Largely due to these challenges, as reflected in the case studies that follow, partnership finance is relatively uncommon in Islamic microfinance. Although, some of the IMFIs analysed in later chapters are using profit and loss sharing partnerships of various kinds, it is still relatively limited and sometimes occurs on an experimental basis.

Murabaha

Murabaha is the most popular and widely used Islamic financing methodology, accounting for over two-thirds of *Shari'ah*-compliant microfinance. This is in large part because it is relatively simple to structure, understand, and implement, particularly when compared with other financing techniques that require more elaborate arrangements. Under *murabaha*, a micro-entrepreneur approaches an IMFI with a request to purchase a commodity, for example a sewing machine. The IMFI purchases the sewing machine at a freely disclosed price and then resells it, after adding a specific profit margin (often referred to as a 'mark-up'), to the micro-entrepreneur, who agrees to buy the sewing machine for the new offered price. The micro-entrepreneur then pays for the equipment in instalments over an agreed period of time. *Bai muajjal* is another financing technique that is very similar to *murabaha*; the only significant difference is that the IMFI is not bound to disclose the cost of the goods and profit mark-up separately to the client.

Murabaha is commonly used to finance the purchase of raw materials as well as machinery or equipment. For this type of arrangement to be *Shari'ah* compliant, the IMFI must own the commodity first and then resell it; the commodity should be a tangible one; and the micro-entrepreneur must know and then agree to the purchase and resale prices. When all these conditions are fulfilled, both parties sign a *murabaha* contract in which all terms and conditions are clearly stated. The collateral can, for example, be in the form of a mortgage on property or a third-party guarantee. Although this model may generate high initial transactions costs, it is easy for all parties to understand and simplifies administration as there are fixed, regular repayments over a specific period of time.

There is some scepticism towards this particular mode of financing; indeed, it has been argued that a fixed mark-up is similar to interest. However, the mark-up is not in the nature of compensation for time or deferred payment;

even though the entire cost has to be incurred because the micro-entrepreneur did not have the necessary funds to make the purchase he or she wanted (Al-Omar and Abdel-Haq, 1996). Rather, the mark-up is (or at least should be) for the recognized service that the IMFI provides. In the previous example, it is for seeking out, negotiating, and purchasing the sewing machine at the best price. If the micro-entrepreneur is unable to pay during the agreed period, the amount of mark-up remains as fixed originally in the contract and does not increase due to the delay, further distancing the mark-up from the time value of money. Moreover, in obtaining the sewing machine, the IMFI is taking a risk: the micro-entrepreneur may not accept the quality or price at which it was purchased and the institution is then stuck with the equipment.

To ensure that this technique is not abused and remains *Shari'ah* compliant, authorities have sometimes felt compelled to stipulate certain procedures. For example, the Bank of Sudan's *Shari'ah* Council issued a *fatwa* (opinion) in 1993 establishing key requirements that have to be met in order for a *murabaha* contract to be legal. These include a borrower submitting an application in detail, describing the commodity to be purchased; the financier buying the commodity and physically taking possession; and the borrower having the right to refuse to accept the commodity when it is offered for sale by the lender. Despite this, as we shall see in the subsequent case studies, there are instances when IMFIs do not always adhere strictly to these procedures and instead employ 'shortcuts', such as asking micro-entrepreneurs to identify the commodity, negotiate with the supplier, and also arrange delivery. For other institutions with robust *Shari'ah* compliance procedures, this arrangement – known as '*murabaha* with agency agreement' – is formalized and subject to its own contractual regulation. After all, IMFIs are in the unique position of balancing *Shari'ah* compliance and financial solvency along with an ethical and religious duty to provide services to as many poor clients as possible; *murabaha* with agency agreement helps some institutions to strike this balance.

Ijarah

Ijarah is similar to leasing. Under this arrangement, a micro-entrepreneur who is short of funds approaches an IMFI to fund the purchase of a productive asset, for example a rickshaw. The IMFI buys the rickshaw and rents it out to the micro-entrepreneur at a price that enables the IMFI to recovers its investment plus a profit. The rickshaw remains in the ownership of the IMFI, which is responsible for its maintenance so that it continues to give the service for which it was rented. The *ijarah* contract is terminated as soon as the rickshaw ceases to give the service for which it was rented or the leasing period comes to an end and the physical possession of the asset and the right of use revert back to the IMFI. However, since it is impractical or too expensive for the IMFI to maintain the rickshaw, more often than not the micro-entrepreneur makes regular payments and becomes the owner of the vehicle once he or she has paid all agreed instalments – in effect, a hire purchase agreement.

In the context of microfinance, an *ijarah* contract has the advantage of not requiring conventional types of collateral, since the commodity or asset being financed serves as collateral itself.

Bai salam

Bai salam is a contract whereby the full price is agreed and paid up-front in cash by the IMFI at the time the agreement is made for an asset or commodity to be delivered at a specific time in the future. The essential purpose is to ease liquidity shortages, most commonly for small farmers, by enabling them to receive advance payment so that they have money to buy inputs to grow their crops and feed their families until harvest time. In such arrangements, the specification and characteristics of the output must be determined as accurately as possible at the time of the contract. Similarly, the price agreed upon should not exceed the prevalent market price. IMFIs are not allowed to sell the products acquired unless they are in physical possession of the goods, and the duration of this transaction is usually a production cycle. *Bai salam* is not particularly popular with IMFIs because there are practical problems in using this instrument to finance large numbers of small farmers; these include taking delivery of the produce, assessing quality, finding sufficient storage space, and arranging sale. A variant of *bai salam* is *istisna*, which is a contract to purchase for a definite price something that can be manufactured or constructed later according to agreed specifications between the parties. It differs from *bai salam* as the full price need not be paid in advance, the contract can be cancelled before manufacturing begins, and the time of delivery is not fixed.

Qard hasan

Qard hasan is a loan targeting the poor or needy that is repaid without interest, mark-up, or share in the venture for which the loan is used. Muslims are urged to provide *qard hasan* to 'those who need them'.[5] This is generally understood to refer to the poorer and weaker sections of society and the money can be used for both productive purposes and 'consumption' needs[6] such as meeting health expenses and school fees (the financing techniques described in much of the preceding discussion are, in the context of microfinance, essentially for business purposes). *Qard hasan* loans are encouraged by Islamic teachings as an effective way of assisting poor persons; indeed, they are preferred to the provision of outright charity.[7] Again, there are similarities with the teachings of other Abrahamic faiths – for example, *gemach* or 'acts of kindness' is a Jewish interest-free loan fund with easy repayment terms. Since *qard hasan* is considered a 'benevolent loan', it is generally interpreted to mean that a borrower cannot be forced to make repayment – in the event that a borrower is unable to repay, the lender must accept the transaction as a charitable act.

Since many poor people prefer to receive cash, which they can use at their discretion, rather than being tied to a particular commodity or transaction, *qard hasan* is both appealing and appropriate in many instances. However, since the borrower repays only the principal in *qard hasan* loans, IMFIs that rely exclusively on this methodology will not be able to cover their operational costs without regular inflows of money, typically from charitable donations. Operational costs also increase in rural, remote, or crisis-struck areas where need is particularly acute. While access to funds from commercial investors for *qard hasan* financing is generally rare, some of the IMFIs described in the following case studies provide *qard hasan* for their poorest clients, or for necessary 'consumption' expenditure, and subsidize the operational costs with the income earned from other, more profitable loans or fund such loans through charitable donations such as *sadaqah* or *waqf*.[8]

Certain Islamic scholars allow the lender also to cover the administrative costs incurred in disbursing the loan. The service charges are not profit; they are actual costs in respect of items such as printing documents and the travel expenses of loan officers visiting borrowers to appraise applications. However, an important condition attached to such charges to prevent them becoming equivalent to *riba* is that the commission or charge cannot be made proportional to the amount or to the term of the loan – in most cases the charge should be the same irrespective of the loan amount. A borrower may also voluntarily choose to pay an extra amount to the lender over the principal amount borrowed (without promising it) as a token of appreciation.

Guarantees

Islamic microfinance providers need to exercise particular care in determining whether they have adequate guarantees in place when deciding to finance a project, as financial penalties for late payment under Islamic law are commonly understood as equivalent to *riba* and therefore impermissible. However, in order to discourage deliberate late repayments, the *Shari'ah* advisory boards of some larger Islamic financial institutions, and increasingly IMFIs as well, have adopted fines for late payments so long as the income raised in this manner is used to fund charitable initiatives.[9]

Broadly speaking, there are two categories of debtors who fail to repay. The first category is someone who defaults by necessity; he or she simply does not have the capacity to repay despite their best intentions. In this instance, Islamic teachings are clear and lenders are encouraged to allow borrowers further time to repay.[10] A second category of debtor is someone who wilfully defaults: that is, someone who refuses to repay even though he or she has the capacity to do so (despite religious teachings that make it incumbent upon Muslims to repay on time[11]). In this instance, an IMFI has the right to seek legal redress based on the agreed contract. This could involve asking a guarantor to repay on the borrower's behalf or to affect the sale or transfer of collateral used to secure the loan.

However, in practice, it can be difficult for an IMFI's loan officers, who are often faced with high caseloads and demanding field visit schedules in challenging weather and terrain, to find the time and resources necessary to distinguish between the two. As IMFIs negotiate the porous border between Islamic ideals and practical limitations, repayment meetings may include negotiations over late or incomplete payments that take into account the client's repayment record, the total amount being temporarily forgiven, and the viability of new repayment timeframes. Pressure for guaranteeing repayment may ultimately rest with loan officers, who must balance fulfilling their job requirements while remaining attentive to client needs.

Savings and *takaful*

Although this discussion focuses on financing techniques, the prohibition of *riba* and *gharar* also impacts upon the provision of savings services and insurance. Since they cannot offer a predetermined rate of return, as this would be equivalent to *riba*, IMFIs that offer savings accounts remunerate the savers on the basis of a share of the institution's profits, if any. Six of the IMFIs described in the following case studies offer savings facilities to their clients on this basis. Some IMFIs also offer *takaful*, which is a *Shari'ah*-compliant alternative to conventional insurance. In *takaful*, which means 'guaranteeing each other' in Arabic, all participants contribute towards a mutual fund and the pool of collected contributions creates a *takaful* account. An IMFI manages the fund and charges an agreed fee to cover operating costs. Any claims made by participants are paid out of the *takaful* reserve and any remaining surplus belongs to the participants, not the IMFI, and is distributed among them at the end of the agreed period.

Conclusions

The need to conform to certain religious principles affects the way in which Islamic microfinance is structured and implemented. While Islam advocates profit-sharing techniques such as *mudaraba* and *musharaka*, most IMFIs consider these too risky and complex to implement and instead favour the simpler cost plus mark-up or *murabaha* technique. While nine of the fifteen Islamic microfinance providers described in this collection of case studies use some type of profit-sharing technique, this is usually only for a minority of their clients and is sometimes on an experimental basis; without doubt, the predominant financing instrument is *murabaha*.

IMFIs can, of course, employ a variety of approaches depending on factors such as the entrepreneurial ability and needs of borrowers, as well as the technical and managerial expertise of the institution. Indeed – and in contrast to interest-based microfinance, which essentially offers one type of loan product – such diversity might even encourage an IMFI to provide more appropriate types of financing to micro-entrepreneurs as well as help it achieve significant scale and outreach. Not all micro-entrepreneurs actually desire or will necessarily benefit from the same type of financing mechanism. An Islamic microfinance provider can employ a variety of *Shari'ah*-compliant financing methods according to the type of activity financed and the economic status, ability, and trustworthiness of potential borrowers.

Thus, for a first-time, relatively poor and inexperienced micro-entrepreneur who wishes to buy a range of items from different suppliers for his or her grocery shop, a *qard hasan* loan may be the most appropriate. *Murabaha* or *ijarah* loans may be more suitable for a small business person wishing to finance the purchase of machinery and equipment. For an experienced entrepreneur lacking only capital for his or her ventures, *mudaraba* may be the most suitable financing mechanism. In more complex ventures that could benefit from capital inputs by both parties as well as technical and managerial input, it may be appropriate to promote a *musharaka* agreement. Such an approach to financing may also promote the financial sustainability of IMFIs, since techniques that have the potential to generate relatively high levels of profit, such as *mudaraba*, are combined with those techniques such as *qard hasan* that barely cover administrative costs but will promote significant scale and outreach.

Apart from *qard hasan* or interest-free loans, which are proposed as an effective way to assist the poorest or most vulnerable, it is worth emphasizing that Islam does not prescribe specific forms of financing; rather, it sets out some broad principles that accommodate various forms and procedures. A new form or procedure of financing cannot be rejected merely because it has no precedent in the past. New forms of financing are acceptable to *Shari'ah* insofar as they do not violate basic principles laid down by the *Qur'an*, the *Sunnah,* or the consensus of the Muslim jurists.

However, this consensus can be elusive: Islamic jurists within a single country, across a region, or even globally have grappled with the interpretation of relevant texts over centuries as economic conditions evolve, and modern Islamic financial products and services continue to require scholarly and juridical input. IMFIs have generally adapted products used by mainstream non-micro Islamic banks for their poor clientele, but this approach does not always suit the needs and financial management strategies of the poor. Resources are slim for innovation in Islamic microfinance, but new, creative financing solutions are urgently needed, particularly for short-term loans for working capital. At the same time, innovative product or service design in Islamic microfinance can be particularly daunting, as IMFIs may not have the in-house *Shari'ah* advisory boards common to regular Islamic financial institutions that provide ongoing and robust support. Due to capacity, funding, or other administrative limitations, many IMFIs are able to seek only periodic external *Shari'ah* compliance audits or they may have to rely on ad hoc guidance.

Notes

1. The *Qur'an* states 'O you who believe! Fulfil all your contracts' (5:1).
2. The *Qur'an* states 'O you who believe! When you deal with each other in transactions involving future obligations for a fixed period of time reduce them in writing' (2:282).
3. There are several passages in the *Qur'an* that strongly condemn the practice of *riba*: 'Those who devour *riba* will not stand except as he stands who has been driven to madness by the touch of Satan ... *Allah* has permitted trade and forbidden *riba* ... *Allah* will deprive *riba* of all blessing' (2:275–6); and also 'O you who believe! Fear *Allah*, and give up what remains of your demand for *riba*, if you are indeed believers. If you do not, take notice of war from *Allah*' (2:278–90).
4. In the Old Testament, for example, it says: 'If thou lend money to any of my people that is poor by thee, thou shalt not be to him as an usurer, neither shalt thou lay upon him usury. If thou at all take thy neighbour's raiment to pledge, thou shalt deliver it unto him by that the sun goeth down' (Exodus 22:25–6). In other words, not only is one not supposed to charge interest, but also if the collateral for a loan is in the form of a necessity like a coat, one must make sure that the borrower can still make use of it when it is needed. There are further references against interest in Leviticus (25:35–7) and Deuteronomy (23:20). Anti-interest sentiment in the West existed as far back as Aristotle and was reinforced by Roman Catholic theologians, such as Augustine and Thomas Aquinas. However, modern Christian and Jewish scholars have generally reinterpreted the term from its original meaning of 'all' interest to 'excessive' interest.
5. There are several verses in the *Qur'an* to this effect: 'Who is he that will give *Allah qard al hasan*? For *Allah* will increase it manifold to his credit' (57:11); 'If you give *Allah qard al hasan*, he will double it to your credit and he will grant you forgiveness' (64:17); and 'Establish regular prayer and give regular charity and give *Allah qard al hasan*' (73:20). *Qard hasan* loans are considered as if they were made to *Allah*, rather than the borrowers, to ease the pain for lenders of parting with their wealth.
6. Ideally, poor people should also be able to access *zakat* and *sadaqah* to meet their consumption needs, although, of course, this is not always possible.
7. The Prophet Muhammad (peace be upon Him) said 'I saw on the gate of heaven written, "the reward for *sadaqah* is ten times and reward for *qard hasan* is eighteen times". So, I asked the angel, how is it possible? The angel replied, "Because the beggar who asked had already had something but a borrower did not ask for a loan unless he was in need"' (Ibn Majah, Volume 3, Book 15, Hadith 2431).
8. *Sadaqah* is voluntary charity while *waqf* is an endowment (usually of a building or plot of land) or a trust set up for charitable purposes. It involves tying up a property or fund in perpetuity so that it cannot be sold, inherited, or donated to anyone. An IMFI could, for example, accept monetary donations, invest the money in property that can be rented out, and use the profits to fund *qard hasan* loans. In contrast, *zakat* cannot be used to fund *qard hasan* or other types of finance agreements.

This is because there is an expectation that loans should be repaid, whereas the proper discharge of *zakat* involves giving up both possession and ownership to that given as *zakat*. The *Qur'an* also stipulates particular categories of *zakat* recipients; *qard hasan*, by contrast, has no restrictions on who may receive financing.

9. For example, the Shariah Advisory Council of Bank Negara Malaysia, the central bank of Malaysia, allows Islamic financial institutions to impose both compensation and late payment charges to act 'as a deterrent mechanism against cases of default by customers in discharging their financial obligation arising from Islamic contracts'.

10. The *Qur'an* states that 'if the debtor is in difficulty, grant him time till it is easy for him to repay' (2:280).

11. The Prophet Muhammad (peace be upon Him) said that 'procrastination (delay) in repaying debts by a wealthy person is injustice' (Bukhari, Volume 3, Book 37, Hadith 486).

Reference

Al-Omar, F. and Abdel-Haq, M. (1996) *Islamic Banking: Theory, Practice and Challenges*, London: Zed Books.

About the authors

Ajaz Ahmed Khan (khan@careinternational.org) is Senior Microfinance Adviser at CARE International, United Kingdom.

Bridget Kustin (bkustin2@jhu.ed) is a PhD candidate in the Department of Anthropology, Johns Hopkins University, Baltimore, United States of America.

Khalid Khan (khalid.khan@akhuwat.org.pk) is Research Associate at Akhuwat, Pakistan.

PART I

Qard hasan: pure Islamic microfinance

The first case, Akhuwat of Pakistan, is probably the 'purest' Islamic micro-finance institution in the collection, possibly the purest anywhere. It is also the largest independent institution in the book, and one of the largest anywhere, but is at the same time one of the simplest.

Virtually all Akhuwat's income is donated, as is all its capital, and its clients pay no interest or profit or any other charges on their loans, apart from a flat non-refundable application fee of about US$2; the main purpose of this is to discourage frivolous requests, and it covers less than 10 per cent of Akhuwat's total costs.

Some global authorities on microfinance are irritated by Akhuwat; they are anxious to show that microfinance can help poor people to better their condition and that it can, at the same time, be a 'sustainable' business, meaning that it is emphatically not a charity. Akhuwat is, of course, not a charity in the usual sense, in that it does not give away its services and does not make grants; it makes loans, which have to be repaid just like loans from any other financial institution. The difference is that the borrowers do not have to pay any interest or any of the other 'profits' or other sums that are charged by other *Shari'ah*-compliant microfinance institutions, and are often very similar to interest charges in all but name.

Akhuwat, however, is something of a hybrid; its loans have to be repaid, but the funds that it lends have either been donated or are non-returnable grants – they are not investments in the usual sense – and Akhuwat can therefore claim to be fully *halal* on both sides of its balance sheet. Additionally, many of its staff work for well below what they could earn elsewhere and there are large numbers of volunteers, the institution pays nothing for the use of mosques or churches for client meetings, and even their clients make significant donations to expenses.

In effect, Akhuwat turns the concept of 'economic man' (or woman) on its head. 'Sensible' people only repay interest-free loans when they have to, particularly if they also owe money to other institutions that charge interest, but Akhuwat's clients repay their interest-free loans as promptly as others, or even more regularly. A significant part of Akhuwat's funds comes from interest-free government loans that are effectively non-returnable so long as Akhuwat continues to use them effectively. These loans are accompanied by grants of between 5 per cent and 10 per cent of the value of the loans to cover operational expenses. Experience worldwide shows that citizens generally regard public money as 'theirs', and do not repay loans that have anything to do with government, but Akhuwat's clients repay loans that have been funded by government as promptly as any others.

The Akhuwat case is followed by 14 others, each of which has in some way adopted a more traditional commercial approach, attempting to cover their costs by securing some form of income from their clients. Some of these are more successful than others, but it is important to remember that a genuine sense of 'brotherhood' (the English translation of *muawkhaat* from which Akhuwat derives its name) can lead to a new, unfamiliar but remarkably effective form of 'business', which is not wholly a charity, nor profit-seeking, but does appear to be able to be 'sustainable'.

CHAPTER 2

Is it possible to provide *qard hasan* and achieve financial self-sustainability? The experience of Akhuwat in Pakistan

Ajaz Ahmed Khan, Muhammad Shakeel Ishaq, Joana Silva Afonso, and Shahzad Akram

Akhuwat was established in 2001 in Pakistan in order to assist poor people to set up and develop their businesses by providing qard hasan *or interest-free loans. It has expanded rapidly to become one of the largest Islamic microfinance organizations in the world. It has 500 branches spread throughout Pakistan with more than 567,000 active borrowers and an outstanding loans portfolio of almost US$77 m. Akhuwat has been very successful in maintaining high levels of on-time repayment, covering operating costs, and raising faith-based contributions from well-wishers as well as voluntary donations from borrowers.*

Keywords: Pakistan, Akhuwat, *qard hasan*, *zakat*, *sadaqah*, faith, voluntary donations

Introduction

Akhuwat is an Islamic microfinance institution established in 2001 in the city of Lahore in Pakistan. It has grown significantly over the last 15 years and now has 500 branches spread throughout the country, including in the remote region of Gilgit-Baltistan in the far north and in the semi-autonomous Federally Administered Tribal Areas (FATA), where it is one of the few microfinance institutions (MFIs) operating. However, the majority of Akhuwat's operations are in Pakistan's most populous province of Punjab, where 397 branches are located. This focus arises partly from the consideration that urban micro-entrepreneurs are underserved by existing microfinance initiatives such as the large government-funded National Rural Support Programme (NRSP), which focus on rural areas.

Akhuwat employs 3,500 full-time staff and has more than 567,000 active borrowers. In terms of the number of active clients, it is the third largest microfinance provider in Pakistan with a market share of 13.1 per cent, after the publicly funded NRSP with 15.9 per cent and Khushhali Microfinance Bank with 13.4 per cent. However, Akhuwat is the largest provider of Islamic

http://dx.doi.org/10.3362/9781780449555.002

microfinance in Pakistan. In terms of geographical coverage, it is the second largest microfinance provider with a presence in 70 districts – only Khushhali Bank, which has a presence in 74 districts, has greater outreach (MicroWatch, 2016).

Akhuwat's mission is to 'alleviate poverty by empowering socially and economically marginalized segments of society through interest-free micro-finance and in the process harnessing their entrepreneurial potential and enhancing their capacity through economic and social guidance'. The organi-zation derives its name from the concept of *muawkhaat*, or 'brotherhood' in Arabic. It is a completely independent not-for-profit organization with no political or religious ties to other bodies. Although it does not keep figures on the faith of applicants, it estimates that a small proportion of all loans – probably 2 to 3 per cent – are given to non-Muslims, usually Christians, although there are some Hindu borrowers as well from the southern province of Sindh. It is a faith-inspired institution but does not undertake *da'wah* or the preaching of Islam. As well as describing the development of the organization, this investigation explains in detail how loans are structured and disbursed and the methods Akhuwat utilizes to raise funds and cover costs.

Products and lending methodology

Akhuwat's primary activity is providing *qard hasan* or interest-free benevolent loans to low income people. *Qard hasan* loans are encouraged by Islamic teachings as an effective way of assisting poor persons;[1] indeed, they are preferred to the provision of outright charity.[2] Akhuwat's loans do not attract any charges apart from a standard application fee of 200 rupees (Rs) or about US$2.[3] The application fee remains the same and does not vary with the size or length of the loan. All loans are repaid in fixed equal monthly instalments over terms of between 12 and 24 months; most commonly, the length of repayment is between 15 and 18 months. Since the annual rate of inflation in Pakistan has varied between 7.2 per cent and 13.9 per cent over the last decade, with the exception of 2008 when it peaked at 20.3 per cent, borrowers are in effect repaying less than they received in real terms. In comparison, other microfinance providers typically charge flat interest rates of between 20 per cent and 30 per cent per annum.

Although Akhuwat's loans are considerably cheaper than those from other microfinance providers, the fact that loans are *Shari'ah* compliant also appears to be an important factor in attracting clients. During interviews with 500 first-time borrowers conducted during April and May 2015, almost two-thirds (62 per cent) said that the main reason why they approached Akhuwat was that the loan was compliant with Islamic teachings, while less than a third (29 per cent) declared that the primary reason was because it was cheaper than other providers.

Since it is not a regulated MFI, Akhuwat is not permitted to accept savings but it does provide other non-microfinance services, including running a health centre in Lahore and implementing regular free distributions of new and recycled clothes and shoes. It also provides free residential education to 59 students at Akhuwat College in Lahore and to 80 students at the Institute of Research, Science and Technology in the city of Faisalabad. Both educational institutions are funded by *zakat* donations and attract students from all faiths from all over Pakistan. Akhuwat is planning to open a university in Lahore in the near future.

Akhuwat's core product is the family enterprise loan, which is provided to establish new businesses – or for expanding existing businesses – and given to individuals in solidarity groups of between three and six people. These can be single-sex or mixed male and female groups of neighbours. The organization does not permit close relatives to form groups. It is by far the most common type of loan product offered by Akhuwat and comprises approximately 90 per cent of all loans. Typically, loans for first-time borrowers are for Rs 15,000 (about US$140), although occasionally borrowers request smaller amounts. Repeat borrowers can access successively larger loans of up to a maximum of Rs 50,000 (approximately US$475). Repayments are made in cash by borrowers at local branch offices. Often one group member will collect repayments from the rest and deposit these at the branch.

Although it is given to an individual, Akhuwat considers the family enterprise loan as 'a loan to the household' and the whole family is made aware of the responsibility to invest wisely and repay. Another family member, normally the spouse but also on occasion a parent or son or daughter, co-signs the loan agreement. The household can hold only one loan at any one time. Akhuwat provides family enterprise loans to support a wide range of retail, manufacturing, and trade activities that generate a regular flow of income. Typically, borrowers tend to be shopkeepers, rickshaw drivers, hawkers, and embroiderers. The case study in Box 2.1 describes a family enterprise loan.

Akhuwat has gradually introduced other loan products to respond to needs identified among existing clients. These include education loans to pay educational fees and to purchase accompanying materials; health loans to finance the cost of urgent healthcare; housing loans to pay for the repair and renovation of houses; marriage loans to assist parents with costs associated with marrying their daughters, including wedding ceremonies and dowries; and emergency loans that are designed to deal with 'unexpected but necessary expenses'. The latter is the only loan that can be held simultaneously with another loan from Akhuwat, and, if approved, it is disbursed within a couple of days after receiving the application. In contrast, the other types of loans generally take up to one month to process and disburse.

Inspired by Islamic teachings that place a particular emphasis on assisting those who are heavily indebted,[4] Akhuwat also provides liberation loans to individuals who have already taken out loans at high rates of interest from private moneylenders and are struggling to repay them. Such practices are relatively common among poor people in Pakistan, particularly to meet the costs associated with marriages or medical treatment, and rates of interest

---

Box 2.1 Using a loan to expand a small business

Nighat is a widow from Dunya Pur, a small town between the cities of Multan and Bahawalpur in southern Punjab. Her husband died in 2006 and she has two sons and one daughter. In order to support her family she started working as a tailor and selling shampoos to villagers. As the latter activity involved travelling alone outside her home, it was criticized by her very conservative extended family. Despite this and the challenges she faced, she persisted and moved on to selling fabric used to make women's clothing as well. She buys cloth from a large bazaar in Multan, which is about 30 miles away, and resells to women in nearby villages who only rarely have the opportunity to travel to larger cities to make purchases directly. In order to develop her business, in 2007 she received a loan of Rs 8,000 (about US$765) from Akhuwat to buy a greater variety of cloth to sell. Although she could have received a larger loan elsewhere, she was attracted to Akhuwat not only because it was cheaper and they did not request formal collateral, but also because it was *Shari'ah* compliant – in her own words, she 'would rather eat only once a day than take an interest-based loan'. Nighat repaid her first loan and has continued to access progressively larger loans to develop her business over the last 10 years or so – she recently received her eighth loan, worth Rs 35,000 (US$330). Nighat now receives orders from boutiques for ready-made women's clothing. She regularly makes voluntary donations to Akhuwat with her monthly repayments so that 'other widows might benefit as she has done'.

---

are generally around 10 per cent per month, although they can occasionally be much higher. Sometimes borrowers are able to pay only the interest charges while the principal remains the same for several years.

When approached to assist, Akhuwat repays the whole amount outstanding to the moneylender in one lump sum payment in the presence of the borrower. The maximum size of a liberation loan is usually Rs 100,000 (US$950), although it can be higher upon the discretion of the executive director. The borrower then repays the loan to Akhuwat in interest-free instalments. Akhuwat carefully scrutinizes each liberation loan application, including verifying loan agreements with the private moneylender and making enquiries with neighbours and local community leaders to ascertain that the debt is genuine. The case study in Box 2.2 describes a loan.

In addition to the various loan products, Akhuwat has developed a mutual support fund to assist borrowers and their families in case of disability or death. When loans are disbursed, borrowers pay 1 per cent of the loan as *takaful* or insurance. In the event of a borrower's permanent disability or death, the outstanding loan amount is waived and the borrower's family also receives a grant of Rs 5,000 (approximately US$50) towards funeral expenses.

Akhuwat markets its services through awareness campaigns in target areas and by word of mouth from existing borrowers. It introduces the programme at a local mosque or church when people congregate for prayers. Interested parties visit their nearest branch office, where loan officers complete an application form. Applicants are also required to present supporting documentation at this stage. Providing that the loan officer believes that the proposal is economically feasible he or she will then visit the loan applicant at their home or business to verify the information contained in the application form and

---

Box 2.2 A liberation loan from Akhuwat

Qudoos works in Lahore as an electrician and rickshaw driver. He is married with five children and estimates that his average monthly earnings are around Rs 25,000 (US$240). His wife works as a labourer and earns about US$75 a month. Unfortunately, in 2012 she became seriously ill with hepatitis C. In order to pay for her urgent medical treatment, and without other options, Qudoos took out a loan of Rs 70,000 (US$670) with a local moneylender. He agreed to pay Rs 5,000 (about US$50) per month as interest at the beginning and thereafter Rs 4,000 a month – these payments did not include the principal. With his wife unable to work, Qudoos struggled to cover household expenses. By October 2014, some two years later, he had paid Rs 112,000 (US$1,070) in interest, while the principal remained the same at Rs 70,000. His relationship with the moneylender became strained and the moneylender was verbally abusive, demanding full repayment of the loan. Qudoos approached Akhuwat and requested a loan of Rs 60,000 (US$570) in order to repay most of the principal and agreed to find Rs 10,000 (about US$100) from his own resources to cover the shortfall. Accompanied by one of Akhuwat's branch staff, Qudoos repaid the moneylender in full and received a document confirming that the loan was settled. One month later, in November 2014, Qudoos began repaying his loan from Akhuwat in 22 equal monthly instalments of Rs 2,727 (about US$25).

---

also to assess the socio-economic status of the applicant to ensure that they belong to Akhuwat's target group.

Applications pass through various stages and are approved only after three or four weeks. For individual loans, a borrower is required to provide three guarantors who are responsible for repayment in case of default – one of these must be a family member to ensure that the family as a whole is aware and supportive of the loan. In line with Islamic teachings, the loan agreement is always clearly written, explained, and signed in the presence of at least two witnesses, who may be guarantors. Signatures and thumbprints of all guarantors are taken in the mosque or church.

For each branch office, loan disbursement generally takes place once a month and between 100 and 150 loans are usually given in any one disbursement event, which is almost always held in the local mosque (occasionally a church is used). Beyond promoting transparency and greater awareness, mosques offer several practical advantages. They possess sufficient space to accommodate the large numbers of borrowers and guarantors that gather for the disbursement ceremonies. They are invariably free during the mornings when the events are held, and they do not charge for using their facilities, which helps keep operational costs to a minimum. In a society in which faith is important, borrowers make solemn promises to invest loans wisely and to repay promptly within a religious environment (Harper, 2012). Each borrower must be accompanied by at least one of the guarantors. Other people present include community leaders and Akhuwat staff. Borrowers are issued with a cheque for their loans which they can cash upon presentation of their national identity cards at branches of local banks.

During the disbursement events, 'social guidance' is often provided by senior staff on the importance of girls' education, community cohesion, protecting and improving the environment, observing traffic rules and local legislation, and adhering to the highest ethical business standards.

After disbursing loans, loan officers continue to visit borrowers on a regular basis to ensure that funds are properly invested and to monitor the performance of the funded activities. Repayments must be submitted at the local branch on a certain fixed date each month. If repayments are not received within three or four days following this date, then loan officers visit borrowers to remind them of their obligations. If repayment is still not forthcoming, a few days thereafter Akhuwat contacts guarantors and asks them to make repayments. This rarely occurs; although exact figures are not kept, from conversations with branch managers, it would appear that guarantors are asked to make repayments for less than 1 per cent of loans. In line with Islamic teachings, there are no financial penalties for delayed repayments.

Although it does not keep detailed records, Akhuwat estimates that it rejects approximately 10 per cent of all applications. The proportion is greater – between 15 and 20 per cent – for relatively new branches, as they receive more applications from first-time borrowers. Apart from calculating that the investment activity will not generate sufficient returns to repay the loan, there are usually two other reasons why applications are rejected. Firstly, applicants sometimes provide misleading information that is uncovered only when loan officers visit the borrower's home or place of business to verify details. Secondly, loan officers sometimes discover that the applicant does not have a good reputation or is considered untrustworthy by others in the local community. In all cases, Akhuwat does not refund the Rs 200 application fee.

Organizational development

Akhuwat has greatly expanded its level of operations since it was established in 2001, as Table 2.1 illustrates. The outstanding loan portfolio at the end of June 2016 was more than Rs 8 bn (almost US$77 m) – more than three times the equivalent figure just two years earlier in 2014. The number of active clients during the same period also increased significantly, from 235,517 to 567,761. Initially, Akhuwat only provided loans to women. After it began lending to men in 2003, the proportion of female borrowers dropped to approximately a third. In recent years, however, the proportion of women borrowers has started increasing once again and was 42 per cent in 2016.

The ratio of repayments overdue by more than 30 days (PAR30) has consistently been below 1 per cent, although Akhuwat only started collecting precise data on delayed repayments in 2008. Over the past eight years, the average loan size increased from about US$150 to US$220.

Despite the fact that its loans are cheaper than those from alternative microfinance providers, Akhuwat is able to consider all the loan applications it receives. There are several reasons why it is not overwhelmed by requests for loans. Firstly, the relatively small size of loans dissuades many

Table 2.1 Key financial indicators for Akhuwat

Year	Outstanding loans portfolio		PAR30 ratio (%)	Number of active loans	Average loan size		Percentage of female clients*
	Rupees	US$			Rupees	US$	
2002	796,400	13,273	n/a	154	9,870	165	100
2003	1,456,501	25,553	n/a	271	9,898	174	30
2004	5,336,141	92,002	n/a	802	10,221	176	30
2005	18,050,490	300,842	n/a	2,862	10,183	170	30
2006	38,003,932	633,399	n/a	6,156	10,540	176	30
2007	50,446,613	840,777	n/a	8,734	10,368	173	30
2008	69,572,549	1,008,298	0.50	12,129	10,752	156	32
2009	95,951,262	1,184,583	0.59	14,599	11,882	147	33
2010	148,566,216	1,747,838	0.84	19,562	11,949	141	34
2011	241,835,425	2,812,040	0.29	31,573	12,231	142	35
2012	761,036,629	8,010,912	0.97	67,337	16,809	177	35
2013	1,550,6C2,201	15,506,022	0.77	163,215	16,215	162	38
2014	2,460,0C9,962	24,849,495	0.48	235,517	17,230	174	38
2015	4,782,4C4,165	46,887,198	0.29	405,939	19,876	195	40
2016	8,046,3C4,716	76,632,330	0.33	567,761	22,571	217	42

Source: Information supplied by Akhuwat, September 2016 (figures as of 30 June each year).
Note: * Approximate figures only until 2007 as Akhuwat did not keep data on the gender of borrowers.

potential clients, particularly as other MFIs and banks offer much larger loans.[5] Secondly, borrowers often have to wait several weeks to receive a loan from Akhuwat whereas other institutions may take only two to three days to process loan applications. Lastly, generally it accepts applications only from people living at a distance of no more than 3 kilometres from its branch offices. These are always located in urban centres, which, as a consequence, excludes most people living in rural areas.[6]

Akhuwat estimates that the majority of its borrowers – approximately three-quarters – are repeat borrowers. Having promptly repaid their loans, sometimes early, borrowers often apply for another, larger loan. Akhuwat reckons that approximately 10 per cent of borrowers do not feel the need to apply for another loan. It also refuses to consider repeat applications from another 10 to 15 per cent of borrowers for a variety of reasons, including evidence that the borrower did not invest the previous loan as agreed, instalments were not repaid on time, or the borrower's identity card is no longer valid.

In a deliberate attempt to 'graduate' successful clients, in August 2015 Akhuwat began a pilot project with the Punjab Small Industries Corporation (PSIC). Although limited so far to Lahore, those clients who have received and promptly repaid three or four loans from one of Akhuwat's projects – the Punjab Chief Minister Self-Employment Scheme – may request a larger *qard hasan* loan of Rs 200,000 (US$1,900) directly from PSIC. Akhuwat provides a recommendation that the client is trustworthy and has a good credit record. So far, 77 clients have graduated to receive loans from PSIC through this initiative.

Occasionally, loan officers discover that borrowers have simultaneously taken another, usually interest-bearing, loan elsewhere. Akhuwat rejects these applications in order to avoid contributing to over-indebtedness. Interestingly, this demonstrates that some borrowers at least are willing to access concurrently interest-based loans as well as Islamic loans.

The challenge of achieving financial self-sustainability

In order to cover its operational costs, Akhuwat receives income from several sources including application fees, grants from institutional donors specifically assigned for administrative costs, *sadaqah* (voluntary charity) donations from well-wishers, returns from bank deposits, and even the sale of books, compact discs, and animal hides. Table 2.2 details these different sources.

Akhuwat charges a non-refundable fee of Rs 200 (about US$2) for each loan application regardless of the size or length of the loan. For the last complete financial year for which details are available, from 1 July 2015 to 30 June 2016, Akhuwat raised more than US$1.13 m from application fees. Between 1 July 2009 and 30 June 2014, the application fee was Rs 100 (US$1), while prior to this borrowers had to become Akhuwat 'members' before they could qualify for a loan. The membership fee between 1 July 2007 and 30 June 2009 was 5.5 per cent of the loan amount, while between 1 July 2002 and 30 June 2007

Table 2.2 Akhuwat's income and expenses

Year	Membership and application fees	Other income	Operational donations	Total income	Total expenses	Cost coverage ratio*	Borrower donations
2001–2	280	16,317	0	16,497	2,792	591	0
2002–3	1,817	1,708	0	3,525	5,271	67	0
2003–4	7,274	302	0	7,576	10,179	74	0
2004–5	29,265	0	0	29,265	33,403	88	0
2005–6	56,629	8,786	0	65,416	79,422	82	0
2006–7	82,373	7,009	0	89,382	137,893	65	0
2007–8	127,976	22,980	0	150,956	190,220	79	346
2008–9	108,969	27,502	0	136,473	206,951	66	150
2009–10	64,791	106,038	83,343	254,171	311,195	82	74,010
2010–11	92,387	210,580	45,732	348,699	699,870	50	144,218
2011–12	204,659	190,190	634,486	1,029,334	1,091,035	94	277,545
2012–13	208,288	311,388	2,021,343	2,541,019	1,994,977	127	569,318
2013–14	325,651	399,510	1,966,411	2,691,572	3,584,806	75	924,696
2014–15	838,238	590,936	3,968,717	5,397,891	4,964,312	109	909,146
2015–16	1,130,420	1,468,506	6,656,673	9,255,600	7,054,083	131	1,451,265

Source: Information supplied by Akhuwat, September 2016 (figures from 1 July to 30 June each year).
Notes: * Calculated by adding all donations (except borrower donations) and service payments to membership and application fees and then dividing by total expenses. All monetary figures are in US$; equivalent data in Pakistani rupees shown in Appendix 2.1.

it varied between 2 and 5 per cent of the loan amount. Before this, there was a standard one-off membership fee payment of Rs 400 (US$6.70).

Akhuwat also receives religiously motivated *sadaqah* and *zakat* (obligatory alms), generally from economically better-off Muslims within Pakistan but also increasingly from the Pakistani diaspora in countries such as the United Kingdom, United States of America (Akhuwat has registered offices in both countries), and the United Arab Emirates. While *sadaqah* may be used as loan capital and also to cover operational costs (the part of *sadaqah* designated to cover operational costs is included in the column 'Other income' in Table 2.2), this does not apply to *zakat*, which instead is only to be used to support those who qualify as *zakat* recipients. Mostly, Akhuwat uses *zakat* funds to pay the educational expenses of students. The organization received more than Rs 154 m (US$1.47 m) in *sadaqah* and *zakat* donations between 1 July 2015 and 30 June 2016 from approximately 1,500 individuals, mostly from Pakistan.

It is clear that significant growth in the last three years has coincided with attracting institutional funding from various regional government bodies. Over a period of one year, beginning in 2013, Akhuwat received Rs 210 m (US$2 m) from the Gilgit-Baltistan Chief Minister Self-Employment Scheme, and in 2014 it received Rs 446 m (US$4.25 m) from the Prime Minister's Interest-free Loan Scheme. In 2015, it received half of an agreed Rs 500 m (US$4.76 m) from the FATA Development Authority and also Rs 200 m (US$1.9 m) of an agreed Rs 500 m (US$4.76 m) from the Technical Education and Vocational Training Authority. However, Akhuwat's largest source of institutional funding has been the Punjab Chief Minister Self-Employment Scheme, from which it has received Rs 5 bn (US$47.6 m) since 2011 and it has an agreement to receive a further Rs 2 bn (US$19 m). Although the exact amounts are not disclosed, each of these agreements includes service payments to cover Akhuwat's administrative expenses (these are included in the column headed 'Operational donations' in Table 2.2). Table 2.3 provides information on Akhuwat's financial position as of the end of June 2016. The end-of-year surplus of unrestricted funds is added to loan capital, while restricted funds become equity.

A differentiating factor of the organization is the fact that borrowers also contribute voluntarily to 'community donation programme' boxes, which are placed in all branch offices. Although listed in Table 2.2 as 'Borrower donations', this income is not used to cover operational costs; instead, it is used only to fund further loans. Had Akhuwat used this income to cover expenses, then its cost coverage ratio would have been above 100 per cent in each of the last five years. From personal observation, it appears that the donations are indeed entirely voluntary. They are made by around a third of the borrowers every time they visit the branch offices to make their monthly repayments, and, judging from the notes visible in the boxes, typically the donations are of very small amounts of Rs 10, Rs 20, or Rs 50 (between 10 and 50 cents).

Table 2.3 Akhuwat's balance sheet and income statement

Balance sheet as of 30 June 2016		
	Rupees	*US$*
Assets		
Cash and investments	1,911,401,586	18,203,824
Outstanding loans	8,067,088,083	76,829,410
Fixed assets	378,532,532	3,605,071
Other assets	58,730,711	559,340
Total	10,415,752,912	99,197,646
Liabilities and equity		
Sundry creditors	119,228,356	1,135,008
Provident fund	11,253,857	107,179
Loans	8,888,446,645	84,651,872
Equity	1,396,824,054	13,303,086
Total	10,415,752,912	99,197,646
Income statement as of 30 June 2016		
	Rupees	US$
Income		
Operating income*	817,644,869	7,787,093
Donations and other income	154,193,218	1,468,506
Total	971,838,086	9,255,600
Expenses		
Operating expenses	690,715,477	6,578,242
Provision for bad loans	1,058,823	10,084
Other expenses	48,904,503	465,757
Total	740,678,803	7,054,083
Surplus	231,159,283	2,201,517

Source: Information supplied by Akhuwat, September 2016 (Akhuwat's financial year is from 1 July to 30 June).
Note: * Operating income includes the fees associated with the loans, and operational donations.

This innovative approach to raising funds was in fact suggested by a borrower who wished to support the organization to reach more clients. When questioned why they donate, the responses from current borrowers reinforce this desire. Mohammed Hashim, from an area called Badami Bagh in Lahore, stated that 'We donate so that other poor people can be helped as we have been, and also so that it may please *Allah*,' while Majeeda Bibi from the same locality remarked, 'We have been helped, and we are happy and willing to donate as well. Hopefully, some other poor person will benefit through our help and offer prayers for us in return.' Clearly, donations are motivated to some extent by faith, but there also appears to be a sense of solidarity with other poor people. During the period 1 July 2015 to 30 June 2016,

Akhuwat raised more than US$1.45 m from voluntary donations from borrowers, which is more than it received from the standard application fee.

During years when the cost coverage ratio was below 100 per cent – that is, the income received from application fees, grants from institutional donors specifically assigned for administrative costs, *sadaqah* donations, returns from bank deposits, and the sale of various items did not meet total expenses – Akhuwat covered the shortfall by using loan capital.

In order to keep operational expenses low, branch offices are usually located in densely populated urban areas. This facilitates monitoring and also ensures that a large number of potential clients are located within a three kilometre radius. Furthermore, staff use public transport or their own motorcycles for travel (they are reimbursed for any expenditure) and branch offices are very small, often consisting of a couple of rooms, and simply decorated with a few items of very basic furniture including a low table – staff and borrowers alike sit on cushions on the floor.

Moreover, Akhuwat's staff are paid less than their counterparts in other MFIs. During their first two to three months, loan officers receive a basic monthly salary of Rs 7,000 (US$67), although this is supplemented with a recovery allowance and, after six months, a project allowance. Their basic salary rises to Rs 12,000 (US$115) per month after one year. Yet, despite the relatively low salaries, staff turnover was just 14.51 per cent in 2015. Staff motivation is partially explained by their religious beliefs; they feel that by working for Akhuwat, they are fulfilling a mission to serve the poor. It is also related to career development opportunities within the organization. Akhuwat has a deliberate policy of selecting less qualified and inexperienced but motivated staff, training them, and promoting from within – the better performing loan officers become branch managers, who in turn can progress to area managers, and eventually to regional managers who might manage over 200 staff with responsibility for more than 60,000 clients. Clearly, this policy of promoting from within has contributed to staff loyalty. The case study in Box 2.3 explains the motivation and career progression of one senior staff member.

Conclusions

In the relatively short space of 15 years, Akhuwat has grown quickly to become the largest Islamic microfinance provider in Pakistan, with an outstanding loans portfolio of almost US$77 m and more than 567,000 active clients served by 500 branches spread throughout the country. It has consistently maintained an extremely low PAR30 ratio of less than 1 per cent.

Equally impressive, Akhuwat has demonstrated that it is possible to provide *qard hasan* loans and cover operational costs. Although it does generate income from the standard fee of Rs 200 (about US$2) that it charges for each loan application, it also receives significant faith-based donations. An interesting feature of the Akhuwat model is the voluntary donations from borrowers.

Appendix 2.1

Table 2.4 Akhuwat's income and expenses

Year	Membership and application fees	Other income	Operational donations	Total income	Total expenses	Cost coverage ratio*	Borrower donations
2001–2	16,800	979,000	0	989,800	167,527	591	0
2002–3	103,550	97,358	0	200,908	300,444	67	0
2003–4	421,900	17,500	0	439,400	590,397	74	0
2004–5	1,755,918	0	0	1,755,918	2,004,160	88	0
2005–6	3,397,768	527,188	0	3,924,956	4,765,332	82	0
2006–7	4,942,398	420,520	0	5,362,918	8,273,607	65	0
2007–8	8,830,361	1,585,636	0	10,415,997	13,125,208	79	20,730
2008–9	8,826,478	2,227,696	0	11,054,274	16,763,039	66	10,338
2009–10	5,507,226	9,013,189	7,084,117	21,604,532	26,451,560	82	5,994,801
2010–11	7,945,254	18,109,893	3,932,944	29,988,091	60,188,779	50	12,258,508
2011–12	19,442,575	18,068,043	60,276,145	97,786,763	103,648,287	94	23,868,857
2012–13	20,828,836	31,138,770	202,134,277	254,101,883	199,497,747	127	54,085,163
2013–14	32,239,431	39,551,505	194,674,651	266,465,587	354,895,769	75	92,469,597
2014–15	85,500,300	60,275,512	404,809,107	550,584,919	506,359,782	109	90,005,532
2015–16	118,694,150	154,193,218	698,950,719	971,838,086	740,678,803	131	152,382,846

Source: Information supplied by Akhuwat, September 2016 (figures from 1 July to 30 June each year).
Notes: * Calculated by adding all donations (except borrower donations) and service payments to membership and application fees and then dividing by total expenses. All monetary figures are in Pakistani rupees.

Box 2.3 Career progression in Akhuwat

Mumtaz Ahmed used to work for the government-established NRSP as a senior credit officer. He received a relatively high salary and a vehicle for his own use. He also benefited from the high social status associated with working for the government in Pakistan. However, while he was reciting the *Qur'an* during the holy month of *Ramadan* in 2005, and in particular reflecting on the verses that warn Muslims against receiving or paying interest, he decided to leave his job because he considered that it was incompatible with his religious beliefs. After a meeting with Dr Amjad Saqib, founder and executive director of Akhuwat, he decided to join Akhuwat as a branch manager, even though this involved a reduction of 40 per cent in his salary and the loss of all the other benefits associated with his previous employment. After receiving training in Lahore, he worked for a short time in Rawalpindi. When Akhuwat expanded to Ghulam Muhammad Abad in Faisalabad, Mumtaz moved there to open the first branch in the city. In 2008, he progressed from branch manager to area manager, and he was promoted to assume his current position of regional manager in 2013. He recently completed 10 years' service with Akhuwat and now supervises 200 employees in 38 branches spread over six areas. As a devout Muslim he feels comfortable working in a faith-based organization and fulfilling a mission to serve the poor.

It is clear, though, that in recent years access to institutional funding from various regional government agencies has fuelled significant growth.

There is evidence to support the claim that the behaviour of some borrowers and donors is motivated by faith, and therefore Akhuwat's model can be replicated among other Muslim majority populations where there is the willingness to donate. In fact, it has already facilitated 16 independent local replications in Pakistan, although they are much smaller.[7]

Notes

1. The *Qur'an* states 'Who is he that will give *Allah qard-al-hasan*? For *Allah* will increase it manifold to his credit' (57:11); 'If you give *Allah qard-al-hasan* ... he will grant you forgiveness' (64:17); and 'Establish regular prayer and give regular charity and give *Allah qard-al-hasan*' (73:20).
2. The Prophet Muhammad (peace be upon Him) said: 'I saw on the gate of heaven written, "the reward for *sadaqah* is 10 times and reward for *qard hasan* is eighteen times". So, I asked the angel, how is it possible? The angel replied, "Because the beggar who asked had already had something but a borrower did not ask for a loan unless he was in need"' (Ibn Majah, Volume 3, Book 15, Hadith 2431).
3. At the time of writing US$1 was equivalent to Rs 105.
4. *Zakat*, for example, can only be paid to deserving individuals or groups who fall into one of the eight categories specified by the *Qur'an* (9:60); these include those who are 'debt-ridden'. Also, Muslims are advised that 'Whoever alleviates the difficulties of a needy person who cannot repay his debt, *Allah* will alleviate his difficulties both in this world and the Hereafter' (Sahih Muslim, Volume 6, Book 32, Number 6250).

5. While Akhuwat's average loan size was Rs 17,230 (US$172) at the end of 2014, the average loan size of Khushhali Bank was Rs 26,115 (US$260), NRSP was Rs 26,696 (US$267), and Tameer Microfinance Bank was Rs 39,588 (US$396) (Basharat et al. 2015).
6. Akhuwat has relaxed this general rule for operations in the mountainous region of Gilgit-Baltistan and accepts applications from borrowers living as far as 20 kilometres from a branch office. At the time of writing, Akhuwat was planning to start working in rural areas as well.
7. These are Harall Bunyad, NAYMET, Kawish, Salamat and Yaseen Welfare Trust, Zaad-e-rah, Muslim Aid, Rukan, Empowerment through Creative Integration, Alkhidmat Foundation, Rural Development Organisation, Decent Welfare Society, Helping Hand, Nur Foundation, the Eissar Trust, Islah Foundation, and Ta-awun.

References

Basharat, A., Arshad, A. and Ali, K. (2015) *Pakistan Microfinance Review 2014*, Islamabad: Pakistan Microfinance Network. <http://microfinanceconnect.info/assets/articles/6a6d84c7346aa2f278887b911b1fe1d7.pdf> [accessed 8 November 2016].

Harper, M. (2012) 'Akhuwat of Lahore: breaking the rules', *Small Enterprise Development: An International Journal of Microfinance and Business Development* 23: 70–81.

MicroWatch (2016) 'A quarterly update on microfinance outreach in Pakistan', *MicroWatch* 39, Quarter 1, January–March 2016.

About the authors

Ajaz Ahmed Khan (khan@careinternational.org) is Senior Microfinance Adviser at CARE International, United Kingdom.

Muhammad Shakeel Ishaq (shakeel.ishaq@akhuwat.org.pk) is Project Manager at Akhuwat, Pakistan.

Joana Silva Afonso (joana.silvaafonso@myport.ac.uk) is a PhD researcher at the Portsmouth Business School, University of Portsmouth, United Kingdom.

Shahzad Akram (shahzad.akram@akhuwat.org.pk) is Chief Credit Officer at Akhuwat, Pakistan.

PART II
The predominance of *murabaha*

This section contains five case studies: START from Kosovo, Mutahid from Afghanistan, Reef Finance from Palestine, Kaah Islamic Microfinance Services (KIMS) from Somalia, and the Islami Bank's Rural Development Scheme (RDS) from Bangladesh.

Four of the institutions are of modest size, and three have under 3,000 clients; they are fairly young, having been established for 10 years or less, but they have not grown as fast as many such institutions. The RDS of the Islami Bank in Bangladesh has over a million clients. The scheme operates throughout Bangladesh and is operated under the auspices of the Islami Bank; it is not a separate institution and, although it has a large number of clients, its share of the Bangladesh microfinance market is very small. This has important implications for the potential role of *Shari'ah*-compliant microfinance in other predominantly Muslim countries.

All these are very different from Akhuwat in that they are intended to cover their costs and, if possible, to make a profit, although only Reef Finance and START were actually profitable at the time the case study material was obtained. START has a small number of clients who borrow on the basis of *qard hasan*, without paying any interest, in the same way as Akhuwat operates for all its clients, but this is only for special cases; their number is restricted because the costs must be covered by the earnings from the main part of the business, which is on the basis of *murabaha*.

In every case, the initial capital has been subscribed in order to facilitate the provision of *Shari'ah*-compliant finance to disadvantaged people, and not for profit, and it is very unlikely that any of them will become profitable enough to repay or multiply the original investment. They are nevertheless commercial businesses – or, in the case of the Islami Bank's RDS, the scheme is intended to cover its operating costs even if the capital is supplied by the parent bank. They are not charities.

Murabaha is the dominating product for all five of these Islamic micro-finance institutions (IMFIs); they adopt a variety of techniques to preserve the formal requirement that the goods they provide to their clients are sold to them on credit rather than being bought with loans on which interest has to be paid, but the actual effect on the clients' and the institutions' cash flows is little different from that of a traditional interest-bearing loan. The profit charge is not increased if repayment is delayed, the institution may reserve the theoretical right to reclaim the goods if payment is not made in full, and it may in theory be responsible for the quality of the goods, but these requirements have little practical effect.

Reef Finance and the Islami Bank's RDS offer *musharaka* to a very small proportion of their clients, which are generally larger and more formal businesses that can keep reliable records of their revenues and their expenses and can thus calculate their profits; like many IMFIs, they may wish and intend to increase this part of their business, but the practical difficulties and the high transaction costs make this very difficult.

CHAPTER 3

Pioneering Islamic microfinance in Kosovo: the experience of START

Ajaz Ahmed Khan and Vehbi Zeqiri

START was established in Kosovo in 2002 by Islamic Relief, one of the largest Muslim faith-based international aid organizations in the world, in order to promote financial inclusion. START offers qard hasan *and* murabaha *loans throughout Kosovo, and since 2013 it has managed to cover operating costs from the income it generates from providing loans. Some borrowers are attracted to START because it offers* Shari'ah-compliant *finance and its identity as a faith-based organization has a positive impact on the motivation of borrowers to repay.*

Keywords: Kosovo, Islamic Relief, *qard hasan*, *murabaha*, self-sustainability, faith

Introduction

In this analysis we examine the experience of an Islamic microfinance institution (MFI), START from Kosovo, which provides loans to low-income borrowers on the basis of *qard hasan* and *murabaha*. As well as explaining the development of the organization and describing in detail how loans are structured and disbursed, we also consider the challenges that the organization faces in achieving financial self-sustainability and explore how faith influences the motivation and behaviour of some borrowers.

Once one of the poorest provinces of the former Yugoslavia, following a period of civil conflict in the late 1990s and subsequent administration by the United Nations, the Republic of Kosovo declared its independence from Serbia in February 2008. It has a population of approximately 2 million, the vast majority of whom (88 per cent) are ethnic Albanians; Serbs constitute 7 per cent[1] of the population while the remaining 5 per cent include ethnic Bosnians, Turks, and Roma. Just 2 per cent of the Albanian population are Catholics while the rest are Muslims. The Serbs are Orthodox Christians.

START was established in April 2002 as an MFI by Islamic Relief Kosova,[2] part of the international aid organization Islamic Relief Worldwide, which has its headquarters in Birmingham, United Kingdom. Islamic Relief Kosova began working in 1999 and initially focused on providing relief and emergency assistance after the Kosovo conflict. With the cessation of open

http://dx.doi.org/10.3362/9781780449555.003

hostilities, the focus moved to the repair and reconstruction of war-damaged infrastructure, including houses, schools, and clinics. In early 2002 it decided to focus on creating income and employment opportunities by providing microcredit and established a registered 'non-banking financial institution' in compliance with local regulations. Rather than responding to an expressed desire for *Shari'ah*-compliant finance among the local population at the time, START was created as an Islamic MFI in order to comply with Islamic Relief's principles as a Muslim faith-based organization.

START is part of Islamic Relief's global *Shari'ah*-compliant microfinance programme that covers 12 countries in Africa, the Middle East, and Asia and reaches approximately 15,000 clients with an outstanding loans portfolio of over £5 m (approximately US$6.5 m). While autonomous and led by a local board of directors in each country that is ratified by Islamic Relief Worldwide, compliance with Islamic commercial law and the standards of the Accounting and Auditing Organization for Islamic Financial Institutions (AAOIFI) is assured through a global *Shari'ah* supervisory arrangement via an external Islamic finance advisory firm. Islamic Relief's Global Microfinance Unit, which is based in the United Kingdom, also supports START through technical capacity building and advice in governance and risk management issues.

START is registered with the Central Bank of the Republic of Kosovo, the national regulatory body. START provides *Shari'ah*-compliant loans to low-income households, according to its mission statement 'regardless of their race, colour, political affiliation, gender or belief', in order to establish new businesses or expand existing ones and to improve living conditions. Most loans are provided for small-scale agriculture and animal husbandry, retail and service activities, as well as the repair and reconstruction of housing. All loan-financed activities must be *halal* or permitted; START will not, for example, support the sale or production of alcohol, tobacco, and pork, or activities associated with gambling and prostitution. START does not currently provide clients with any additional training or technical services.

Organizational development

Direct lending began in April 2002 and was initially restricted to rural areas in the municipality of Skenderaj (also known by its Serbian name Srbica) in north-central Kosovo; this was one of the areas most affected during the 1998–9 Kosovo conflict. During subsequent years, START increased its geographical coverage to provide loans in the neighbouring municipalities of Drenas (Glogovac), Malisheva, and Vusthtrri (Vučitrn). Beginning in 2007, loans were provided further afield in areas surrounding the cities of Peja, Prizren, and eventually the capital Prishtina. At present, it provides loans in rural and urban areas throughout the country. START's head office is in Prishtina although it also uses a field office located in the town of Drenas in central Kosovo.

START currently employs a total of 15 full-time staff. There are five full-time loan officers, three who deal with *qard hasan* or benevolent loans, and two who deal with *murabaha* or cost plus profit loans. The additional staff are the executive director, deputy director, credit manager, finance manager, legal officer, legal assistant, human resources and administration officer, data entry and support officer, and two receptionists. Staff turnover is relatively low and the majority of staff have been with the organization for several years. It is worth noting that most staff are practising Muslims and it is clear that faith plays a very positive role in staff motivation and loyalty. Many of the staff said that they felt more comfortable in an environment where their religious observance is understood and accepted. Some also revealed that they regularly work extra hours without pay and are reluctant to leave the organization, especially since there are relatively few opportunities to work in a religious environment in Kosovo.

START was the first *Shari'ah*-compliant MFI in Kosovo and is a member of the national microfinance network called the Association of Microfinance Institutions in Kosovo (AMIK); this comprises 10 members[3] and includes most, although not all, of the larger and more established microfinance providers. Altogether there are 18 MFIs operating in Kosovo, accounting for approximately 7 per cent of the value of all loans disbursed in the country. Most of these were established immediately after the end of the conflict in 1999 by international aid organizations including Mercy Corps, the International Catholic Migration Commission, and World Vision. However, the vast majority of loans are disbursed through eight commercial banks.

Although START has been operating continuously for more than 14 years, it remains a relatively small MFI; in 2015 it disbursed a total of 1,190 loans with an average loan size of 1,786 euros[4] (approximately US$2,000). In terms of outstanding loans portfolio, it is the sixth largest MFI among AMIK's 10 members. All the other MFIs, apart from one that was established in 2011 and inspired by START,[5] are not *Shari'ah* compliant and charge effective interest rates varying between 28 per cent and 34 per cent per annum on a declining balance. START's executive director is a member of the board of AMIK and the organization has a good reputation within the microfinance sector in Kosovo.

Approximately one-third of START's loans are currently given to women. When the organization was first established, the proportion was more than two-thirds, but this has decreased as the focus is now no longer just on widows. Although loans are not distributed on the basis of religion, the overwhelming majority of the borrowers are Albanian Muslims. There is, however, also a small number of borrowers – no more than 1 per cent – who are ethnic Serbs, Bosnians, Roma, and Croats. The slightly disproportionate number of Albanian Muslim borrowers is likely accounted for by the location of START's operations; in particular, its initial loans were concentrated exclusively among Albanian Muslim communities in central Kosovo.

Table 3.1 provides key financial indicators and illustrates how START has developed since it was established in 2002.

Table 3.1 Development of key financial indicators for START

Year	Outstanding loans portfolio (euros)	PAR30 ratio (%)	Number of loans	Average loan size (euros)	Proportion of female clients (%)
2002	141,026	0	214	871	70
2003	281,020	1	500	968	20
2004	396,694	2	708	993	18
2005	542,922	2	950	996	26
2006	709,403	3	965	1,079	22
2007	837,987	4	1,228	1,094	18
2008	885,209	4	1,375	1,160	21
2009	843,080	5	1,393	1,142	24
2010	754,745	4	1,129	1,205	23
2011	1,196,967	3	829	1,878	21
2012	1,755,467	6	938	1,848	24
2013	2,066,810	6	1,097	2,041	20
2014	2,477,199	6	1,320	1,901	27
2015	2,120,343	6	1,190	1,786	30
2016*	2,385,752	4	821	1,788	27

Source: Information supplied by START, September 2016.
Note: * Data as of end June 2016. All other figures are given for calendar years

Approximately, 40 per cent of START's active clients are repeat borrowers, while 60 per cent are first-time borrowers. The outstanding loans portfolio at the end of June 2016 was almost 2.4 m euros (approximately US$2.69 m), which is more than three times the equivalent figure in 2010. During the same period, the portfolio at risk ratio greater than 30 days (PAR30) varied between 4 per cent and 6 per cent. In 2015, a total of 1,190 loans were disbursed by START. Of these, 976 were *qard hasan* loans while 214 were *murabaha* loans. However, the average size of *murabaha* loans was more than double the average loan size of *qard hasan* loans: 3,470 euros (US$3,887) compared with 1,417 euros (US$1,587). The expansion of operations is largely due to the fact that START received funding of US$3 m in six equal instalments of US$500,000 from the Islamic Development Bank (IDB) between 2011 and 2013. The money is not repayable as long as START continues to use it to 'provide *Shari'ah*-compliant finance to economically disadvantaged sectors of the population'. However, if START does not manage the fund according to the terms of the agreement, the funds must be repaid to the IDB and will then be given to another similar organization in Kosovo.

Since it was established in 2002, START has provided almost 15,000 loans, serving more than 8,000 clients. However, the majority of borrowers (64 per cent) have only ever taken out one loan, although it is also apparent that different members of the same family have taken out a loan that is then used by the household. Since they are cheaper than alternative interest-based loans, and for some because they are *Shari'ah* compliant, there is a strong demand for START's loans and a long list of clients whose applications have been approved but not yet disbursed due to a lack of funds.

At the same time, for several reasons the organization is not overwhelmed by applications. Firstly, it has been very conservative in marketing its services. Secondly, many people want cash rather than specific goods and are reluctant to access the larger *murabaha* loans. This is partly because they want money for consumption purposes but also because sometimes borrowers prefer to buy goods from suppliers who charge lower prices and do not issue invoices and therefore they avoid paying value added tax (VAT). Lastly, in order to fulfil its social development mission, START insists on collecting a wide range of information on the social and economic background of clients. This includes the amount and sources of income earned by all household members, as well as the viability of their businesses. Combined with the relatively low loan ceilings of 1,500 euros (US$1,680) for *qard hasan* loans and 5,000 euros (US$5,600) for *murabaha* loans, compared with the maximum of 25,000 euros (US$28,000) for the microfinance sector as a whole, this dissuades many potential applicants and explains why the number of repeat borrowers is relatively low – only 24 per cent of clients have taken out three or more loans.

The methodology of *qard hasan* and *murabaha* loans

From 2002 until 2010, START provided only *qard hasan* loans and charged an administrative fee of 50 euros (US$56); this increased to 60 euros (approximately US$65) in 2008, regardless of the size or length of the loan (the local currency has been the euro since 2002). Those considered to be from the poorest economic categories, which includes widows, do not pay the administrative fee. All loans are provided on an individual basis and generally for a period of one year, with 12 equal monthly repayments, although if clients are considered to be extremely poor then the repayment period is extended, in exceptional cases to up to 30 months. The administrative fee is collected in cash from borrowers when the loan contract is signed and it reflects the administrative costs that START estimates the organization incurs to process an 'average' loan application. *Qard hasan* loans do not attract any additional charges – borrowers simply repay the amount received. The case study in Box 3.1 describes one such loan.

At the very end of 2010, partly in response to the fact that the income generated from a relatively small number of *qard hasan* loans was insufficient to cover the organization's operational costs and hence achieve financial self-sustainability, and partly in response to demand for larger loans from slightly less poor people, START also started providing *murabaha* loans. While *qard hasan* loans have a specific focus on assisting those individuals whose income falls below the national poverty line, *murabaha* loans are given to individuals whose income is above the national poverty line. Households that live on

---

Box 3.1 Using a START loan to establish a small business

Shefkije is 57 and from Prishtina. She lives with her extended family, which includes her husband, two sons, two daughters-in-law, and two grandsons. The family lost their home, belongings, and livelihoods during the Kosovo conflict. Afterwards, Shefkije established a small business working from home, producing and selling traditional pies and chutney. She needed money to develop her business but was reluctant to apply for an interest-based loan because of her Muslim faith. After learning of its services, Shefkije approached START and requested a loan of 1,000 euros (US$1,120) to repair her kitchen at home. The repairs included new tiling and work surfaces to make the area where she worked cleaner and more hygienic. After promptly repaying the loan she applied for a second loan to purchase equipment to cook more efficiently and on a larger scale. She is currently with her fourth loan and her business has grown to employ other members of her family. Both her daughters-in-law help with the cooking while her sons purchase all ingredients and supplies and are also responsible for delivering orders throughout the city.

---

less than 1.75 euros (US$2) per day are categorized as poor while those living on less than 1.25 euros (US$1.40) per day are considered extremely poor. According to the World Bank Group in Kosovo (2015), 29.7 per cent of the population in Kosovo lives under the national poverty line.

For *murabaha* loans, clients select the items they wish to purchase and the place where they wish to buy them from. START's loan officers then visit the supplier and purchase the items by paying in cash; the invoice is in the name of the client, not START. The client is responsible for arranging transport of the items and taking delivery from the supplier. The procedure is relatively straightforward and inexpensive when there is just one supplier and a single product, such as an item of machinery, which is to be bought and delivered. Indeed, for most *murabaha* loans, only one supplier is involved. However, it becomes slightly more complicated and costly when borrowers require items from several different suppliers. Despite this, START does not charge a higher mark-up even when its officers are required to visit and buy a range of items from more than one supplier.

All loans attract fixed monthly repayments. The profit mark-up for *murabaha* loans is a flat rate of between 5 per cent and 6 per cent, which is equivalent to about 11 per cent on a declining balance basis. This is still considerably cheaper than alternative interest-based loans. Thus, a *murabaha* loan of 3,000 euros (US$3,360) repayable over one year attracts 12 equal monthly instalments of 265 euros (US$297); the total amount repayable is 3,180 euros (US$3,564). In comparison, a similar sized loan from a local interest-based MFI that charges an effective interest rate of between 28 per cent and 34 per cent would be much more expensive, with total repayments of between 3,900 and 4,080 euros (US$4,368 to US$4,570). To ensure that the procedures are *Shari'ah* compliant, the financial software that START utilizes will not permit certain steps: for example, the agreement cannot be printed out and signed until such time as START has paid for the purchase of the goods. The case study in Box 3.2 describes a *murabaha* loan in which all the items were bought from one supplier.

Box 3.2 Buying raspberry plants with a *murabaha* loan

Mirand is 21 and from the capital city of Prishtina. He lives in a two-bedroom apartment with four other family members – a younger brother and sister as well as his parents. Mirand worked for some time as a waiter. However, after visiting a local grocery store and seeing how well packaged raspberries were selling, he decided, with help and advice from an agronomist, to plant around one hectare of land with raspberry seedlings. He approached START for a loan because, in his own words, 'it is the only financial institution offering financial products based on Islamic values and principles'. He requested that the organization purchase 10,000 bare root raspberry seedlings on his behalf from a local nursery. START paid 5,000 euros (US$5,600) for the plants and added a profit mark-up of 5 per cent, so that the plants cost Mirand 5,250 euros (US$5,880). The items were delivered to his smallholding and he planted all the seedlings in April 2015. The first yield of 3.5 tonnes in August 2015 exceeded his expectations and the following month he harvested another 4.8 tonnes. His main cost is paying for labour to harvest the raspberries by hand. However, the cost of labour is relatively low and the wholesale price of 1.8 euros (US$2) per kilogram means that from his September harvest alone his sales totalled 8,640 euros (US$9,700). He has made all his repayments comfortably so far and, as the loan is repayable over 18 months, has put funds aside to meet repayments during the winter months when he is unable to harvest. His intention in 2016 is to increase the area of land he has under cultivation.

Prior to introducing *murabaha* loans, START consulted with its external auditors and tax authorities about how such loans might be viewed by the government in an environment which, despite the high proportion of Muslims, is largely unfamiliar with Islamic finance. The advice that START received was that it might be construed simply as the buying and reselling of products and therefore categorized as trade and liable to VAT. This would mean clients having to pay a mark-up of around 16 per cent and would make the loans, in START's opinion, too expensive. To preclude this possibility, START uses the term 'trade financing' on all loan documents. It received an opinion or *fatwa* from a well-known local Islamic scholar confirming that the procedures it employs and use of the term 'trade financing' are *Shari'ah* compliant. START uses the term *murabaha* when discussing these loans with clients and the wider public. For reporting purposes, START identifies the income earned from *murabaha* loans as 'profit' and the Central Bank equates this with interest earned by other financial institutions.

All borrowers require two personal guarantors and an item of movable collateral (such as a vehicle), except those borrowers who request less than 1,000 euros (approximately US$1,120); in the latter case, only one guarantor and an item of movable collateral is required. Loans used to be disbursed in cash at START's office in Drenas. However, since 2009, all loans have been disbursed by bank transfer. Conscious not to contribute to over-indebtedness, which is increasingly an issue in Kosovo (Pytkowska and Spannuth, 2013), START does not provide loans to clients who have outstanding loans elsewhere. It checks an applicant's indebtedness as well as his or her credit rating by accessing information held by the Credit Register of Kosovo (CRK) – every financial institution licensed by the Central Bank of Kosovo must submit loan data to the CRK within 48 hours of disbursement.

Table 3.2 START's income and operational expenses

Year	Income from qard hasan (euros)	Income from murabaha (euros)	Operational expenses (euros)	OSS ratio (%)
2002	4,600		75,936	6.06
2003	25,100		132,105	19.00
2004	34,400		142,762	24.09
2005	44,775		143,634	31.17
2006	46,675		151,796	30.75
2007	72,300		145,297	49.76
2008	80,220		128,239	62.55
2009	81,180		175,180	46.34
2010	64,920	692	126,801	51.74
2011	34,770	20,603	113,793	48.89
2012	43,860	52,876	135,248	71.52
2013	47,340	93,505	130,820	107.66
2014	63,480	122,042	153,640	120.75
2015	57,600	126,571	162,985	115.70
2016*	41,520	54,805	91,500	105.27

Source: Information supplied by START, September 2016.
Note: * Data as of end June 2016.

The challenge of achieving financial self-sustainability

The operational self-sustainability (OSS) ratio has gradually risen since START was established. START finally managed to cover all operational expenses from the income it earns from disbursing loans in 2013; the OSS ratio increased further in 2014 to 120.75 per cent and was 115.70 per cent in 2015. Prior to 2013, START was dependent upon an annual subsidy from its parent organization, Islamic Relief Worldwide, in order to cover the shortfall in income. It is worth noting that operational costs reached a high of 175,180 euros (approximately US$196,200) in 2009, but these fell in subsequent years as START decided to reduce staff salaries on average by between 15 and 20 per cent. The revised salaries are still competitive, though, and comparable to those received by staff in peer organizations. Certainly, the introduction of *murabaha* loans in 2011 has generated more income for START. Despite the fact that such loans are also operationally more complex and require specialized staff, START earns more from *murabaha* loans than from *qard hasan* loans. Table 3.2 details the income earned by START from all loans as well as annual operational expenses since 2002.

As can be seen in Table 3.3, which presents a summary of the balance sheet and income statement as of the end of June 2016, START had positive equity of 682,209 euros (US$764,074) and a net income of 48,060 euros (US$53,827).

In response to demand from clients and in order to further increase its financial self-sustainability, START is keen to diversify the types of financial

Table 3.3 START's summary balance sheet and income statement

	Amount (euros)
Balance sheet as of 30 June 2016	
Total assets	2,944,983
Total liabilities	2,262,774
Total equity	682,209
Income statement as of 30 June 2016	
Total financial income	144,928
Total operating expenses	91,500
Net income	48,060

Source: Information supplied by START, September 2016.

products that it offers, for example by introducing profit- and loss-sharing arrangements such as *musharaka* and *mudaraba*, *ijarah* or leasing, and *bai salam* or a contract for a deferred sale – these would likely enable it to generate greater income. However, it is unable to do so until legislation governing the operations of MFIs in Kosovo is changed. While they are far from unsupportive, the lack of knowledge and awareness of Islamic finance among the regulatory authorities, particularly with regard to promoting anything other than straightforward *qard hasan* loans, presents a challenge for START. Therefore, in addition to providing loans, START has been involved in raising awareness of Islamic finance in Kosovo – it organized three courses, each one lasting 40 hours, which were attended by around 50 finance professionals, and the executive director of START regularly speaks at local microfinance conferences. Three separate non-governmental organizations from neighbouring Macedonia and Montenegro have also visited START, at the instigation of the IDB, to analyse its operations and procedures.

The influence of faith on the motivation and behaviour of borrowers

As the two case studies presented earlier highlighted, it is apparent that some borrowers are attracted to loans from START precisely because they are *Shari'ah* compliant. Khan and Phillips (2010) interviewed 170 clients and found that more than a third of START's borrowers – 38 per cent to be exact – approached the organization for a loan primarily because it was compliant with their religious beliefs, with more than half of those interviewed – 55 per cent – stating that the Islamic nature of the loans had been a very important factor in their decision. However, local staff suggest that some borrowers are inclined to exaggerate the importance of religion and in fact apply for a START loan simply because it is cheaper than alternative interest-based loans. The same staff members did concede, however, that due to their religious beliefs a sizeable minority will *only* take *Shari'ah*-compliant loans and that this number is increasing as the number of practising Muslims grows and people become aware that such loans are available. Anecdotal evidence suggests that the number of practising

Muslims in Kosovo is still relatively small but increasing as people are more willing to openly embrace the culture and traditions of their past in the newly independent state. Several borrowers mentioned that they had previously taken out interest-based loans due to the lack of an alternative, but that they would be taking out only *Shari'ah*-compliant loans in the future now that they were available.

In line with Islamic teachings,[6] START does not apply any financial penalties to borrowers for late repayment – the outstanding debt remains the same. Despite this, borrowers do not appear to be tempted to delay repayments and the PAR30 is currently 4 per cent; this is similar to, and in several cases lower than, that of other interest-based MFIs that charge penalties for late repayment – most organizations commonly charge 0.5 per cent of the outstanding loan amount per day. Instead, in the relatively small number of cases when START's borrowers do not repay on time, loan officers call them by telephone to remind them that their repayment is overdue. Most borrowers then repay at this stage within a few days. If borrowers are late with their repayment instalment by more than one week, loan officers will visit them at their homes or business premises to ascertain the reason for non-repayment. If the loan officers establish that the borrower is experiencing difficulties and is unable to repay, then START, again inspired by Islamic teachings that encourage lenders to wait and grant borrowers extra time to repay,[7] simply waits without taking any further action.

At the beginning of 2014, however, START started using the services of private enforcement agents to enforce repayment in the very small number of cases where it was established, following a series of visits and consultations, firstly that borrowers were unwilling rather than unable to repay and secondly that they were also more than 180 days late in repaying. In such cases, all the charges incurred by the private enforcement agents are paid by borrowers; START recovers only the amount of the original debt owed without any penalty or late repayment charges. START has been extremely reluctant to seek legal redress, particularly since it can take months before local courts reach a verdict and even longer to enforce judgment.

There are a number of possible reasons why borrowers repay promptly, even when there is no financial penalty for late repayment. It is apparent that some borrowers feel obliged to repay loans because their religious values dictate the timely fulfilment of their contracts or repayment of debts.[8] Khan and Phillips (2010) found that 21 per cent of START's borrowers professed religious obligation as the prime motivation for repayment. Indeed, this extends to situations when a borrower passes away. In such circumstances, the policy of START is to write off any outstanding debt. However, it has invariably been the case that relatives of deceased borrowers have come forward and assumed responsibility for repaying any outstanding debt. On some occasions, particularly when relatives were poor, even village leaders have assumed this duty.[9] The majority of borrowers, though – 74 per cent to be precise – viewed repayment as a moral obligation and a matter of personal principle that one should not default on a contract.

Several staff and borrowers also noted that the repayment of debt was a cultural tradition among the Kosovar Albanian population.[10] What is significant is that exactly half of the borrowers asked stated that START's identity as a faith-based organization had a positive impact on their motivation to repay. Several also suggested that they wanted to support START as it was one of very few organizations providing *Shari'ah*-compliant loans in Kosovo and they wanted it to succeed. Borrowers did not exhibit any of the skepticism that has affected some Islamic finance providers elsewhere that the loans were not authentic or 'fully Islamic' and were instead simply 'interest-based loans rebranded' (Alim, 2014).

Local staff, while admitting that faith and cultural tradition do influence repayment, also stressed the importance of borrowers wishing to maintain their access to 'cheap' loans – as already highlighted, loans provided by START are far less expensive than those provided by other MFIs and commercial banks. Staff also felt that borrowers were motivated by the legal and financial consequences of default, something that several borrowers also acknowledged. Default would mean that their loans would remain outstanding on records held by the CRK, and would hinder their possibilities of obtaining credit elsewhere in the future. Indeed, such consequences lead to relatively high repayment rates across all MFIs in Kosovo.

It is also apparent that repayment is relatively high because START carefully selects and analyses loan applications and, as outlined previously, quickly addresses delayed repayments, with programme staff immediately visiting borrowers who do not repay promptly. Furthermore, in order to identify trustworthy borrowers, START has sometimes sought the assistance of local community or religious leaders, finding that such association with and, on occasion, pressure from local leaders can encourage borrowers to repay their loans on time. However, in most areas of Kosovo the relationship that START has established with local community leaders in identifying and selecting trustworthy borrowers and ensuring prompt repayment has been more effective and extensive than their relationship with religious leaders. Nevertheless, religious leaders have been effective, particularly in areas where they are well respected and religious observance is comparatively high.

Notes

1. Official government statistics record a lower figure as not all Serbs submit census data.
2. 'Kosova' rather than 'Kosovo' is the spelling most frequently used by the local Albanian population.
3. For further details, see AMIK's website at <www.amik.org>.
4. At the time of writing, 1 euro was equivalent to US$1.12.
5. Timi Invest is much smaller than START and, using local capital, attracts investors on the basis of profit and loss sharing.
6. The majority of Islamic scholars regard any charge on late payment as *riba* or usury and therefore *haram* or unlawful.

7. The *Qur'an* states: 'If the debtor is in difficulty, grant him time till it is easy for him to repay' (2:280).
8. Muslims are encouraged not to delay what is due to others nor take too long to pay it. Indeed, the person to whom the money is owed has the right to demand his or her money and to cancel the contract for the remaining time. The Prophet Muhammad (peace be upon Him) said 'procrastination [delay] in repaying debts by a wealthy person is injustice' (Sahih Bukhari, Volume 3, Book 37, Hadith 486).
9. It is the belief of Muslims that the soul of a believer is held hostage by his debt in his grave until it is paid off (Sahih Tirmidhi, Hadith 1078). In addition, it is reported that the Prophet Muhammad (peace be upon Him) refused to lead funeral prayers until the debt of the deceased man was repaid (Sahih Bukhari, Volume 3, Book 37, Hadith 488).
10. Under the Code, or *Kanun*, of Leke Dukagjini, which is the body of 'customary law' that has influenced the way in which Albanians have traditionally conducted their lives, a pledge must never be broken. In more recent years, staff conceded that the influence of the Code had weakened.

References

Alim, E.A. (2014) *Global Leaders in Islamic Finance: Industry Milestones and Reflections*, Singapore: John Wiley & Sons.

Khan, A.A. and Phillips, I. (2010) *The Influence of Faith on Islamic Microfinance Programmes*, Birmingham: Islamic Relief.

Pytkowska, J. and Spannuth, S. (2013) *The Risk of Over-indebtedness of MSE Clients in Kosovo: Results from a Comprehensive Assessment*, Luxembourg: European Fund for Southeast Europe.

World Bank Group in Kosovo (2015) *Country Snapshot, April 2015*, Prishtina: World Bank.

About the authors

Ajaz Ahmed Khan (khan@careinternational.org) is Senior Microfinance Adviser at CARE International, United Kingdom.

Vehbi Zeqiri (vehbi.zeqiri@start-finance.org) is Executive Director of START Microfinance Institution, Republic of Kosovo.

CHAPTER 4

The Islami Bank Bangladesh's Rural Development Scheme: 'need-based banking rather than greed-based micro-banking'?

Mohammed Kroessin

The Rural Development Scheme was started in 1995 and is operated as a separate rural poverty alleviation programme by the Islami Bank Bangladesh, the nation's largest Islamic banking institution and its most profitable private commercial bank. The scheme serves just under a million people in more than 18,000 villages throughout the country, and has almost 3,000 staff. Eighty per cent of its clients are women. The scheme is operated through groups in a similar way to the Grameen Bank, but the group meetings also use religious capital to leverage social development outcomes. Recoveries are over 99 per cent, although the scheme is not profitable because of its high transaction costs, but it continues to expand, which allows the bank to build a loyal future customer base.

Keywords: Bangladesh, Islami Bank, *murabaha*, rural poverty, urban poverty, *bai-muajjal, musawamah,* Grameen Bank, BRAC, social collateral

Over a quarter of Bangladesh's population of 150 million lives below the poverty line. The situation of the poor is made worse by the acute rural–urban economic disparity coupled with illiteracy and a lack of public healthcare and sanitation facilities. The country's economy is primarily agrarian with the vast majority living in rural areas. But the agricultural sector produces less than 20 per cent of the country's gross domestic product (GDP) whilst employing nearly half of the total labour force, whereas textiles and shipbuilding have become more important in recent years. Without investments, the agricultural sector is unable to provide any further scope for employment, resulting in an influx of the rural poor towards urban areas. Rural areas are therefore characterized by stagnant agriculture and inefficient cottage industry. Underemployment and unemployment are widespread, with vast human resources remaining unutilized due to lack of education, training, and investment and business opportunities, especially in rural areas. While the microcredit market is saturated, access to *Shari'ah*-compliant microfinance in the Muslim-majority country remains limited. The reasons for this are unclear but it appears that a growing number of affluent middle-class consumers have

http://dx.doi.org/10.3362/9781780449555.004

developed a demand for Islamic finance products that is not reflected in the micro-segment. Most Islamic products remain located within the secular development discourse, although the presence of *'shudh'* ('bank interest' in Bangla) is a concern for a small number of borrowers.

This is the context within which the Islami Bank Bangladesh Limited (IBBL) operates. It was founded with the major objective of supporting the establishment of an Islamic economy for balanced economic growth by ensuring the reduction of rural–urban disparity and the equitable distribution of income.[1] In view of the above, IBBL branches have been encouraged to invest their deposits in their respective areas, and in particular for the 'economic upliftment' of rural people. Accordingly, the Rural Development Scheme, the IBBL's Islamic microfinance programme, was introduced to cater for the investment needs of the agriculture and rural sector and to promote employment and other income-generating activities to alleviate poverty.

Origins, history, and mission of the Islami Bank

The IBBL's Rural Development Scheme (RDS) is perhaps the oldest and largest commercial Islamic microfinance programme in the world. As the first fully fledged Islamic bank in South Asia, the IBBL was founded in 1983 with start-up capital provided by the Jeddah-based Islamic Development Bank, a number of public and private banks and institutions from the Middle East, and key figures from the Bangladeshi business community.

The RDS is delivered as part of the IBBL's statutory and regulatory commitments to finance small and medium enterprises (SMEs), as required by the Bangladesh Bank, the central bank, for private commercial banks (PCBs). This segment of the banking industry has experienced massive growth since the roll-back of the nationalization of the finance sector, particularly since the pro-capitalist Ziaur Rahman (1977–81) and Ershad (1982–90) regimes. State-owned financial institutions focusing on industrial or agricultural lending are categorized as development finance institutions, while the well-known Grameen Bank, BRAC, and other microfinance institutions (MFIs) are not scheduled with the Bangladesh Bank and their operations are more flexible.

Although legally a PCB and supervised by the Bangladesh Bank, the IBBL sees itself as broadly a 'development finance institution', particularly with regard to its microfinance operations. This vision is, however, hampered by the fact that the IBBL is a scheduled bank and is therefore tightly regulated by the Bangladesh Bank in terms of outreach and capital adequacy and cannot compete with MFIs on equal terms.

For a number of years, the IBBL was, in profit terms, the largest private commercial bank in Bangladesh, double the size of the second largest bank. IBBL claims that it finances approximately 20 per cent of Bangladesh's exports and that a quarter of the foreign remittances received by the country are channelled through the bank; this makes it a significant player, particularly

Table 4.1 IBBL financial information

	Bangladeshi taka (millions)	US$ (millions)
Authorized capital	20,000.00	256.09
Paid-up capital	16,099.90	206.14
Equity	47,845.33	612.62
Reserve fund	27,879.72	356.97
Deposits	615,359.21	7,879.12
Investment (including investment in shares)	629,631.27	8,061.86
Foreign exchange business		
Import financing	343,668	4,400.36
Export financing	224,236	2,871.14
Remittances	321,066	4,110.96

Note: Figures as of 31 December 2015.

because 'manpower' exports and the ready-made garments industry play such an important role in the way in which Bangladesh has defined its own development success story. Its commercial success is also noteworthy because, compared with the state-owned banks, the IBBL, with just over 300 branches operated by some 11,000 staff in 2014, has only a fraction of their retail banking or venture capital exposure but manages nevertheless to be very profitable – so much so that it was the highest corporate tax payer in recent years. Table 4.1 provides key financial data on IBBL.

While the IBBL is a commercial bank, its objectives are wide-ranging. IBBL public documents state that the bank's stated mission is to:

> establish Islamic Banking through the introduction of a welfare oriented banking system and also ensure equity and justice in the field of all economic activities, achieve balanced growth and equitable development through diversified investment operations particularly in the priority sectors and less developed areas of the country. To encourage socio-economic upliftment and financial services to the low-income community particularly in the rural areas.

In an effort to realize its mission of development within an Islamic framework, the IBBL has two arms that carry out welfare and social development work: the Islami Bank Foundation and the RDS.

The Islami Bank Foundation, a charitable subsidiary of IBBL, runs a number of projects throughout the country that are archetypically Islamic in nature: education including *Madrassas*, free or highly subsidized healthcare, relief work, and Islamic propagation. Interestingly, it also provides financial hardship grants and runs an income-generation scheme through *qard hasan* or interest-free loans; these are separate from and in addition to the RDS microfinance programme.

In contrast to the social development dimension of the mission statement, the IBBL's financial vision is expressed in its annual reports in more technical terms:

> Our vision is to always strive to achieve superior financial performance, be considered a leading Islamic bank by reputation and performance.

> Our goal is to establish and maintain the modern banking techniques, to ensure the soundness and development of the financial system based on Islamic principles and to become [a] strong and efficient organization with highly motivated professionals, working for the benefit of people, based upon accountability, transparency and integrity in order to ensure stability of financial systems. We will try to encourage savings in the form of direct investment. We will also try to encourage investment, particularly in projects which are more likely to lead to higher employment.

The Rural Development Scheme's operational philosophy

While the Islami Bank's commercial lending is considerable and is geared around a policy of import substitution and job creation, the RDS is development-focused and works through outreach via the branch network to access a particular segment of the Bangladeshi economy and population: the rural poor. The Urban Poor Development Scheme (UPDS) also delivers microfinance in one branch in the Gandaria area on the outskirts of Dhaka and serves the local slum population. Despite the huge number of urban poor, this remains until now the only UPDS operation. This is partly because the IBBL's business strategy is to capture the SME market share in the capital, so most urban branches are located in middle-class areas or business districts. But it is also the IBBL's – and particularly their microfinance operation's – avowed objective to contribute to rural development. Overall, of the IBBL's nearly 300 branches, two-thirds are located outside the main urban centres, and most of them provide microfinance through the RDS.

Interestingly, although microfinance schemes are plentiful in the NGO sector in Bangladesh, commercial banks have been much less engaged. This is perhaps because the regulatory requirements for commercial banks compel them to administer microfinance programmes from their branches at district capital level, adding considerable transaction costs to branch-based outreach. In contrast, development finance institutions such as Grameen, BRAC, and ASA are allowed to base themselves directly at village level, which makes their services cheaper to deliver.

The RDS is deemed an important part of the bank's work, particularly vis-à-vis the IBBL's claim to being a welfare bank. In 2010–11, the IBBL had the largest loan portfolio focused on poverty alleviation among private and foreign banks. According to the Bangladesh Bank, IBBL disbursed more than Tk (Bangladesh taka) 2.29 bn (US$29.25 m) during the period, which is around 53 per cent of the total disbursement by the 40 PCBs and foreign commercial banks (FCBs) in the non-state banking sector. PCBs and FCBs together disbursed a total of Tk 4.05 bn (US$51.74 m), of which PCBs disbursed Tk 3.38 bn (US$43.18 m) and FCBs Tk 0.67 bn (US$8.56 m).[2] The bank's welfare credentials were underlined in a newspaper interview with the IBBL's managing director, Muhammad Abdul Mannan:

> Islami[c] banking always encourages using funds for reducing [the] gap between rich and the poor rather than resource centralization to a selected group of people. We always try to emphasize on need-based banking rather than greed-based banking.[3]

While essentially economic in nature, the RDS also has a strong social development approach, focusing on the promotion of Islamic values and religious practice. One of the aims of the RDS is to develop 'moral values' and create awareness about social rights and responsibilities. To this end, in the weekly meetings with clients, field officers deliver lectures on different topics from an Islamic perspective. An internal IBBL document states:

> At a very basic level the disbursement of collateral-free loans in certain instances is an example of how Islamic banking and microfinance share common aims. Thus Islamic banking and microcredit programmes may complement one another in both ideological and practical terms. This close relationship would not only provide obvious benefits for poor entrepreneurs who would otherwise be left out of credit markets, but investing in micro-enterprises would also give investors in Islamic banks an opportunity to diversify and earn solid returns. (IBBL, 2007)

This is also indicative of the dual aim of the RDS: on the ideological side, the promotion of Islamic ideals; and, on the commercial side, the selling of what is at best a marginally profitable product for the bank, which can earn much more in its foreign exchange or export finance businesses.

Since its launch in 1995, the RDS has worked with almost 5 million people. In 2015, the scheme provided microfinance services to nearly 1 million people in over 18,000 villages throughout the country (see Table 4.2). The programme embodies the ambitions of the more welfare-focused leaders of the IBBL, who would like the bank to be more of a development finance institution. Yet the commercial realities show that the programme is still only a small part of the bank's operations, despite a considerable year-on-year growth of between 50 and 100 per cent in the past few years. The overall volume of the RDS over the last few years has hovered around the 3 per cent mark. Also, despite the importance given to the RDS by most senior staff, the board envisages a slowing down of the expansion of the programme to a rate of 20 per cent in the coming years as it requires subsidies that may not be sustainable at such a scale and pace of growth.

Table 4.2 RDS operational information

Area coverage	
No. of branches handling the scheme	251
No. of villages (total no. of villages in the country is about 87,000)	18,810
No. of districts (total no. of districts in the country is 64)	64
No. of centres	28,740
No. of groups	177,796
No. of active clients (currently receiving finance)	560,357
Total no. of members (awaiting finance but participating in other activities including savings)	940,989
Percentage of women members in the scheme	79%
Average no. of members per centre	33
Financial statement (RDS and MEIS)	
Cumulative disbursement (since inception)	Tk 123,447.24 bn (US$1,576,476,297)
Present outstanding	Tk 19,262.58 bn (US$245,865,076)
Overdue	166.23 bn
Percentage of recovery	99.14%
Balance of members' savings (including centre fund)	6,617.04 bn
Staffing	
No. of field officers	2,478
No. of project officers	217
No. of zone officers	17

Note: Figures as of 31 December 2015.

The RDS also graduates successful clients into a Micro Enterprise Investment Scheme (MEIS) before moving them into a branch-based SME banking-focused service.

The Rural Development Scheme's lending and loan recovery modalities

The RDS portfolio is centrally managed by the IBBL Rural Development Division, which is headquartered in Dhaka, and is operated out of the IBBL branch network, which selects suitable villages within a 10 kilometre radius from the branch location with microfinance services provided off site. Selection criteria are:

- easy access for RDS loan officers, who are usually equipped with motorcycles;
- the presence of agriculture and other off-farm activities, as the RDS targets only the economically active;
- the prevalence of low-income people as defined in the target group parameters set out below.

After the primary selection of a project area consisting of four to six villages, the RDS officer conducts a detailed baseline survey to identify the target group and the types of economic activities in those areas. The branch involved has to ensure that at least 400 eligible participants can be identified in the selected area for service delivery to be operationally feasible.

People who have a loan from other MFIs or who are known to have defaulted are not eligible to become an RDS member. This means that the RDS reaches a particular client group which is currently underserved, either due to geography – although this is unlikely given the proliferation of microfinance in Bangladesh – or due to their unwillingness to engage with interest-based microloans.

Target group

The RDS, notably, is not serving the poorest of the poor and a number of minimum eligibility criteria – centred on asset ownership – exist:

- farmers with a land holding of no more than 0.5 acres;
- sharecroppers with consent from the landowners;
- people engaged in off-farm activities having no land or up to a maximum of 0.5 acres;
- people or farmers permanently residing in the selected villages;
- people with a derelict pond that is eligible for investment for re-excavation and fish cultivation;
- destitute women and distressed people, who will be provided with an investment for dairy cows, poultry, ducks, goats, etc. and other suitable off-farm activities for generating supplementary income.

Upon selection, small groups are formed consisting of five members, preferably of similar occupations. The members of the group select their group leader and deputy group leader to co-ordinate the group's activities. A senior branch official then visits to give formal recognition to the group and issues them with passbooks for the group bank account.

To support the RDS's operational efficiency, groups are formed into a 'centre' made up of a minimum of two to a maximum of eight groups. The group leaders under a particular centre select a centre leader and deputy centre leader from amongst themselves to co-ordinate the centre activities, which usually operate out of the centre leader's homestead. The centre has to conduct regular weekly meetings that are recorded in a resolution book along with signatures of the members; members who do not know to how to sign are encouraged to acquire some basic literacy skills. Attendance of the centre meetings is the first requirement for becoming a member of the scheme.

The centre meetings are conducted by the RDS field officers according to the following agenda:

- discussion of different Islamic topics such as moral values, social rights, and responsibilities;

- collection of investment instalments, personal savings, the centre fund, and other payments;
- appraisal and approval of investment proposals, and other discussions.

Investment clients are selected from the group members in the centre meeting and supplied with application forms and other related papers by the RDS officer, who also carries out the loan appraisal. On finalization of the investment application, the list of the selected clients, supported by their applications, is submitted to the branch manager for approval.

Each member of the group has to provide a guarantee against the investment of other members of the group, following the Grameen social collateral model; this holds all members responsible for recovering the defaulted amount and/or loss, if any. Clients are allowed to take an initial maximum investment of Tk 10,000 (US$145) eight weeks after they enrol as active members in the group. The highest amount of investment under the scheme is Tk 100,000 (U$1,450). While Grameen and others have since dropped the group guarantee, the RDS still operates it in principle, although the practice is interpreted through the Islamic requirement to be lenient to the debtor. RDS leadership believes that the mix of solidarity lending and instilling Islamic values assists the RDS to recover 99 per cent of all loans.

The scheme has been designed according to the *Shari'ah* principles of Islamic finance and primarily utilizes a cost plus sales contract called *bai-muajjal* or *musawamah*; this is similar to *murabaha* apart from the fact that there is no requirement to disclose the profit margin. There are 45 weekly deferred repayments. A one-off mark-up of 10 per cent on the sales price is set with 2.5 per cent waived for regular timely repayments. In pricing terms, this makes the *bai-muajjal* a slightly more attractive microfinance product compared with income-generating loans offered by, for example, the Grameen Bank, which charges an interest rate of 20 per cent per annum. While this is not a major difference, discerning clients who want to avoid *shudh* do find this a viable alternative.

Profit- and loss-sharing schemes such as equity investments (*mudaraba*) or full business partnerships (*musharaka*) were also introduced on an experimental basis in 2007, but the administration was deemed to be too cumbersome for most clients' accounting skills and too risky. These schemes exposed the bank to fraud due to the increased moral hazard when clients have to determine and declare the profit or loss that the investment or joint venture has generated. This is despite senior IBBL management statements that emphasize their eagerness to offer profit- and loss-sharing schemes, as such methods, in their eyes, represent the essence of Islamic finance.

However, a *musharaka* product remains available but is mainly offered to MEIS clients who have been graduated through the RDS and are engaged in more formal businesses. This product requires the development of basic accountancy skills and also physical collateral.

In investment under the RDS in *bai-muajjal* mode, where the goods' cost, quality, or suppliers cannot be determined earlier, the proposed goods

Table 4.3 Investment categories, durations, and ceilings

Sector	Duration	Ceiling of investment (BDT/Tk)	Equivalent (US$)
Crop production	1 year	25,000	318
Nursery and commercial production of flowers and fruit	1 year	50,000	635
Agriculture implements	1 to 3 years	50,000	635
Livestock	1 to 2 years	50,000	635
Poultry	1 year	35,000	445
Fisheries	1 to 2 years	50,000	318
Rural transport	1 year	20,000	254
Rural housing	1 to 5 years	50,000	635
Off-farm activities	1 year	50,000	635

are purchased and debited to the IBBL purchase account. After delivering the goods to the clients, the investment amount is adjusted in the IBBL purchase account. When the bank officials cannot go to the market to purchase the goods, the bank nominates a buying agent who hands over the goods to the client and notifies the bank. Only in exceptional circumstances does the RDS appoint the client as the agent, but group leaders may do so and can act on behalf of the IBBL if its staff cannot take physical possession of the goods. The bank also has a well-staffed *Shari'ah* secretariat that undertakes audit and spot checks to ensure that *Shari'ah* non-compliance risks are identified and dealt with effectively.

For most trades, the investment amount, along with the mark-up, has to be paid back by the clients in 45 equal weekly instalments per annual investment cycle, subject to the following maximum limits. Longer periods apply to some types of investment (see Table 4.3).

No physical collateral is required against investments under the scheme as the entire RDS has been designed around the concept of social collateral, which is practised within the IBBL's social development objectives. The strict group and centre structure and the social mobilization element are essential for the high recovery rate of over 99 per cent, but so is the fact that service users are carefully selected by bank officials. Besides, each member of the group gives a personal guarantee for other members of the same group and the members are jointly liable and responsible for the repayment of investments.

On the basis of the list submitted by the field officers, the Investment Committee of the IBBL branch carefully scrutinizes the applications and sanctions the investment at branch level. The Investment Committee consists of the manager, project officer, and field officer. After the investment is sanctioned, the branch completes the documentation formalities and then disburses the amount with the help of the investment officer and field officer.

In all cases, the branch must ensure strict adherence to banking and *Shari'ah* compliance policies.

The performance of investments under the scheme is fully supervised by the Rural Development Division at head office level but the branch has to take responsibility for the investment as well as recovery. To ensure good financial performance – in 2015 the scheme achieved a 99.14 per cent recovery rate – the field officers intensively supervise the client, which further strengthens the pressure of the group collateral approach. This means that the RDS is very labour intensive and therefore high in transaction costs, given the relatively small loan sizes.

Each member of the group has to deposit a minimum of Tk 2 (about US$0.25) per week into the centre fund. This fund is kept by opening a *mudaraba* savings account in the name of the respective centre, and it is utilized for the welfare of the members by way of an interest-free or *qard hasan* loan for emergency spending needs on the basis of the decision of the centre in the weekly meeting; this is similar to the practice of other MFIs. Any unused savings are subject to the IBBL's profit payout on *mudaraba* investments.

One field officer looks after a client portfolio of up to 400 clients, while an additional assistant officer or officer is engaged in the branch as a project officer to supervise the activities of the field officers. One or more officials in each zonal office is assigned as an RDS zone officer to supervise the scheme activities of the branches within the zone. The zone officers visit the branches in their respective zones at least twice a year. Moreover, head office officials also visit branches to inspect field activities once a year.

Weekly, monthly, quarterly, and annual statements of the performance of the RDS at each branch are submitted to the Bangladesh Bank and the Microfinance Regulatory Authority so that activities can be monitored and evaluated regularly.

Shari'ah compliance

As an Islamic bank, the IBBL's RDS is also under the purview of its internal *Shari'ah* governance framework, which is operationalized by the IBBL *Shari'ah* Secretariat and overseen by the *Shari'ah* Supervisory Committee (SSC). The SSC is responsible for framing and implementing policy for *Shari'ah* compliance in the bank. As per the Islamic banking guidelines circulated by Bangladesh Bank, the SSC is represented by 12 members consisting of prominent Islamic scholars with adequate knowledge of *Fiqh ul Mu'amalat* (Islamic commercial law), renowned lawyers, and eminent economists. The SCC of the IBBL gives opinions and guidelines to implement and comply with *Shari'ah* principles in all activities of the bank, particularly in the modes of investment. The SCC is governed by by-laws approved by the board of directors.

As part of the major responsibilities of the SSC, *Shari'ah* inspections are also conducted in all the branches under its direct supervision to ensure

Shari'ah compliance in all activities of the bank, including the operations of the RDS.

The IBBL is also the founding member of the Islami Banks Consultative Forum and the Central *Shari'ah* Board for Islamic Banks in Bangladesh, which includes PCBs and also state-owned banks. It does not, however, extend to any other Islamic MFIs apart from Islamic Relief Bangladesh, as the Islamic microfinance sector is still very small.

Sustainability

The IBBL's RDS is still relatively small as far as the IBBL's balance sheet is concerned and is only marginally profitable at best. However, the bank's management has targeted the RDS as one of its intended growth areas, particularly because, after 'graduation', new customers can be introduced to the more commercially focused products the bank has to offer. Since the RDS is embedded operationally within the branch structure of the IBBL, it is difficult to ascertain operational sustainability data as the overheads are not included in the operating expense figures; a publication by the Asian Development Bank (Charironenko and Rahman, 2002) makes a very brief assessment of the RDS, concluding that 'it is unclear whether or not IBBL's microfinance activities are sustainable'. However, the *raison d'être* for the IBBL's RDS, which has been operational since 1995, is important. While it might be a loss-leader or part of the bank's corporate social responsibility programme due to its close links with the Islami Bank Foundation, it also appears to serve a broader religious purpose – that of the Islamization of society through its economy, similar to the ideological commitments that underpin other development strategies.

Beneficiaries

The typical IBBL RDS client is a smallholder in a rural part of Bangladesh, with financing eligibility criteria centring on landownership. There is an upper landownership limit of 0.5 acres of cultivable land, although sharecroppers are also eligible. The RDS targets the 'able-bodied and industrious' rural poor rather than those the programme sees as the 'hard-core poor', who do not possess any assets, business acumen, or vocational skills and are not economically active – despite the RDS's overtly pro-poor ambitions.

The typical client should also be engaged in small off-farm activities in rural areas. Seventy-nine per cent of clients are female, although the MEIS, established in 2005, offers a higher credit ceiling and therefore attracts mainly male entrepreneurs.

The Rural Development Scheme: material or spiritual growth? Or both?

In spite of the Islamic terminology, the RDS is very closely based on the Grameen Bank model of social collateral lending, and its technical development has been led by a former Grameen employee. But the RDS has made the group lending approach its own, by bestowing Islamic legitimacy on it through the use of scriptural references. 'The cardinal principle of the Rural Development Scheme,' an internal document states, 'is the "Group Approach". *Allah* loves those "who conduct their affairs by mutual consultation"' (*Qur'an* 42:38). For all decision-making activities, this mutual consultation is given high priority.'

Importantly, as noted above, the scheme carries an Islamic educational dimension for the clients; in the weekly meetings officiated by RDS field officers, discussion of different Islamic topics is given priority over the collection of instalments and personal savings. The RDS's approach is seen as an enhanced microcredit model that does not just address material needs but also clearly has a spiritual dimension. With the clients organized into centres, each meeting starts with a recitation from the *Qur'an* and concludes with *Dua* (supplication) led by the IBBL officer and a collective chanting of the 18 commandments, listed in Box 4.1 below.

The RDS commandments are taken from Grameen's '16 Decisions', albeit with some changes. These changes primarily seek to Islamize the '16 Decisions' by stressing the need to rely ultimately on *Allah* (commandments 1 and 5) – in contrast to the Grameen self-reliance model – while, for example, the family planning element that is integral to Grameen is deemed as un-Islamic and hence has been removed.

This type of Islamic education, while not in itself problematic within the context of the social mobilization of clients in a Muslim-majority country, may be problematic for the small number of clients from the Hindu community. In these cases, Hindu ethical teachings are utilized in the motivational dimension of the RDS. The bank targets non-Muslims as clients in order for it to be seen as impartial.

At the same time, the RDS management is also keen to plug into the Western mainstream discourse by relating the scheme to rural development. This is also relevant because the development field in Bangladesh is very obviously dominated by the big brands such as Grameen and BRAC. By branding the RDS in English, couched in the ubiquitous language of rural development, the IBBL clearly seeks a connection with this wider field. At the local level, the RDS uses the Bangla term '*unnayan*', which means development – an expression also utilized by secular organizations. Intentionally, there is no use of Arabic or Islamic terminology, although other IBBL bank products are clearly labelled as Islamic.

Moreover, the IBBL is very sensitive about branding and creating associations through what is acceptable in official policy terms. Most of its regular non-micro commercial financial products are labelled in clear Islamic terms, such as the IBBL '*Murabaha* savings account', in order to appeal to the large consumer base that values *Shari'ah* banking. This is a difficult strategy for the IBBL because the state of Bangladesh is committed to Islamic finance but the current Awami League government is hostile to Islamic political movements. This may be dangerous

---

Box 4.1 The 18 commandments for RDS members

The members of the RDS memorize and utter loudly the 18 decisions at the centre meeting in order to implement them in their practical lives. The decisions are memorized after becoming a member and before any investment. This is considered a precondition of RDS investment.

We shall:

1. seek help of *Allah*, the Almighty, in all conditions of life, speak truth, and lead an honest life;
2. order others to do good deeds and prohibit them from doing bad deeds;
3. be law abiding, not do illegal work, and not allow others to do the same;
4. not remain dependent on others, rather stand on our own feet;
5. bring prosperity to our family, *Insha'Allah*;
6. grow vegetables in the surroundings of our house, eat plenty of them, and enhance our income by selling the surplus;
7. during the plantation season, plant as many seedlings as possible;
8. not remain illiterate, and establish a night school if necessary;
9. arrange education for the children;
10. help each other and try to rescue any member of the centre from danger, if any;
11. give preference to others, compete in good deeds, and encourage others in this;
12. build and use sanitary latrines, but, if this is not possible, build latrine digging holes;
13. drink water from the tube well, or otherwise drink boiled water;
14. keep our children and environment clean;
15. take care of our health and eat a balanced diet;
16. not take or give any dowry at our sons' and daughters' weddings and tell others that this creates a social problem;
17. follow discipline, unity, courage, and hard work in all areas of our lives;
18. keep our promises (*Wadah*) to others, not embezzle the deposit (*Amanah*), and never tell a lie.

Source: IBBL (n.d.).

---

for the IBBL, which is regarded as being close to the opposition Jamaat-e-Islami political party.

In this sense, the vision for development has been recast by the IBBL. While its commercial banking operations are driven technically by Islamic ideology and offer retail banking products that, judging by their commercial success, resonate with the wider public, it is in fact its rural development work that is explicitly committed to *Shari'ah*-compliant social development. Through an emphasis on Islamic values, prayer, and fasting, which become part and parcel of receiving a loan, the scheme is creating its own power relationship with clients. Given the saturation of microfinance, this makes the RDS an interesting consumer choice, and it has the added advantage that the most popular product is slightly cheaper than credits from comparable conventional MFIs.

Hence, the IBBL combines a range of features that make it not only a commercially very successful financial institution but also a social development agency by using programmatic interventions that are designed to promote economic development based on social transformation led by *Shari'ah*-compliant financial inclusion.

Notes

1. For further information, see IBBL's website at <www.islamibankbd.com/rds/index.php>.
2. *The Financial Express*, 'IBBL disbursement tops poverty alleviation drive', 6 June 2011.
3. Ibid.

References

Charironenko, S. and Rahman, S.M. (2002) *Commercialization of Microfinance*, Manila: Asian Development Bank.
IBBL (2007) 'Grameen Bank vs RDS of the IBBL', internal document, Dhaka: Rural Development Division, Islami Bank Bangladesh Limited (IBBL).
IBBL (n.d.) 'Rural Development Scheme', internal document, Dhaka: Islami Bank Bangladesh Limited (IBBL).

About the author

Mohammed Kroessin (mohammed.kroessin@irworldwide.org) is Head of Islamic Microfinance, Islamic Relief Worldwide. Note: this chapter is written in a private capacity and does not necessarily reflect the views and opinions of Islamic Relief Worldwide. Mohammed worked with the IBBL's Rural Development Scheme during his PhD research in 2008.

CHAPTER 5

Providing an Islamic alternative: the experience of Mutahid in Afghanistan

Hashmatullah Mohmand

Mutahid is a wholly owned subsidiary of MISFA, the Microfinance Investment Support Facility for Afghanistan, and was established in 2011. It was started because a survey by MISFA showed that there was a strong demand for Islamic financial products that was not satisfied by existing microfinance institutions that provide interest-based loans. It has been wholly financed by MISFA, using donated funds from a number of sources. Mutahid operates in six of Afghanistan's 34 provinces, focusing on Kabul and the north-east of the country. Since its establishment it has served almost 14,000 clients. Mutahid offers both conventional interest-based loans and Islamic loans. In mid-2015, there were 2,000 clients who had received Islamic loans, of whom about 7 per cent were women.

Keywords: Afghanistan, Murabaha, MISFA, *salam, ijarah*

Introduction

This case study describes the origins and evolution of Mutahid, a microfinance institution (MFI) sponsored by the Microfinance Investment Support Facility for Afghanistan (MISFA), to test and demonstrate the feasibility of *Shari'ah*-compliant microfinance in Afghanistan. It documents the effectiveness and overall lessons learned during the development, pilot, and implementation phases of providing *murabaha* loans on both an individual and a group basis. It also identifies key differences in the nature, processes, and results of the *murabaha* product compared with interest-based loans. Mutahid's staff from the main office in Kabul and from the Taimani and Chaman branches in Kabul and Herat provinces were interviewed in some detail for the purposes of this case study. Fifteen clients in Kabul and Herat were also interviewed. These clients had a variety of businesses, including beauty parlours, grocery shops, bakeries, carpentry workshops, garments and clothing shops, mobile phone and phone credit retailers, electric equipment suppliers, tailors, and painters and decorators.

   MISFA is an apex organization that was established in 2003 as a vehicle through which the Afghan government and international donors could channel technical assistance and funding to build Afghanistan's microfinance

http://dx.doi.org/10.3362/9781780449555.005

sector. Two key objectives in MISFA's strategic plan (2013–15) were to strengthen microfinance sector leadership and to promote inclusive finance in Afghanistan, including through research, development, and innovation.

MISFA commissioned a study to assess the demand for Islamic financial products; this was conducted by the Afghanistan Public Policy Research Organization in August 2011 in Herat, Jalalabad, Kabul, and Mazar-e-Sharif. The research found that there were strong and widespread objections to paying interest on loans, and also support for Islamic financial arrangements from religious leaders and community elders. One of the recommendations of the study was for MISFA and its partner MFIs to consider developing and piloting an Islamic product. MISFA decided to design and then to introduce the Islamic microfinance product with Mutahid, considered one of its more progressive MFI members and one that had in fact been started by MISFA itself.

Mutahid Development Finance Institution

Mutahid Development Finance Institution was established in April 2011 and is a subsidiary of MISFA. Mutahid, which means 'united', was formed in order to combine and consolidate the best components of six earlier MFIs into one organization, and to salvage the significant investments that had been made in these six institutions during the period prior to 2011. Mutahid itself has only ever received funding from MISFA since it was established and it generates income from disbursing loans. MISFA is considering establishing Mutahid as an independent entity and, at the time of writing, the by-laws and articles of incorporation are being developed. In the future, Mutahid will look for other sources of funding.

Mutahid aims to offer financial services and create opportunities for Afghan entrepreneurs, through an operationally self-sustainable and innovative development finance institution. Mutahid provides microfinance services in six provinces, namely Kabul, Herat, Mazar, Kunduz, Takhar, and Badakhshan. It offers five types of loans: *murabaha* group loans, *murabaha* individual loans, conventional interest-based individual loans, conventional interest-based group loans, and loans for small- and medium-sized enterprises. Only the first two categories are *Shari'ah* compliant; the remainder are interest based. As of the end of June 2015, Mutahid had 13,952 active clients of which 3,310 were women. The total number of *murabaha* clients was 1,956, of which 141 were women. All the clients for both *murabaha* and conventional finance are managed by 277 staff members of whom 152 are women.

Mutahid supplies 5 per cent of the Afghan microfinance market, based on the size of its outstanding loan portfolio. Its gross loan portfolio amounted to AFN (Afghanistan afghani) 403 m, or about US$6.72 m,[1] at the end of the second quarter of 2015. This represents an increase of 44 per cent compared with the corresponding period in 2014. The portfolio at risk greater than 30 days (PAR30) decreased from 3.8 per cent in January 2014 to 2.5 per cent in

January 2015. The increase in the gross loans portfolio and decrease in PAR30 indicate that there is a high potential to attract new clients in 2016 and beyond. The positive growth continued despite an overall recession in Afghanistan's gross domestic product (GDP), which contracted from 14.4 per cent in 2012 to 2 per cent in 2014. Mutahid's *murabaha* product loan portfolio was AFN 63 m (US$1.05 m), or 15.5 per cent of its total portfolio.

Murabaha loans

MISFA supported the development of Mutahid's and Afghanistan's first *Shari'ah*-compliant microfinance loan product. After much consideration and consultation, Mutahid decided to offer *murabaha* finance. Under this arrangement, Mutahid purchases whatever tangible assets the client requires from appropriate suppliers and then resells them to the client at a predetermined price with the addition of a profit margin or mark-up. The client is then required to repay Mutahid in specific instalments.

The main advantage of *murabaha*, when compared with other modes of Islamic finance, is that it is fairly easy for all parties to understand and manage – it is, in fact, very similar to a conventional trading transaction made on credit. The profit rate is fixed during the term of the finance, and the client knows the amount of profit mark-up and the amounts and timing of the instalments at the time of signing the contract. It also ensures that loans are used only for the purpose that is stated by the client.

Mutahid offers two kinds of *murabaha* product. Initially, it launched the *murabaha* individual loan in Herat in January 2013 and in Kabul some three months later. In January 2014, it launched the *murabaha* group loan in Kabul, in Herat in November 2014, and in Mazar-e-Sharif, Kunduz, and Takhar provinces in May 2015. The group *murabaha* loan is similar to the individual *murabaha* product but differs in that it does not require property collateral. MISFA provided the resources to research and develop the policy and operational details of both types of *murabaha* product. The number of *murabaha* clients in Herat and Kabul was 211 and 1,745 respectively as of the end of June 2015. This number had increased by an average of 20 per cent per quarter since January 2015.

Although the Islamic products are integrated into Mutahid's operations, the group and individual *murabaha* borrowers are serviced by a special team of field staff who are separate from the staff who service the other, more numerous clients who are using non-Islamic products. As of the end of June 2015, MISFA had provided a total of AFN 517 m, or just under US$6 m, to finance the development of the *murabaha* products, their staffing, and the loan portfolio itself.

Mutahid's *murabaha* loan products were the first *Shari'ah*-compliant microfinance products to be offered in Afghanistan, and Mutahid was the first organization to receive approval from the Afghanistan Scholar Council (ASC), an independent entity of Islamic scholars supported by the government of

Afghanistan. After the product development and policy documents for the *murabaha* loan products were developed, they were submitted to the ASC for review and approval. The documents included proposals for *bai salam* or advance purchase and *ijarah* or leasing as well as for *murabaha*. The ASC approved the *murabaha* and *bai salam* products after a 20-day reviewing process, and recommended some changes for the *ijarah* product, which would have to be resubmitted for later approval. Mutahid's management decided to postpone the launch of the *ijarah* product and launched the *murabaha* product in Herat and Kabul. Mutahid also formed its own internal *Shari'ah* supervisory board to review and monitor the *murabaha* products to ensure that they continued to adhere to *Shari'ah* rules and principles.

Loan approval and disbursal procedures

The application and approval procedures for Mutahid's individual and group *murabaha* loans are similar. When a client visits Mutahid, he or she first approaches the customer service officer, who fills out a 'comprehensive financial service form'. This form has 10 sections which are divided into two categories. The first category records the client's personal information, including the home address, contact details, enterprise information, financial position, and the financial service requested. The second category follows the checklist of eligibility (see Box 5.1), which is reproduced below. Some business owners are illiterate – particularly women – but Mutahid's staff assist clients in completing the necessary documentation and also explain loan details and procedures.

The following flow chart (Figure 5.1) summarizes the process, from the moment a client approaches Mutahid to the delivery of the asset that is being financed.

A *murabaha* individual loan can be from a minimum of AFN 50,000 to a maximum of AFN 250,000 (about US$830 to US$4,130) in the first cycle, depending on a client's financial capacity. The maximum loan for the second cycle and beyond is AFN 500,000 (approximately US$8,330). Individual borrowers must provide a title deed of a property as collateral and must also have one guarantor who agrees to pay the debt in case the client defaults. They must also provide copies of their business registration documents. The loan must be approved by Mutahid's Credit and Risk Assessment Committees. In the case of a new client, the branch manager must check formally in writing with local MFIs to ensure that clients do not borrow from two MFIs simultaneously. Each individual *murabaha* loan transaction takes an average of between five and 10 working days to analyse and complete. The paperwork at Mutahid can be completed within four to five days, but it takes longer to complete the attestation process and for the client to obtain title deeds and other documents.

Murabaha group loans are given to groups of between two and six members. The loan limit for group loans is from a minimum AFN 10,000 to a maximum of AFN 50,000 (about US$160 to US$830) per group member in the first cycle.

Box 5.1 Eligibility criteria checklist

1. Client is not an employee of MISFA or Mutahid.
2. Client agrees to approved amount if reduced (from initial loan requested) and has no outstanding amount due.
3. Client has own or a relative's national identity document.
4. Financing request is for own enterprise only; applicant's age is between 18 and 60 years; applicant is in good health.
5. If group borrower: group has to have two to six client members; one-third must be above 30 years old.
6. If group borrower: members must agree to guarantee each other's loans.
7. Any relationship with MISFA or Mutahid staff must be disclosed.
8. Checks must be carried out with *Shura* (community leaders), *Wakil* (head of district council), and neighbours.
9. Client's enterprise must not be in the exclusion list, such as liquor or gambling; client's residence and enterprise must be verified.
10. Residence must be checked by sight of electricity or cleaning bill.
11. If individual borrower: title deed must be checked.
12. Guarantor must have a fixed enterprise premises, and must be capable of repaying the loan.
13. Guarantor has ID; guarantor's residence and enterprise must be verified.
14. Guarantor must not be a relative of the client or of Mutahid or MISFA staff.

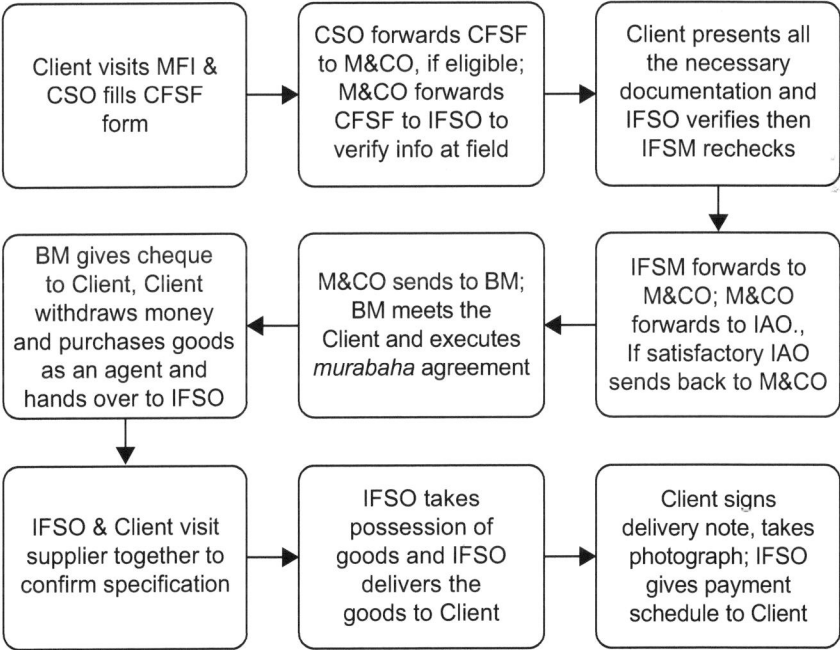

Figure 5.1 The *murabaha* process from client approach to asset delivery
Note: AM = Area Manager; BM = Branch Manager; CFSF = Comprehensive Financial Service Form; CSO = Customer Service Officer; IAO = Internal Audit Officer; IFSM = Islamic Finance Service Manager; IFSO = Islamic Finance Service Officer; M&CO = Monitoring and Compliance Officer; MFI = Microfinance Institution.

After the first cycle has been satisfactorily completed, the loan ceiling can increase by AFN 20,000 or US$330 per cycle up to a maximum amount of loan for each group member of AFN 100,000 (about US$1,670); this will amount to a total of AFN 600,000 (US$10,000) for six group members. Group *murabaha* loans do not need Credit Committee approval or the title deed of a property; the clients guarantee each other and only one other external guarantor is needed. Approval takes between three and six working days depending on the group members' ability to submit the necessary documents.

The approval of initial and subsequent group *murabaha* loans depends on previous loan repayment history and fulfilment of Mutahid's loan utilization policy. If one group member's loan repayment has been delayed for more than 30 days in 12 months, or if two loan repayments are delayed for more than seven days in 12 months, then subsequent loan applications are rejected. Similarly, if loan repayment is delayed for more than 12 days in 12 months, or one loan repayment is delayed by more than seven days in 12 months, no increases are allowed in loan sizes.

The approval process for conventional interest-based loan products is shorter than for *murabaha* for several reasons. The Islamic finance service officer (IFSO) is not involved, and there is no need to verify product specifications and quotations, to purchase products, sign delivery agreements, or take photographs of the products. Only two guarantors are needed when the loan amount is higher than AFN 40,000 in the first cycle. The client is usually able to obtain a loan within three to five days, but in certain cases finding two guarantors may delay the process. The mark-up or profit rates for both *murabaha* and conventional interest-based products are 15 per cent. However, an extra administrative expense of 2 per cent is charged for conventional interest-based loans. The profit margin on the *murabaha* products amounts to an annual equivalent of 26.6 per cent if the loans were based on fixed interest.

Comprehensive policy documents have been produced for the *murabaha* loan product; these provide step-by-step guidance to Mutahid's staff members. Process flow diagrams and application tracking systems track the flow of the complete transaction, so that staff members can be held accountable for each stage of the overall client support process.

IFSOs are responsible for collecting loan repayments from *murabaha* borrowers. They receive monthly summarized lists of the clients showing each client's loan repayment status. The maximum loan repayment period is 12 months, and the IFSOs are key to ensuring that *murabaha* loans are repaid promptly. They generally telephone the clients two to three days before each repayment is due, or visit them personally to remind them to make their loan repayments. The procedure for loan repayments is similar for both Islamic and conventional loans. If clients do not make a payment on time, the usual approach is to call the guarantors, since, in most cases, they are close friends of the borrowers.

Murabaha group clients deposit their repayments in 'express pay' machines that are available in different locations in Kabul; they can also pay through their mobile phones. This mobile service is provided by Roshan telecommunications company using the M-Paisa system, but most clients prefer the former method as they receive a paper receipt. Individual clients make their repayments by depositing the money in a designated local bank.

Client perceptions about *murabaha* and conventional products differ in Kabul and Herat. A third of borrowers who were surveyed in Kabul and two-thirds of those in Herat stated that they would be totally unwilling to take conventional loans on religious grounds. On average, over half of all clients took this position; the difference between the two cities may be caused by the more conservative religious attitudes in Herat. Half of the individual loan borrowers and a third of those who had taken group loans complained about the lengthy loan approval process, but group borrowers were much more satisfied with the procedures for second and subsequent loans. The majority of group and individual borrowers were satisfied with the loan repayment methods. Most of the borrowers of both group and individual *murabaha* loans said that they planned to take out further loans.

The case studies in Boxes 5.2 and 5.3 describe the contrasting.

Approximately 7 per cent of the *murabaha* clients in Kabul and Herat are women, compared with 21 per cent of conventional clients. The main reason for this is that most women are involved in part-time, informal home-based businesses and they do not buy large quantities of supplies from regular suppliers in the same way as most male business people do. They prefer to receive cash loans so that they can buy raw materials as and when they need them – with *murabaha* loans they have to buy the full amount of the raw materials being financed at the time they get the loan. It has also been suggested that fewer women take out loans from Mutahid because the 15 per cent mark-up is too high for their small part-time, home-based businesses. Women may also find it harder to find qualified guarantors, and they often want to start new businesses rather than expand existing ones. Mutahid is generally reluctant to lend for start-ups because of the high failure rates.

It is often the case that male borrowers use their wives or other female relatives as channels for microfinance loans, in order to benefit from the preference that some institutions give to female borrowers and also to avoid being identified as multiple borrowers from more than one institution. Mutahid's stringent procedures for loan appraisal minimize this practice.

Not many very poor people apply for *murabaha* loans. Out of a total of 1,956 *murabaha* clients, only 35 – less than 2 per cent – have taken the minimum amount of AFN 16,000 (approximately US$270). In contrast, a slightly higher proportion of borrowers of conventional interest-based loans have taken this amount. The average loan at Mutahid is AFN 28,900, or nearly US$500; regardless of whether the loans are Islamic or not, many extremely poor people may prefer not to borrow because they believe, probably correctly, that getting into debt is more likely to hurt than to help them.

Box 5.2 Mutahid's approach to recovering an unpaid loan

Hussain approached Mutahid for an individual *murabaha* loan of AFN 200,000 (approximately US$3,30) to expand his bread-baking business in Herat. He received the goods and his business flourished. Initially he paid the instalments on time but after three months he started to delay his payments and after five months the repayments stopped altogether. He had sold his business without informing Mutahid and had disappeared. The Mutahid IFSO responsible visited his home but his wife was not willing to co-operate. The officer also visited Hussain's guarantor, but he was not willing to repay either. It transpired that Hussain had closed his business premises and had left Afghanistan for Iran. The officer and the local Herat branch manager then called on the guarantor who had provided a title deed as collateral. After several visits by Mutahid staff, the guarantor made three payments in order to avoid losing his house. He was not able, however, to repay the remaining four instalments. The guarantor, with the support of Mutahid's staff, then visited the local community leader and other members of Hussain's group. Through continuous dialogue and consultation over a period of three months, the community as a whole finally agreed to collect the necessary money out of charity for Hussain's family. Eventually, Mutahid successfully recovered the full debt. This strict approach may have caused some hardship for the borrower's family and the guarantor, but it demonstrates the efforts Mutahid's staff are willing to make to recover loans, and the strength of community commitment to avoid the stigma of unpaid debts. After this incident, Mutahid introduced a more detailed assessment of the assets of potential clients and guarantors.

Box 5.3 Business success following a *murabaha* loan

Khawani was only 14 years old when his father was killed. Subsequently, Khawani and his family sought refuge in Pakistan. When they returned to Afghanistan in 2003, Khawani found employment as a truck driver and earned enough income to support his family. However, as the transport industry started scaling down with the gradual withdrawal of foreign troops from the country, Khawani opened a grocery shop near his home but lacked capital to buy and stock a variety of items. He was approached by a Mutahid loan officer who was publicizing their services. In order to conform with his religious beliefs, Khawani decided to opt for a *murabaha* loan and received AFN 200,000 (approximately US$3,30). After investing his loan he believes that his business has improved. 'When I received the loan, my working capital increased from US$6,000 to almost US$10,000 and so did my profits. My daily sales are more than AFN 10,000, of which 20 per cent is net profit.' According to Khawani, his monthly net profit exceeds AFN 60,000 (approximately US$1,000). He is now 28 years old and has three sons and a daughter. He can afford to send two of his school-aged children to a private school in the hope that they will be able to get a good education and complete their studies, in contrast to Khawani, who only managed to study until fourth grade.

Marketing and modifications

Various marketing techniques have been used by Mutahid to increase the general public's awareness of the *murabaha* product. IPSOs call regularly on potential clients and distribute leaflets to shops and homes, and, as might be expected, most clients find out from friends or relatives. Mutahid also puts up poster advertisements, and its staff meet members of urban district councils and local religious leaders or *mullahs* and tell them about their Islamic loans. *Mullahs* are very influential, as some clients visit them to seek advice on the type of loans they should access. Approximately a third of *murabaha* clients who were surveyed said that they had rejected conventional interest-bearing loans after consulting their *mullah*.

Mutahid measures its branches' performance against an annual work plan, and each branch manager prepares a monthly plan with weekly and monthly targets for each loan officer. The targets include the number of new *murabaha* clients it aims to attract, the value of funds to disburse, and the number of potential clients to visit in order to promote new clients for *murabaha* loans. MISFA itself, as the parent and owner of Mutahid and as the initiator of the Islamic loans, assesses and monitors loan disbursement and collection on a monthly basis. MISFA also carries out an annual evaluation and makes specific recommendations for the improvement, marketing, and management of loans.

As may be clear from the above description of the loan approval processes for both the individual and the group *murabaha* loans, the procedures were in need of simplification. A number of changes were introduced in 2014 and 2015 to reduce the paperwork involved and loan-processing times, but also to motivate more clients to apply. The number of guarantors was reduced from two to one, and clients were required only to obtain and submit one rather than three separate attested property valuations. It is also no longer always required that property dealers should do the evaluations, or that the location and value should always be attested by district council members. One of Mutahid's IFSOs, along with her or his team leader, can now ask a client's neighbour to do this, and then the local *mullah* can attest to the home's location and valuation.

A major change has also been made to the process whereby Mutahid ascertains the value of the goods that its *murabaha* clients want to purchase with their loans. IFSOs used to have to get quotations from three different suppliers and then select the lowest bid. This stage of the process has been handed over to the clients. Each client acts temporarily as an 'agent' of Mutahid, in order to maintain the formal requirement of *murabaha* that goods should first be purchased by the financial institution and then resold to the client. The client selects the best quotation from a supplier whom he or she already knows, and passes this information to Mutahid. The client then ceases to be an agent and reverts to their normal role. Mutahid then purchases the specified goods from that particular supplier and resells them to the client.

Mutahid's *murabaha* lending has been extended from two to six provinces over the last two years. The loan portfolio and the number of clients have both increased. The *murabaha* product processes have been greatly simplified, and clients are more satisfied with the streamlined application procedure and associated services. The customer base is growing, and Mutahid's Islamic supervisory board ensures that its activities are aligned with Islamic rules and principles. They are also trying to reach down to poorer and more vulnerable people, particularly women. The *murabaha* products are filling an important niche in the microfinance market for clients who, because of their religious convictions, will access only *Shari'ah*-compliant services.

Note

1. The US$ – Afghani exchange rate fluctuates, but the rate used in this case study is AFN 60 = US$1.

About the author

Hashmatullah Mohmand (hashmatullah.mohmand@misfa.org.af) is Knowledge Management Specialist at Microfinance Investment Support Facility for Afghanistan (MISFA).

CHAPTER 6

The *murabaha* syndrome: Reef and Islamic microfinance in Palestine

Ajaz Ahmed Khan and Mohammed Elayyan

Reef Finance is a microfinance institution from Palestine that was established in 2008. It aims to improve the livelihoods of rural Palestinians by providing financial services. It has expanded quickly and now has nine offices in the West Bank and Gaza serving almost 3,000 clients and an outstanding loans portfolio of over US$9 m. The vast majority of its loans are made on the basis of murabaha *and most borrowers are small-scale farmers.*

Keywords: Palestine, Reef Finance, West Bank, Gaza, *murabaha, manfa'a, musharaka*

Introduction

Reef Finance is an Islamic microfinance institution (MFI) from Palestine. In this investigation we explore the development of the organization and describe in detail how its loans are structured and disbursed. We draw upon information provided directly by Reef Finance and by Sharakeh, the Palestinian Network for Small and Microfinance, and gathered through extended interviews and discussions with the staff and borrowers of Reef Finance, as well as other microfinance providers in Palestine, during the first half of 2016.

Although the first microloans in Palestine were provided in the 1980s by non-governmental organizations and funded largely by grants from international aid organizations, it was not until the Palestine Monetary Authority (PMA) assumed responsibility for licensing and overseeing the operations of banks and MFIs in 1995 that the provision of microfinance increased significantly. At the beginning of 2016 there was a total of 16 banks and 10 MFIs in Palestine. However, despite at least 80 per cent of the population being categorized as Muslims, Islamic microfinance has limited outreach and offers only a narrow range of services. Reef Finance is the only fully fledged Islamic MFI and there are just two Islamic banks: the Arab Islamic Bank and the Palestine Islamic Bank.

Although there are three other MFIs that provide Islamic loans, in each case only a minority of the organization's borrowers access Islamic finance. Palestine for Credit and Development (Faten), the largest MFI in Palestine

http://dx.doi.org/10.3362/9781780449555.006

with an outstanding loans portfolio of US$82.7 m and 31,575 active clients, started providing Islamic loans in 2005 and approximately 19 per cent of its clients access Islamic loans. The equivalent figure for the Palestinian Development Fund (PDF), which started Islamic lending in 2000, is 28 per cent, and approximately 10 per cent of the clients of the Arab Center for Agricultural Development (ACAD) access Islamic loans, which it first promoted in 1995. In contrast to MFIs, banks in Palestine are not permitted to simultaneously offer Islamic and interest-based services. As of the end of December 2015, the outstanding Islamic loans portfolio of both MFIs and banks was US$761 m, which constituted 13 per cent of the overall loans portfolio in Palestine. The vast majority of these loans – 93.4 per cent – were provided on the basis of *murabaha* (cost plus profit mark-up), while 3.9 per cent were categorized as *ijarah* (leasing) and 1.2 per cent as *istisna* (a contract to produce something specific with deferred delivery). Only 1.5 per cent of loans were classified were *mudaraba* (profit and loss sharing).

Organizational development

Reef Finance has its headquarters in Ramallah, which is the administrative capital of the Palestinian National Authority, and it has branch offices in Hebron, Nablus, and Gaza, with smaller offices in Jenin, Tulkarm, Yatta, Qalqilyah, Salfit, and Khan Younis. It was registered as a not-for-profit company on 2 July 2007 with the Ministry of National Economy. Reef Finance's parent company, the Palestinian Agricultural Relief Committees (PARC), signed an agreement on 30 August 2007 with the Netherlands Representative Office, which provided a grant of US$2,747,385 to establish the organization. It started lending in February 2008. PARC is the largest shareholder, with 91.47 per cent of the total number of shares. There are 25 other shareholders, mostly rural savings and credit co-operatives, but also eight individuals.

Reef means 'rural' in Arabic and the primary activity of Reef Finance is providing loans to small-scale farmers and others living in rural areas in the West Bank and Gaza. In common with all other MFIs, the organization is not permitted to accept savings and it is regulated by the PMA. Reef Finance employs 36 full-time staff, including 20 loan officers, and one part-time staff member. It is also a member of Sharakeh, which has eight leading MFIs as its members and a collective outreach of approximately 70,000 clients.[1] Reef Finance's objective is 'to improve the living conditions of rural Palestinians by providing 'high-quality financial services to both individuals and co-operatives'. It estimates that 98 per cent of its clients are indeed rural – a higher proportion than any other member of Sharakeh.

The number of loans disbursed annually by Reef Finance has increased steadily; at the end of 2015, Reef Finance had an active portfolio of 2,934 loans provided for both productive and consumption purposes and an outstanding loans portfolio of US$9,001,534 (the fifth largest of Sharakeh's eight members). More than half of all loans – 57 per cent – were provided in the West Bank and the remaining 43 per cent in Gaza. The majority of loans (1,939 or 77 per cent)

Table 6.1 Development of key financial indicators for Reef Finance

Year	Outstanding loans portfolio (US$)	PAR30 ratio (%)	Number of active loans	Average loan size (US$)	Percentage of female clients
2008	1,106,198	4.26	88	12,570	9
2009	2,905,263	2.91	479	6,065	16
2010	3,511,528	9.41	769	4,566	18
2011	5,605,955	13.33	1,085	4,669	13
2012	6,892,282	9.96	1,715	4,019	14
2013	8,577,289	8.00	2,511	3,416	17
2014	8,698,759	8.50	2,800	3,107	16
2015	9,001,534	7.65	2,934	3,068	16

Source: Internal data supplied by Reef Finance, January 2016.

were categorized as being for enterprise purposes. The remaining 23 per cent were given for the repair and renovation of housing, paying educational fees, and personal loans for purchasing household items. Table 6.1 details the development of key financial indicators since operations began in 2008.

More than half of active loans (1,559 or 53 per cent) were below US$4,000. The relatively high average loan size of US$3,068 is somewhat misleading because Reef Finance has disbursed a number of very large loans to agricultural co-operatives. For example, in October 2015 it provided a loan worth US$300,000 to buy an olive oil press for a group of four agricultural co-operatives comprising 80 members. The vast majority of loans are given to individuals; less than 2 per cent of loans are given to agricultural co-operatives. As a comparison, the average loan size for Sharakeh's eight members is US$2,100.

Approximately 30 per cent of Reef Finance's active clients are repeat borrowers, while the remaining 70 per cent are first-time borrowers. In recent years, the organization has significantly expanded operations – the outstanding loans portfolio at the end of 2015 was slightly above US$9 m, which was almost three times the equivalent figure in 2010. The portfolio at risk greater than 30 days (PAR30) ratio has varied from a low of 2.91 per cent in 2009 to a high of 13.33 per cent in 2011 – sudden rises can occur when the movements of both borrowers and loan officers are restricted due to political reasons. In such circumstances, Reef Finance sometimes suspends and reschedules repayments until the political situation improves – this happened, for example, in 2014 during the conflict in Gaza. The proportion of female clients has remained relatively constant at around 16 per cent.

Types of loans and lending methodology

Reef Finance markets its services in villages and interested borrowers approach the organization directly to make an application. It publicizes its loans as Islamic loans. Applications are analysed by loan officers and always followed up by on-site field visits to verify the information provided. As well as examining the capacity of an applicant to invest productively, loan officers also consult with neighbours and local community leaders to assess a borrower's reputation and trustworthiness.

Reef Finance also conducts checks with the Credit Registry of the PMA to assess the levels of indebtedness and creditworthiness of both applicants and their guarantors. It pays a monthly fee of US$300 for this service and this permits the organization to make up to 600 enquiries per month. It does not approve applications from borrowers who have loans outstanding elsewhere. Generally speaking, Reef Finance permits loans with monthly repayments of up to 30 per cent of a borrower's estimated income, although it will increase this proportion to 50 per cent for those with secure employment in the private or public sectors. The PMA has stipulated that financial indebtedness should not exceed 50 per cent of an individual's income. Those applications considered feasible by loan officers are forwarded and assessed by a credit committee. While around half are approved without any modifications, others are approved but for lower amounts and a small minority are rejected.

Reef Finance has four categories of loan: personal loans up to a maximum amount of US$3,000; housing loans up to US$7,000, which are typically used for the repair and renovation of homes; trade loans that can be no higher than US$10,000; and agricultural loans for a maximum amount of US$15,000. While Reef Finance does provide loans of up to US$50,000, loans greater than US$15,000 are given only to agricultural co-operatives or partnerships of two or more borrowers. Slightly more than half of all loans – 56 per cent – are provided for agricultural activities, typically the construction of greenhouses and the purchase of sheep, cows, and poultry. Emphasizing the organization's rural focus, this proportion is the highest of any Sharakeh member. A very small proportion of loans – just 2 per cent – are provided for manufacturing, while 19 per cent are given for services and trade. Almost a quarter of loans – 24 per cent – are for housing, education, and consumption purposes. Productive loans are repaid typically over a period of 30 months.

The vast majority of loans that Reef Finance provides – approximately 95 per cent – are on the basis of *murabaha* or cost plus profit mark-up. The organization prefers this methodology because it considers that by purchasing and delivering equipment, inputs, or other items there is less chance that the loan will be diverted for 'non-productive or consumption' purposes, which may happen with a cash loan. In fact, the overwhelming majority of Islamic loans provided by ACAD, Faten, and PDF are also on the basis of *murabaha*. Reef Finance also provides finance on the basis of *manfa'a* (literally 'benefit' in Arabic) for university students. *Manfa'a* refers to the benefit that the recipient derives from the use of a tangible asset or service, in this case the teaching provided by the university. Under this arrangement, Reef Finance pays the student's matriculation fees directly to the university and signs an agreement with the student for repayment of the cost of the fees plus an arrangement charge.

Table 6.2 Duration of loans and profit mark-up

Amount (US$)	Maximum length	Annual profit mark-up (%)
1–1,000 (exclusively for students)	12 months	4.5
1–2,000	24 months	12
2,001–5,000	24 months	12
5,001–7,000	36 months	9
7,001–10,000	36 months	8
10,001–15,000	36 months	7
15,001–30,000	36 months	6–7
30,001–50,000	48 months	4–6

Source: Internal data supplied by Reef Finance, January 2016.

The mark-up that Reef Finance charges varies according to the size of the loan, as detailed in Table 6.2. With the exception of one-year *manfa'a* loans of up to US$1,000, which attract a profit mark-up of just 4.5 per cent and which form a very small proportion of the overall number of loans, the profit mark-up is greater for smaller loans as Reef Finance believes that these incur higher administrative costs.

Although categorized as *murabaha*, Reef Finance has a unique policy among MFIs in Palestine of not funding the total cost of the proposed investment; instead, borrowers must also contribute in terms of providing assets or other inputs. Typically, Reef Finance will fund approximately 80 per cent of the total cost of the venture, while the borrower must fund the remaining 20 per cent from his or her own resources. For example, Reef Finance might purchase and delivery healthy, vaccinated chicks, but the borrower must purchase sufficient feed and ensure that the birds have a safe, hygienic, and secure area where they can be housed and kept warm at night. Reef Finance favours this approach because it considers that a borrower is more committed to the success of the venture if he or she has made a financial or in-kind contribution. Furthermore, borrowers must make a cash payment to Reef Finance of up to 25 per cent of the mark-up. For example, if the *murabaha* mark-up during the first year amounts to US$200, then a borrower might be asked to pay up to US$50 immediately once the loan agreement is signed.

Reef Finance's staff estimate that approximately two-thirds of borrowers approach the organization specifically because they are more comfortable with *Shari'ah*-compliant finance. They consider that the remainder are attracted to their loans because they are relatively cheaper than those offered by most other MFIs. For a loan worth US$2,000, Reef Finance charges a profit mark-up of 12 per cent per year or US$480 over 24 months. Sharakeh's other members typically charge flat rates of 18 per cent per annum on a similar sized loan, which would mean interest payments of US$720 over two years. Crayne et al. (2014) also observed a strong disposition towards Islamic finance. During interviews with 612 micro, small, and medium enterprises in the West Bank and Gaza, they found that 49 per cent of them expressed a preference for Islamic financial products and only 28 per cent were willing to use interest-based loans to finance their businesses. Interestingly, 34 per cent of those interviewed still expressed a preference for Islamic loans even if they were more expensive than interest-based loans.

ACAD, Faten, and PDF all started providing Islamic loans in response to a demand from a significant minority of clients who were reluctant to access interest-based loans for fear of breaching their religious beliefs. Some of Reef Finance's staff are also motivated to work for the organization for faith-based reasons, particularly in areas such as Hebron and Qalqilyah, where religious practice is stronger. Certainly, some staff have remained loyal to the organization despite the fact that they receive lower salaries than their counterparts in other MFIs and the organization does not have a policy of rewarding employees with bonuses based on the number of loans staff may disburse or for ensuring high rates of loan recovery.

Reef Finance has an agreement with the Al-Takaful Insurance Company whereby, in the event of a borrower's death or serious injury or illness that prevents him or her from working, the outstanding loan amount is waived and whatever part of the loan that has already been repaid is gifted to the borrower's spouse or next of kin. In order to access this service, when loans are disbursed borrowers pay US$1.54 for every US$1,000 loaned as *takaful* or insurance.

In common with other MFIs, Reef Finance uses a mix of personal guarantees, guarantor salary transfers, and promissory notes to secure their loans. The number of personal guarantors required depends upon the size of the loan. For loans below US$2,000, Reef Finance requires just one personal guarantor; for loans between US$2,001 and US$5,000, it requires two personal guarantors, one of whom must have a salaried income; for loans between US$5,001 and US$7,000, it requires two guarantors, both of whom must have salaried incomes; while for loans between US$7,001 and US$10,000, it requires three personal guarantors. Only for larger loans above US$10,000 does it request physical collateral such as property, vehicles, or even gold.

For those loans that are approved, Reef Finance purchases the specific items requested by borrowers and asks a selected supplier, often one identified by the borrower, to deliver these to the borrower's place of business. As a matter of good practice, it always collects prices from two or three different suppliers before making a selection based on cost and quality. The loan officer is always present when delivery takes place and hands a cheque to the supplier once the borrower confirms that the items are exactly of the quantity and quality requested. The vast majority of suppliers are paid by cheque; only a relatively small proportion of around 5 per cent are paid through bank transfer. It usually takes around one or two weeks for a loan to be processed, approved, and disbursed.

The procedure for acquiring and delivering items is relatively straightforward and inexpensive when there is just one supplier and a single product, such as a greenhouse, which is to be bought and delivered. Indeed, for most *murabaha* loans, only one supplier is involved. However, it becomes slightly more complicated and costly when borrowers require items from several different suppliers. Occasionally, and in order to satisfy borrowers and avoid selecting an item that the borrower might not accept, Reef Finance has even bought the same item, for example sheep, in small numbers from several different suppliers. Despite this, it does not charge a higher mark-up even when it is required to visit and buy a range of items from more than one supplier – the level of mark-up is determined by the size of the loan rather than by the amount of work involved. In order to ensure that it buys healthy livestock and poultry, Reef Finance often requests a veterinarian to accompany the loan officer when visiting suppliers. The case study in Box 6.1 describes a *murabaha* loan provided by Reef Finance.

Importantly, Reef Finance has been able to make use of its position as a frequent buyer of particular items to negotiate price discounts with suppliers. For example, since it receives many requests to purchase greenhouses, it has signed contracts with two greenhouse suppliers and has managed to negotiate discounts of between 7 and 10 per cent, which it passes on to borrowers. The greenhouses consist of a metal skeleton frame with plastic sheeting and

---

Box 6.1 A *murabaha* loan from Reef Finance to purchase sheep

Zaher and his wife Shifa have five children and live in a semi-rural community around 10 kilometres from the city of Ramallah. They received a *murabaha* loan from Reef Finance in November 2014 in order to purchase 17 sheep. Zaher and Shifa feel uncomfortable paying interest and approached Reef Finance specifically because it provides *Shari'ah*-compliant finance. They identified a local farmer with a reputation for selling good-quality sheep. The loan officer who had analysed their application visited the supplier together with a veterinarian, and after they were satisfied that the animals were healthy, negotiated a sale price. Reef Finance agreed a price of US$8,000 with the supplier to buy and deliver 17 sheep. Since the profit mark-up was 8 per cent per annum or US$640, Zaher and Shifa made a down payment of US$160 or 25 per cent of the mark-up. They were then committed to pay Reef Finance a further US$9,120 in equal monthly instalments over the next 24 months. The loan officer who had analysed their application was also present when the delivery took place, at which time he presented a cheque to the supplier for US$8,000. Reef Finance agreed with the supplier that if any of the animals was subsequently found to be unhealthy in the next two to three months, they could be exchanged at no extra cost. Zaher and Shifa did in fact return two of the sheep two months later and these were replaced with healthy sheep by the supplier. In respect of their contribution to the venture, the couple have a small enclosure next to their home where the animals are housed and also constructed new pens on the ground floor where pregnant sheep and those that have recently given birth are housed. They also bought several sacks of specialist feed for the sheep using their own savings. There is public pasture a few minutes from their home where the animals are kept during the summer months. On average, the sheep produce two lambs per year that can be sold for between US$200 and US$300 each at around two months old. Zaher and Shifa have built up their flock and currently have 37 sheep as well as 12 goats. They prefer to sell the sheep at the Muslim festival of *Eid-al-Adha* when prices are higher. On a weekly basis they also produce and sell yoghurt. Taking out the loan has increased their income.

cover one '*dunam*' or 1,000 square metres of land. Typically, they cost in the region of US$9,000; however, Reef Finance can generally purchase them for around US$8,350. Furthermore, by participating in the process of sourcing supplies, it can also ensure that the borrower benefits by using good-quality inputs (and even have them exchanged if they are not of the required quality), thereby reducing one of the risks of business failure.

Repayments are on a monthly basis and are generally made through post-dated cheques deposited with Reef Finance; one cheque corresponds to each repayment. A small proportion of repayments – around 10 to 15 per cent – are made in cash at branch offices. Agricultural loans may attract a grace period of between one and three months. In line with Islamic teachings,[2] Reef Finance does not apply any financial penalties to borrowers for late repayment – the outstanding debt remains the same. Despite this, borrowers do not appear to be tempted to delay repayments and the PAR30 ratio is currently 7.65 per cent. Although some of Sharakeh's other members have lower ratios – for example, Vitas has a PAR30 ratio of just 0.30 per cent, Faten 1.68 per cent, and ACAD 4.1 per cent – other members have similar ratios to Reef Finance: for example, Asala has a PAR30 ratio of 6.6 per cent, and UNRWA 8 per cent. In contrast to Reef Finance, though, Faten charges 0.065 per cent per month for late repayments on its Islamic loans, while the rate PDF charges depends on what it has agreed as the *murabaha* mark-up – for example, if the mark-up is 5 per cent, then the penalty would be 5 per cent of the overdue amount per month.

When Reef Finance's borrowers do not repay on time and there are insufficient funds in their accounts for the post-dated cheques to clear, loan officers call them by telephone to remind them that the cheques have 'bounced' and to immediately deposit funds into their account. At this stage, most borrowers do then deposit enough cash into their accounts for the cheques to clear. If borrowers are late with their repayment instalment by more than one week, loan officers will visit them at their homes or business premises to ascertain the reasons for non-repayment. If loan officers establish that the borrower is experiencing difficulties and is unable to repay, then Reef Finance, again inspired by Islamic teachings that encourage lenders to wait and grant borrowers extra time to repay,[3] simply waits without taking any further action. The organization may even reschedule loan repayments, allowing the borrower more time to repay. However, in the event that Reef Finance considers that a borrower has wilfully defaulted on a loan, the organization's lawyer will telephone the borrower and inform them that they have seven days to make repayments otherwise they will contact the police. The consequences can be serious, as it is a felony to write a cheque and not have sufficient funds in an account to support that cheque; this can be punished by 90 days in prison. Reef Finance may also contact a guarantor's bank and make arrangements to receive funds to cover the missed repayments from the guarantor's monthly salary payments.

A very small proportion of loans – approximately 2 per cent – are given in cash in cases when in-kind lending is not possible, for example when suppliers are located outside the West Bank and Gaza. A similar proportion are given

---

Box 6.2 A *musharaka* partnership for a greenhouse business

Mustafa sought a *musharaka* partnership with Reef Finance in May 2014 in order to purchase damaged greenhouses which he repairs and rehabilitates before reselling them. Mustafa buys the greenhouses from local farmers in and around Ramallah and even from areas in Israel. He was against taking an interest-based loan because of his religious beliefs. Mustafa and Reef Finance both contributed US$10,000 to the venture. They opened a joint account in a Jordanian Bank where the funds were deposited and the money could be used only for purchasing used greenhouses. They initially agreed to divide any profits from the enterprise equally: that is, in accordance with their capital contributions. However, after the partnership began, Reef Finance agreed to allocate 75 per cent of the profits to Mustafa as he was managing the project and undertaking all the work. At the end of three months, they brought the partnership to a close with Reef Finance making a profit of US$580, in addition to its capital investment of US$10,000, an amount far greater than it would have earned through a *murabaha* loan.

---

on the basis of *manfa'a*. In response to demand from borrowers, Reef Finance is planning in the future to provide *ijarah* (leasing) and *bai salam* (forward selling) loans as well. Reef Finance has experimented with four *musharaka* or profit- and loss-sharing loans. It made a loss on the first three loans provided in 2010–11 (which might explain its reluctance to increase such loans), but a profit on the last, which was given in 2014 (see Box 6.2).

Covering operational costs

Reef Finance operates in a challenging environment. Both borrowers and staff suffer from restrictions on their movements and Gaza in particular has been affected by conflict. As a consequence, the organization sometimes reschedules repayments. However, despite various operational, economic, and political challenges, Reef Finance moved quickly to achieve financial sustainability and within five years of starting operations the income earned from loans was greater than operational expenses, as detailed in Table 6.3. It has a strong balance sheet, as shown in Table 6.4, with a net income of US$252,581.

Conclusions

Despite operating in a very challenging political and economic environment, Reef Finance has expanded quickly since it was established and has an active portfolio of almost 3,000 clients and an outstanding loans portfolio of over US$9 m. Since 2012 it has managed to cover operating costs from the income it earns from disbursing loans. Its services are popular with borrowers and a significant proportion of them are attracted to *Shari'ah*-compliant finance.

The vast majority of Reef Finance's loans are provided on the basis of *murabaha*; although this approach does require additional efforts from staff in terms of identifying the items to be bought, liaising with suppliers, and

Table 6.3 Reef Finance's income and operational expenses

Year	Income earned from loans (US$)	Operational expenses (US$)	OSS ratio (%)
2008	80,320	517,652	13
2009	237,149	594,959	37
2010	454,641	712,525	48
2011	571,564	721,925	68
2012	802,499	722,411	109
2013	1,077,491	986,301	109
2014	1,181,632	1,082,649	109
2015	1,326,099	1,143,300	118

Source: Internal data supplied by Reef Finance, January 2016.

Table 6.4 Summary balance sheet and income statement for Reef Finance

	Amount (US$)
Balance sheet	
Total assets	10,556,975
Total liabilities	3,497,080
Total equity	7,059,895
Income statement	
Total financial income	1,395,881
Total operating expenses	1,143,300
Net income	252,581

Source: Information supplied by Reef Finance, January 2016.
Note: Figures as of 31 December 2015.

arranging delivery, it also offers certain advantages. By delivering inputs rather than cash, there is, of course, a greater likelihood that the loan will be invested productively. Reef Finance uses its position as a frequent purchaser to negotiate discounts with suppliers, which it passes on to borrowers, and it also ensures that the items bought, particularly livestock, are of good quality (and can be exchanged if need be), thereby increasing the likelihood that the loan will be repaid and reducing the risks of business failure.

Reef Finance adheres to Islamic teachings and does not apply any financial penalties to borrowers for late repayment; it will often restructure repayments should a borrower encounter difficulties. In contrast to the manner in which *murabaha* loans are generally provided, Reef Finance does not fund the total cost of the proposed investment but instead insists that borrowers must contribute in terms of providing assets or other inputs. Indeed, it seems that the organization is keen to promote the economic well-being and development of borrowers; in the longer term, it has plans to become a specialist Islamic rural bank that can offer clients a range of financial services.

However, our analysis of Islamic microfinance in Palestine has also highlighted more general issues. With the vast majority of loans provided on the basis of *murabaha*, sometimes with the profit mark-ups inversely proportional to the size of the loan, and with differing *Shari'ah* interpretations on issues such as charging penalties for late repayments, there is scepticism among some members of the general public as to whether the services on offer are 'genuinely Islamic' and not simply 'repackaged interest-based loans'. Despite some distrust, though, there are few signs that Islamic finance providers are looking to develop new products or diversify their portfolios. In order to regulate the operations of Islamic banks and ensure *Shari'ah* compliance, the PMA introduced legislation in March 2013. As a result, Islamic banks must establish a *Shari'ah* supervisory committee to oversee the operations and the development of products. The committee must consist of at least five but no more than nine people who have knowledge of *Shari'ah*, banking, and economics. Although in the past there has been no such obligation on MFIs, this will change as they will also be required to establish a *Shari'ah* supervisory committee from 2017.

Reef Finance and other Islamic microfinance providers have focused almost exclusively on utilizing *murabaha* because it is relatively straightforward to structure, understand, and implement; indeed, Islamic microfinance in Palestine has become synonymous with *murabaha* – a tendency that Yousef (2004) has called the '*murabaha* syndrome' in Islamic finance. Furthermore, with relatively limited financial resources, it is likely that they will continue to favour this approach because it is less risky and costly than methodologies such as *mudaraba* and *musharaka* that require greater organizational input. Certainly, access to additional financial resources and technical expertise will encourage Islamic microfinance suppliers in Palestine to provide more profit- and loss-sharing loans; however, one suspects that this may not be sufficient, and it needs to be accompanied by a change in institutional outlook as well.

Notes

1. More information can be found at the organization's website <www. palmfi.ps>.
2. The majority of Islamic scholars regard any charge on late payment as *riba* or usury and therefore *haram* or unlawful.
3. The *Qur'an* states: 'If the debtor is in difficulty, grant him time till it is easy for him to repay' (2:280).

References

Crayne, R., Tawil, I. and Lechner, D. (2014) *MSME Finance in the Palestinian Territories: An Analysis of Supply and Demand*, Cologne: ICON-INSTITUTE GmbH & Co. KG Consulting Gruppe.

Yousef, T.M. (2004) 'The *murabaha* syndrome in Islamic finance: laws, institutions and politics', in C.M. Henry and R. Wilson (eds), *The Politics of Islamic Finance*, Edinburgh: Edinburgh University Press.

About the authors

Ajaz Ahmed Khan (khan@careinternational.org) is Senior Microfinance Adviser at CARE International, United Kingdom.

Mohammed Ibrahim Elayyan (mohammed@palmfi.ps) is Projects Co-ordinator at Palestinian Network for Small and Microfinance (Sharakeh), Palestine.

CHAPTER 7

The experience of Kaah Islamic Microfinance Services in Somalia

Abdi Abdillahi Hassan

Kaah Islamic Microfinance Services (KIMS) was started in 2014 by Kaah Express, a large international funds remittance company based in Mogadishu. KIMS offers murabaha *and* ijarah *financial products, and it has a particular focus on serving young men and women who want to start or to develop small businesses. By 2016, KIMS had extended its savings and loan services to over 4,000 people, to a total value of over US$3 m.*

Keywords: Somalia, Somaliland, *Shari'ah*-compliant, *murabaha*, *ijarah*, Mogadishu

Somalia has been devastated by over two decades of civil war. Most Somali institutions have collapsed and much of the country's economic and social infrastructure and assets have been destroyed. In the absence of a formal commercial banking sector, remittance companies enable the Somali diaspora to remit around US$1.3 bn annually to their families in Somalia. The country's economy has been largely sustained through the rearing of traditional livestock and remittances from the diaspora. The telecommunications industry has expanded, but in general Somalia's economy has been defined by conflict. The 2012 *Africa Human Development Report* estimated annual per capita income to be US$284,[1] much lower than the sub-Saharan African average of US$1,300 and one of the lowest in the world. An estimated 73 per cent of the population lives in poverty, 61 per cent in the towns and cities and 80 per cent in rural areas, and about 43 per cent of the population lives on less than US$1 a day. Somaliland and Puntland in the northern and eastern parts of the country have regained some peace and stability, while security challenges remain in central and south Somalia. Somaliland withdrew from the Somali republic in 1991 and declared itself to be an independent state, and comparatively has experienced solid economic growth in recent years. Puntland is also beginning to recover from the years of fighting, as are the recently declared autonomous regions of Jubaland and Galmudug.

Islamic finance and microfinance are new concepts in Somalia in general. Before the civil war, most services and industries were government-run and independent financial institutions were forbidden. Islamic financial systems

http://dx.doi.org/10.3362/9781780449555.007

have only recently been adopted in Somaliland, and in the rest of Somalia they remain at a very early stage.

Business history

Kaah Express is a leading international money service business that operates in over 40 countries and serves hundreds of thousands of customers each month. It has an extensive network of agents worldwide, as well as a fully developed network of branches and agents in Somalia, through which money transfer services can be accessed in many of the towns and larger villages in the Somali territories. Kaah Express supports the transfer of millions of dollars a year, most of which flows from the global Somali diaspora to Somalia. In 2013, Kaah Express conducted a nationwide market study on microfinance and found that less than 5 per cent of the Somali demand for microcredit was being met. The research identified over 2 million potential enterprise credit clients who required tens of millions of dollars of finance. Over 60 per cent of these potential customers were either existing or potential micro-entrepreneurs between the ages of 18 and 35.

Kaah Express's management recognized that the successful introduction of *Shari'ah*-compliant microfinance services, operated through its substantial existing branch network, could make an important contribution to the economic development of Somalia. In 2013, they registered Kaah Islamic Microfinance Services (KIMS) to offer *Shari'ah*-compliant financial services across the Somali territories. KIMS launched lending operations in March 2014 as the first full-service for-profit microfinance institution in Somalia. It is registered as a non-banking financial institution in all the jurisdictions where it operates (Somaliland, Puntland, and South and Central Somalia), and as such is licensed to offer both credit and deposit services as well as money transfer and insurance (*takaful*) products.

KIMS prioritizes enterprise financing through *Shari'ah*-compliant products but also facilitates personal savings with particular attention to women and youth. Women and young people are generally marginalized in Somali society; they have high unemployment rates and have historically faced difficulties in accessing financial services. Poor people's exclusion from the financial system is a major factor contributing to their poverty. In recognition of this market gap, KIMS provides Islamic loans and savings services to poor but economically active people.

A typical client is a young Somali man or woman who lacks finance for starting or expanding a small business. KIMS' clients are engaged in a wide range of activities such as small-scale retail, farming, livestock, fishing, electrical installation work, tailoring and dressmaking, plumbing, shampoo and soap making, building, metal work, shoe making, and fabric design, including tie-dye, printing, and embroidery.

Starting operations in Somaliland, KIMS has now expanded to Puntland and South and Central Somalia and currently operates 10 branches in eight cities and towns. KIMS' branches are housed within and utilize Kaah Express's existing infrastructure and network of agents, enabling the company to operate much more cost-effectively than more typical micro-finance operations. In Somaliland, it has offices in Borama and Burao and two in Hargeisa; in Puntland, it has offices in Bosaso and Garowe; and in South and Central Somalia, it has offices in Kismayo and Beledweyne and two in Mogadishu.

KIMS has over 50 staff that fill various positions including senior managers, loan officers, logistics officers, and administrative and finance officers. Three-quarters of the staff are under the age of 35, and 30 per cent of them are women. The staff had little or no previous experience in Islamic microfinance and they have been trained and coached in order to enable them to perform effectively in their new roles. KIMS is governed by a board of directors with diverse backgrounds. Under the board's supervision and control, KIMS is managed by experienced individuals who have been actively involved in the financial sector for the past two decades.

The performance of KIMS

KIMS has developed, tested, and launched two Islamic microfinance products – namely *murabaha* and *ijarah* – and one savings product; these have all been well received by the community. KIMS' focus is solely on the provision of enterprise finance and a linked savings product. The institution does not provide finance for consumption activities.

KIMS currently provides both individual and group loans. Individual enterprise clients are typically established businesses such as retail shops and traders. KIMS provides group loans through joint liability groups, informal groups of four to 10 individuals who come together for the purpose of receiving loans from KIMS. Generally, the members are engaged in similar types of non-farm economic activities and include existing businesses as well as start-up projects. The members offer a joint undertaking to KIMS to guarantee each other's loans. Group members are also expected to provide support to each other in carrying out work-related and social activities.

Since its launch, KIMS has financed over 4,000 clients with a total loan value of over US$3 m. It has an active client base of over 2,000 and an active portfolio of more than US$1.5 m. KIMS has also mobilized over US$100,000 in savings, which is a combination of compulsory and voluntary savings. Seventy per cent of KIMS' clients are young people aged between 18 and 30 and over 50 per cent are women.

KIMS' enterprise finance clients have grown rapidly and the organi-zation considers that the provision of sustainable financing to this group has provided significant economic benefits to local communities. KIMS estimates that its loans have helped create around 4,000 new jobs across Somalia. Surveys of clients have found that, on average, one new worker is hired for every business financed by KIMS. Through prudent client selection and strong follow-up mechanisms, KIMS has achieved a repayment rate of 99 per cent. Unlike some microfinance providers in Somalia, KIMS has aimed from the outset to be commercially viable.

Current Islamic finance products

KIMS' *murabaha* and *ijarah* loan sizes range from US$500 to US$25,000, with *murabaha* forming the majority of loans provided.

For *murabaha* loans, KIMS and the client agree on the asset to be financed, including an agreed mark-up. KIMS buys the asset, with free and clear title. The client then pays KIMS for the cost of the asset and the agreed profit in a series of instalments, or as a lump sum payment, depending on the specific agreement with KIMS. The client and KIMS have to define and agree on the specification of the goods, their cost price, mark-up, and payment schedule, including dates. Any risk of the asset losing value during the transaction is shared between the two parties, and the client has to receive the asset immediately. The case study in Box 7.1 describes finance received through a *murabaha* arrangement.

Although borrowers are not always successful in their business ventures, KIMS does not penalize them for late payments but attempts to reschedule loans, as the case study in Box 7.2 describes.

In *ijarah*, or leasing, the transfer of ownership takes place at the end of the contract and is pre-agreed between KIMS and the client. Once the agreed rental payments have been made, ownership of the asset is transferred to the client for no charge, or for a token price or other figure that is agreed at the beginning of the contract, or the transfer of ownership may be gradual. This arrangement is suitable for micro-entrepreneurs who need to acquire fixed assets or equipment.

KIMS purchases the required assets and rents them to the client, who pays the rental costs at regular intervals. The client is the lessee and is responsible for taking good care of the asset; KIMS as the lessor monitors the use of the equipment. *Ijarah* is not generally practical for groups since problems arise in sharing the use of assets. *Ijarah* has two advantages from the point of view of the financing institution: the risk of default is reduced because the asset can be reclaimed if the scheduled payments are not maintained; and ownership of the asset is transferred legally to the client only when the final instalment is paid.

Table 7.1 summarizes the main features of the two different types of financing that KIMS provides to its clients.

One of the objectives of KIMS is to encourage its clients to save. Every client is required to deposit 3 per cent or more of the amount borrowed, and they are also encouraged to continue making voluntary savings with KIMS as they service their loans. Each client is provided with a savings account with

---

Box 7.1 A *murabaha* arrangement for a retail business

Sahra is a 30-year-old business woman. She started her business in 2014. She was in financial difficulties at that time so she contacted KIMS and qualified for a loan in May 2014. She has borrowed a total of US$2,200 from KIMS. Sahra has a shop in Hargeisa, where she sells a variety of drinks, basic foods, household cleaning items, and cosmetics. Sahra has successfully completed two loan cycles of US$500 and then US$700 and she is currently repaying her third loan of US$1,000. Average loan cycles are six months; the mark-up is 8 per cent for six months or 16 per cent per year on the loans. Sahra keeps daily records of her business income and expenditure and calculates her profits every month. Sahra estimates that she has around US$6,800 worth of capital in stock; she sells US$1,600 of goods per month and she calculates her profit to be US$700 per month. Sahra has no biological children; however, seven of her nephews and nieces, who are orphans, are dependent on her, and six of them go to school. Sahra employs three workers – one full time and two part time – in order to run her business. She is the main breadwinner for her family and all of her direct family members are financially dependent on her.

Box 7.2 Financial difficulties and the rescheduling of loans

Sahra (not the same woman described in Box 7.1) applied for a loan from KIMS in January 2015. She is a single mother with three children, and there are also four other adult members of her family living with her who depend on her financially. She is the sole breadwinner in her whole family. Sahra started her business in Sheikh Omar village, a suburb of Hargeisa. She took out a loan of US$300 plus mark-up to establish a small clothes shop. At first it appeared that the business was running smoothly and she paid her instalments regularly. Later on she faced financial difficulties that caused her to miss the payment dates of several instalments. The loan officer dealing with the case contacted her about the delays and she finally admitted having financial difficulties. She told him that her sales had dropped and as result her profits had declined. There is still US$108 outstanding, and the loan has been rescheduled several times, but the issue remains unresolved. However, her total debt has not increased as there are no late penalty charges. KIMS has contacted her guarantor and negotiations are under way in order to pay the outstanding balance. The file will be closed only when the last repayment has been made.

Table 7.1 The features of *murabaha* and *ijarah*

	Murabaha	Ijarah
Mark-up	16% per annum	12% per annum
Calculation method	Flat	Flat
Grace period	0	0
Repayment frequency	Variable, depending on cash flow of clients. Usually 3 to 12 instalments	Variable, depending on cash flow of clients. Usually 9 to 24 instalments
Cash collateral	10% upfront	12% upfront
Term	6 to 12 months	9 to 24 months
Guarantee	Personal guarantee	Personal guarantee
Credit insurance	1% upfront	1% upfront

Kaah Express for this purpose. KIMS' customers have the right to withdraw their savings when they have successfully repaid an outstanding loan. If a client requests a repeat loan, the outstanding savings balance remains in the savings account and the customer is required to deposit a new amount for additional savings.

KIMS is actively seeking to increase its pool of voluntary savings through financial education programmes that promote the importance of savings to populations across the country. Building a sustainable base of deposits in Somalia remains constrained by the lack of low-risk investment options such as treasury bills in the country. Furthermore, the country's dislocation from capital markets makes access to regional or international fixed-term deposit products challenging.

As structured, KIMS' Islamic microfinance programmes face a range of operational challenges, including identifying assets, price negotiation, and the distribution of goods from wholesalers, all of which have a significant impact on administrative costs, due to the extra work they entail.

Furthermore, some Islamic scholars have criticized *murabaha*, stating that the fixed profit rate is similar to a fixed interest rate; they argue that it is not truly in the spirit of Islamic *Shari'ah*. Other Islamic scholars, however, disagree and have approved the *murabaha* product, stating that the profit added to the price of the commodity is an acceptable fee to compensate the financier for identifying, buying, and then reselling the required commodity at the best price. KIMS' management incline to the latter view, and their religious advisers have confirmed that this is acceptable. KIMS continues to explore the viability of introducing other Islamic products, such as profit- and loss-sharing arrangements, but the priority for a new microfinance institution is to reach financial sustainability prior to the introduction of such higher-risk products. Also, given the limited availability of appropri- ately priced financial services in the Somali market, KIMS' low-income business clients have expressed strong satisfaction with KIMS' current product range.

Table 7.2 summarizes the financial position of KIMS at the end of June 2016, and its operations for the preceding 12 months. The figures are approximate, and are rounded to the nearest US$1,000.

The loan application process

To be eligible for a loan, applicants must be citizens of Somalia or Somaliland, they must complete the application form correctly, and they have to be 18 years old or older. They must already own a business activity or be willing to start one, and they must not be close relatives of other members in the same group, or relatives of KIMS' staff.

In general, the community has a high opinion of KIMS' services, because of the institution's marketing and outreach campaigns and its long-standing reputation for providing safe and efficient remittances.

Table 7.2 The financial position of KIMS

Uses of funds/assets (US$)		Sources of funds/liabilities (US$)	
Cash and bank balances	952,000	Clients' savings	107,000
Clients' accounts outstanding	1,063,000	Accounts payable	77,000
Less cumulative allowance for bad debts	(21,000)		
Net outstanding	1,042,000		
Vehicles	12,000	Equity and reserves from earlier surplus	1,980,000
Computers and office equipment	29,000		
Software	129,000		
Total	2,164,000	Total	2,164,000
Income (US$)		Expenditure (US$)	
Sales on *murabaha* and *ijarah*	1,175,000	Wages and salaries	56,000
Costs of goods sold	1,075,000	Consultancy fees	19,000
Gross margin	100,000	Promotion, communication, and events	6,000
Grant income	258,000	Rent	6,000
Account opening fees	1,000	Administration, and other costs	16,000
Total income	359,000	Depreciation	6,000
		Provision for bad debts	10,000
		Total expenses	119,000
		Profit	240,000

When a potential client becomes aware of KIMS from the media, other clients, or from contact with a KIMS loan officer, he or she picks up a KIMS leaflet, a loan information sheet, and loan application form from a KIMS branch or a Kaah Express agency. He or she fills in the application form and gives it to a KIMS staff member. A KIMS' credit officer then visits the group or individual, appraises their activities, and checks with the customer the exact loan amount needed. The client then identifies the specific items needed from the wholesale supplier and negotiates the price, and, if the appraisal is positive, the credit officer forwards the application with his or her recommendation to the loans committee, which approves or rejects the application. The client then has to identify a guarantor; this is a trustworthy person who will be able to cover the outstanding value of the loan if the client fails to repay. Once the loan is approved, the logistics team takes over. They purchase the required items from the wholesaler and resell them immediately with the agreed mark-up to the client. KIMS has built strong relationships with reputable suppliers to get discounts. When the client gets a quotation from a supplier, KIMS' logistics officers renegotiate with the supplier or identify another supplier who can provide the items at a lower price. Any discount provided to KIMS by the supplier is then deducted from the client's loan amount (cost) rather than being added to KIMS' profit.

If the loan is rejected, the credit officer calls the client and provides feedback on the decision, and sometimes the committee recommends the loan officer meet the customer for further clarification. If the customer and guarantor are not known to the KIMS management team and credit committee, the committee may then meet the applicant and guarantor in order to obtain further information.

Advantages of the KIMS microfinance model and future developments

KIMS benefits from Kaah Express's substantial operational infrastructure and agent network, enabling significant cost savings and rapid national reach. This model for delivering services has enabled KIMS to expand to meet market demand much more quickly than conventional 'bricks and mortar' microfinance institutions. KIMS has also integrated mobile money services into its operation, enabling its enterprise loan clients to repay their loan in instalments via their mobile phones, using the 'Zaad' mobile money service, which saves both clients and KIMS significant time and money. The mobile money service is in fact widely used by KIMS enterprise clients. KIMS is in the process of installing a new, fully automated, Islamic core banking management information system that will enable the company to increase the scale of its lending services quickly and efficiently.

KIMS has an aggressive expansion plan under implementation; this includes increased service provision in its current locations, as well as the opening of branches in new locations and the development of new loan products. It has, for example, recently launched a new small- and medium-sized business loan product called KIMS Pluz, which is now available in Hargeisa, Beledweyne, and Mogadishu. Rural lending is also being gradually ramped up with significant expansion in service provision planned.

KIMS has successfully been awarded and has managed more than US$3 m in donor grant funding since its inception in 2013, and it has additional grant funding in the pipeline. Given the significant unmet demand for financing from potential clients, KIMS plans to move away from donor funding as its only source of funds. In the medium term, KIMS is planning to open up its equity base to socially driven investors. It will strive to attract value-adding organizations that can contribute capital, knowledge, and expertise that enable it to become a leading financial services provider in the Horn of Africa.

Note

1.   This is the most recent year for which reliable data is available.

Reference

United Nations Development Programme (2012) *Africa Human Development Report 2012: Towards a Food Secure Future*, New York: United Nations Publications.

About the author

Abdi Abdillahi Hassan (ahassan113@yahoo.com) is the Public Relations and Marketing Manager for Kaah Islamic Microfinance Services.

PART III

Institutions providing a range of Islamic financing arrangements

The third section consists of four cases: PASED and Ebdaa from Sudan and Al Amal and Kompanion from Yemen and Kyrgyzstan respectively. Nowhere in the world is totally peaceful, but these three countries are – or have been until very recently – in considerable turmoil. War and civil disorder are prime causes of poverty; microfinance has been promoted as a tool for the alleviation of poverty, and is part of the accepted armoury of instruments for assisting 'post-conflict' communities. Hence it is appropriate that Islamic microfinance institutions should be active in such places.

The fact that their services are needed does not in itself make their operations easy. At the time of writing, Al Amal is operating not in a 'post-conflict' situation but in an actual war zone, and the boundaries between war and peace are by no means clear. The case shows how the institution has adapted to the war, and it includes a story of a client whose business was destroyed by the war but is being rebuilt with assistance from Al Amal.

PASED has evolved from a donor-promoted project that was originally set up in Port Sudan to assist refugees from warfare in neighbouring Eritrea, and is now a profitable institution. This is sadly a rare example of an aid project that has successfully made the transition into a profitable business, which can compete on level terms with numerous more commercially oriented microfinance institutions that have come up in the same territory.

Neither Ebdaa nor Kompanion are profitable, but both were established by social investors whose ultimate objective was at the very least to create 'sustainable' institutions that could survive from their own earnings even if they might not yield a profit to their original investors. Kyrgyzstan is not at war but is far from stable, politically or economically; Kompanion appears from the case study to be 'investment ready' in that it could be profitable if it had the necessary funds to bring its operations up to and above the break-even level; potential investors may be discouraged by the political situation, but it is likely that funds will become available.

Similarly, Ebdaa Bank operates in the Kordofan in Sudan, one of Africa's most drought-prone and poverty-stricken areas, but it has nevertheless successfully introduced an effective profit- and loss-sharing finance system for local farmers, which is both *Shari'ah* compliant and profitable for both parties. Ebdaa also has the potential to be profitable as an institution; it was only established in 2014, and its management has chosen to expand its coverage rather than aim for immediate profits.

All four institutions in this section thus demonstrate that Islamic microfinance can be profitable, even in very difficult circumstances, and that people will put up with the sometimes tortuous arrangements that are required to achieve *Shari'ah* compliance, even if alternatives are available.

CHAPTER 8

Al Amal Microfinance Bank in Yemen: financial services in times of war

Abdullah Al-Kassim

Al Amal Microfinance Bank was established in 2008 as a joint venture between the Government Social Fund and the Arab Gulf Fund for Development. It has some 40,000 active borrowers with an outstanding portfolio of US$13.4 m, and 93,000 active savings accounts with balances totalling about US$12 m. The bank operates 18 branches throughout the country, and uses mobile services and agents to extend its outreach. It also offers business training and other non-financial services to its clients. The ongoing war in Yemen has seriously affected the bank's clients and its financial results, but Al Amal continues to operate.

Keywords: Yemen, Islamic, *murabaha*, *takaful*, *ijarah*, conflict, *mudaraba*, savings

Al Amal Microfinance Bank, known as AMB or simply Al Amal, was established in 2008 as the first bank of its kind in Yemen and the Middle East and North Africa (MENA) region in accordance with the priority given by the government to tackle poverty and reduce unemployment. Its goal is to provide sustainable financial services to small and micro-entrepreneurs who are excluded by mainstream banks. AMB is a joint collaboration between the Yemeni government's Social Fund for Development, which owns 45 per cent, the Arab Gulf Programme for Development (AGFUND), which owns 35 per cent, and private sector shareholders who own the remaining 20 per cent. The bank is regulated and supervised by the Central Bank of Yemen. Al Amal had a market share of 36.5 per cent of the Yemeni microfinance sector at the end of 2014. The total number of loans disbursed reached 124,186 with a total disbursed portfolio of US$46 m. Women account for 56.1 per cent of the number of borrowers and young people account for 28 per cent. Although Al Amal has been affected by the political crisis which began in 2011 and is ongoing, it has managed to increase its number of active borrowers to 40,511. By July 2015, the bank had opened 241,736 regular savings accounts, a further 18,937 savings accounts for children under the age of 18, and 42,380 for young people. The bank has about 260 employees and 18 branches in eight main cities, which cover about 75 per cent of the Yemen population.

http://dx.doi.org/10.3362/9781780449555.008

Al Amal enjoys a good local, regional, and international reputation, and has become one of the key microfinance actors in the MENA region in general and in Yemen in particular. It has won six international awards, including the Islamic Microfinance Challenge 2010, sponsored by the Consultative Group to Assist the Poor, which aims to develop viable business models that provide microfinance products compatible with Islamic law or *Shari'ah*. In addition to providing financial services, Al Amal has implemented government- and donor-funded cash assistance programmes for the poor, such as cash for work and conditional cash transfer schemes. It also launched mobile banking and mobile branch banking services, and these, along with the 417 authorized agent service points, have enabled it to cover most rural areas. In May 2013, the bank opened the Al-Amal Foundation for Training and Entrepreneurship, the largest in the MENA region; this aims to help Al Amal integrate its financial and non-financial services. This, together with the Al-Amal Entrepreneurship Club, aims to provide clients with technical, vocational, and administrative skills so that they can meet the requirements and needs of the labour market and can exchange ideas with one another. In both urban and rural areas, the bank offers a variety of credit and savings products, *takaful* (*Shari'ah*-compliant insurance), national and international money transfers, and social cash transfer disbursements. All services are *Shari'ah* compliant and are available to all bank clients.

AMB's credit products are broadly classified into three major categories:

- Al Amal microfinance products, including solidarity group, individual, and seasonal loans;
- Al Amal partnership products, including partnership, welfare, and pensions;
- Al Amal investment products, including small- and medium-enterprise investment using *murabaha* and micro-leasing or *ijarah* methodologies.

All of the loan products are governed by Islamic lending principles. They bear no interest and vary in their design and delivery mechanisms. A service fee is charged to cover the costs of administering loans. From its beginning, Al Amal has worked to build methodologies that will cover the financing of risks, whose repayments are paid in accordance with the cash flows of the project, not from their capital.

Al Amal has also introduced low-cost savings products specifically designed for savers with low incomes, and for other poor, disadvantaged, and underserved segments. These include regular savings, child savings, term deposits, current accounts, youth savings, and investment funds. All are implemented on the basis of *mudaraba*, in which the saver is entitled to a share of Al Amal's profits rather than a fixed rate of return.

In order to minimize its own and its clients' costs, Al Amal uses agents for many of its transactions, including for identifying and acquiring goods for sale under *murabaha* contracts, and for some disbursement and recovery services. AMB has a specially equipped vehicle that acts as a mobile branch, bringing its services to remote places; the vehicle is used for receiving and examining loan applications, and for savings deposits and withdrawals and cash disbursements and recoveries.

The most widely offered *Shari'ah*-compliant loan contract is *murabaha*, an asset-based sale transaction that is used to finance raw materials or goods for sale. Typically, the client requests a specific commodity for purchase, which AMB procures directly from the market and subsequently resells to the client, after adding a fixed 'mark-up' for the service provided. Al Amal may contract the client as an 'agent' on its behalf to procure the commodity directly from the market. However, ownership and responsibility for the commodity lie strictly with AMB until the client has paid in full. In most cases, clients repay in equal instalments. The mark-up is distinct from interest because it remains fixed at the initial amount, even if the client repays after the due date. To be *Shari'ah* compliant, AMB must own the commodity before selling it, the commodity must be tangible, and the client must know and agree to the purchase and resale prices.

There are two ways in which these *murabaha* transactions may be carried out. Al Amal may use the agency approach known as *alwakala alnaqdeyyah*. Instead of giving the cash to the client as in conventional interest-based lending, it contracts a person to procure the commodity directly on its behalf from the market. AMB then takes over the commodity and delivers it to the client. The ownership and responsibility for the commodity remain with Al Amal until the client has received it and has signed the contract. Alternatively, Al Amal may enter into a partnership with the supplier, and will then contract an agent to deliver the commodity to the client. Agents may be relatives or friends of the client, in which case they are usually not paid for this service, or they may receive a small fee from the client, which amounts to US$2.50 or US$4.50 depending on the loan size. The case study described in Box 8.1 is an example of a *murabaha* contract.

Al Amal uses *ijarah* or leasing contracts for financing the use and acquisition of equipment and machinery. The duration of the lease and related payments is determined in advance to avoid uncertainty. For the transaction to be considered Islamic and not a sale with camouflaged interest, the *ijarah* contract must specify that the ownership of the asset and responsibility for its maintenance remain with Al Amal. When all the agreed leasing or *ijarah* payments have been made, the item may be sold to the client at a mutually agreed price, or, in theory at any rate, it can be returned to the AMB. Typically, Al Amal purchases equipment such as sewing machines, blacksmith and carpentry tools, vehicles, and taxis, and then leases them to the clients who pay agreed monthly instalments. The case study in Box 8.2 describes an *ijarah* contract.

For leasing transactions, the client who wishes to rent an asset submits an application including a price quotation from the supplier addressed to AMB. The loan officer completes a feasibility study to ensure that the item will generate enough income to cover the repayments. The client then pays 10 per cent of the asset value upfront and signs the rental agreement, and Al Amal buys the asset.

Box 8.1 Using a *murabaha* contract for an ice cream business

Mohammed Sultan is physically disabled; although he has suffered many hardships, he has developed a business selling ice cream to schoolchildren. He applied to Al Amal for a loan, and received YR (Yemeni rials) 150,000, or about US$750,[1] to improve his cash flows. The actual cost of the goods that Al Amal purchased for him was YR 147,000; the balance of YR 3,000, about US$15, was the profit in the *murabaha* contract. He repaid this loan over 10 months, and then decided to expand his business further and to appoint sub-distributors. He borrowed YR 750,000 – about US$3,750 – to buy push-carts for the sub-distributors; the cost was YR 730,000 and the YR 20,000 balance – US$100 – was Al Amal's profit. He repaid this over 18 months.

Box 8.2 Buying a sewing machine on an *ijarah* contract

Neamah lives with her husband and eight children in a very small house. They had no income except the little that she could earn with her very old sewing machine. She needed a new, better sewing machine to work more efficiently and feed her family, but did not have sufficient funds. After learning of the Empowering Women's Programme, which Al Amal runs in partnership with the German Aid Agency GIZ and AGFUND, she approached the bank for a loan. AGFUND finances the loans and covers half the loss in case of default, while GIZ pays the profit on the loans and covers the balance of 50 per cent in case of loss. Neamah took out a one-year loan for YR 30,000 (about US$150) under the programme, from the bank's Al Mukalla branch. She has been able to buy a new sewing machine and is now able to take on more work. She has been able to attract new clients and generate more income.

The client then pays rent according to the agreed schedule; AMB follows up any missed payments but does not impose any fines for delays. After all the rental payments have been made, Al Amal sells the asset to the client.

Al Amal makes loans on an individual and a group basis. For individuals, it makes a thorough analysis of the proposed business venture, and borrowers receive loans based on their past performance, their credit histories, the viability of their business propositions, and the quality of their references. Individual borrowers must provide collateral and their loans also have to be co-signed. AMB ensures that the guarantors are respectable and that their guarantees are on the basis of friendship and personal knowledge. The credit officers try to build close long-term relationships with their clients, and the individual loans are designed to be flexible and to match the exact needs of the clients. Potential clients for individual loans already have a good knowledge of financial products and solid experience with their enterprise.

Al-Amal Solidarity Group loans are provided to groups of men or women with approximately equal economic status who live in the same neighbourhood. The group members serve as guarantors for each other. This product is for clients who have small home-based or similar businesses but lack collateral or individual guarantors. The groups must demonstrate their willingness to guarantee each other's loans, but, unlike many microfinance groups elsewhere, they do not have regular meetings and Al Amal deals with the members individually, not in the context of group meetings.

Potential clients form groups of four to seven members for urban group loans and seven to 20 members for rural group loans. They submit their loan applications jointly. Each member of the group is responsible for his or her own loan repayment, but members agree to guarantee each other's loans. Collateral and co-signers are generally not required for group loans, since the peer pressure and a collective sense of responsibility generated by the group take their place. The group members also perform tasks that are typically performed by the bank's staff; they screen their fellow members carefully and they decide whom to accept into their group. AMB carries out only a minimal loan analysis; instead, it relies on peer assessments by group members of each other's businesses. AMB does, however, check online that prospective clients are not indebted to other microfinance institutions (MFIs), using the Yemen Microfinance Network. Among those benefiting from group loans are young entrepreneurs who might not possess formal collateral.

Al Amal 'sharakat' or partnership loans are for salaried people who work in either the private or the public sector, to meet domestic finance and consumption needs. The loans can be used for businesses, for house maintenance, education, or consumption, and they must be guaranteed by the employer along with two co-workers. Al Amal individual loans are for people who have small or micro-enterprises. They can be used for businesses, for home and vehicle maintenance, education, and consumption, and must be guaranteed with a cash deposit, jewellery, or a commercial guarantee authenticated by the commercial court.

One per cent of the value of all loans is deducted for the *takaful* or micro-insurance fund to cover the risk of a client being unable to repay a loan. Outstanding loan balances are covered from this fund if the client dies, suffers a severe disability or illness, or loses his or her business activity before having fully repaid a loan. An additional amount of YR 20,000 (about US$100) is paid to the client's family to assist in covering funeral expenses if the client dies. Yemen's difficult security and health situation makes this all the more necessary, and the *takaful* fund also protects clients from losses from theft, fire, or violence. The case study in Box 8.3 provides one example of how the *takaful* fund was used.

Al Amal has three different types of clients: groups, individuals, and partnerships. Approval criteria include objective factors such as nationality, age, and earning capacity as well as subjective assessments of applicants such as their reputation, their frankness during discussions, their manners, and their transparency. Al Amal finds out whether an applicant is an active customer of another financing programme or has substantial debts. Close family members are not allowed to be in the same groups, and one person cannot be part of more than one group at any one time. Loan officers have three meetings with applicants to evaluate the applicants' circumstances, business, cash flow, and ability to pay. If they are approved, proposals are then put to the Branch Credit Committee, which is composed of the branch or area manager, group credit specialists, and at least 75 per cent of the loan officers in each branch. Like many other MFIs, Al Amal makes extensive use of guarantees to manage credit risk.

Box 8.3 Benefiting from the *takaful* fund after a fire

Mohammed received a loan of YR 2,000,000 (approximately US$10,000) from Al Amal to expand his grocery shop. However, some months later, and as his business was going well, disaster struck and his shop was burned down; nothing was left but ashes. He nervously approached the Al Amal bank branch where he got his loan in order to make a repayment, but when he told the branch manager that his business had burned down, the manager assured him that the bank waives loans for any client who loses their business in that way. Mohammed was very surprised, since, to his knowledge, banks do not usually act in this way. He was even happier when the branch manager said that he could apply for another loan. He did so, and took out a loan for YR 3,000,000 (about US$15,000), which enabled him to revive his hopes and rebuild his business.

There are detailed guidelines as to the selection of guarantors, such as the requirement that one guarantor should not provide more than two guarantees.

Loans of below US$250 make up 79 per cent of all loans and are approved at the branch; loans of between US$250 and US$1,000 make up 18 per cent of loans and are approved by the area manager; and loans of between US$1,000 and US$2,500, which constitute 2 per cent of all loans, go to the operations manager. Only 0.3 per cent of loans are in the highest classification – from US$2,500 to US$4,000 – and these have to be approved by the executive director, who has commented: 'Suggesting the right amount of financing for our clients is like helping them choose the right shoes to buy. It is bad for them if it is too big, and also if it is too small.'

Yemeni society is very conservative, and consequently Islamic finance has become the predominant financial philosophy in microfinance. Most low-income clients are afraid to break Islamic law and to receive or pay *riba*, or interest, because it is forbidden in Islam. Frequently, the first question clients ask is: 'Is the bank *Shari'ah* compliant?' The pressure for *Shari'ah*-compliant finance comes first and foremost from the clients, and this is supported by the country's Central Bank.

The process by which a product is deemed to be *Shari'ah* compliant differs among institutions, many of which will use more than one method. They may hire a specialist organization for *Shari'ah* certification, they may rely on government supervision, or they may appoint an external or internal *Shari'ah* adviser. Al Amal chose to rely on the rulings of the Central Bank. This lack of standardization has an important influence on clients' perceptions of a product's authenticity and their acceptance; this is particularly important for low-income Muslims who may rely more heavily on local imams, who may themselves not be well versed in finance or Islamic financial principles, than on specialist private sector advisers or the government's *Shari'ah* board. This causes a number of problems, particularly in a country such as Yemen that has many doctrines and sects, each of which has its own views, and where there is no readily accessible or universally accepted national *Shari'ah* board.

The approximate accounts in Tables 8.1 and 8.2 show the financial position of Al Amal at the end of 2014, before the war that devastated the country and inevitably damaged the financial position of the bank.

Table 8.1 Al Amal's approximate income and expenditure

	Amount (US$ millions)
Income	
Profit from advances to clients	3.52
Less cost of customer deposits	0.72
Net finance income	2.80
Deposit income from banks and financial institutions	6.30
Fees from clients	0.08
Fees from social transfer services	0.52
Other income	0.70
Total income	10.4
Expenditure	
Wages and salaries	2.00
General and administration expenses	1.60
Zakat (state charity) cost	0.50
Total expenses	4.10
Net profit	6.30

Note: Figures cover the period from 1 January 2014 to 31 December 2014.

Table 8.2 Al Amal's approximate balance sheet

	Amount (US$ millions)
Assets – uses of funds	
Cash and bank balances	0.80
Deposits with banks and financial institutions	49.0
Loans and advances to clients	13.4
Accounts receivable from clients	3.40
Property and equipment	0.90
Total assets	67.5
Liabilities – sources of funds	
Client savings balances	10.0
Client long-term deposits	1.50
Other borrowings	19.0
Paid-up equity capital	19.0
Retained profits and reserves	18.0
Total liabilities	67.5

Note: Figures as of 31 December 2014.

The bank's resources grew by almost 40 per cent from 2013 to 2014, and at that point the portfolio at risk greater than 30 days (PAR30) was less than 0.5 per cent.

Al Amal relies for its funding on equity and donor funding, in spite of the conflicts that Yemen has been going through, which have obviously created an unattractive investment environment. The major sources of funding and investment include a number of credit lines, some of which can be used to lend as Al Amal wishes while others are for loans to specified types of enterprise and clients. These include a US$2 m loan from Silatech, a Qatar-based fund that focuses on youth; a variable fund from the USA-based crowdfunding platform Kiva; funds worth US$1.4 m from Shamil Bank of Yemen and Bahrain, designed to create jobs in new small enterprises; a loan of US$1 m from Al-Asmakh Foundation; and loans for US$1 m from Capital Secretariat, which Al Amal matches, to support job creation. Finally, the SANAD Fund for MSME (micro and small and medium enterprises), a Luxembourg-based fund initiated by KfW, the German development bank, has also committed a US$3 m fund to provide credit for entrepreneurs. These funds do not generally demand a financial return; they require that any profits should be reinvested in similar new enterprises. The funds have formally to be repaid over a period of between two and five years, but it is possible for them to be rolled over for longer terms; foreign currency risks are usually carried by the lenders.

Al Amal emphasizes savings as a way of reaching more clients, to create a savings culture, and to diversify its own sources of liquidity. At the end of December 2014, as can be seen from the accounts summarized above, the balances in its different types of savings accounts amounted to about US$11.5 m, and by the end of July 2015, despite the increasing hostilities, it had over 93,000 active savings accounts with a savings portfolio totalling more than US$17 m. Savers earn a return on their savings on the basis of *mudaraba* or as a share in the profits of the bank.

Al Amal has taken a number of precautionary measures in order to enable the bank itself and its clients to cope with the political crisis, and it has also explored other mechanisms beyond savings to reduce its reliance on donors as sources of liquidity. The bank has also launched a private investors' fund to target social impact investors, both inside the country and abroad. One result of the hostilities is that there are increasing numbers of low-income people who need either to start their own micro-enterprises or to find employment with others.

The armed conflict in 2015 forced some international financing agencies to suspend their businesses with Yemen, and many international funding markets are closed and fund transfers into the country suspended. In response to these events, Al Amal has adopted a new crisis management methodology called 'Value at Risk'. This means that it continues its activities at a minimal level in spite of the risks. Loan risks have naturally increased in the uncertain environment, and clients' demands for loans have been affected

---

Box 8.4 Jameel's experience of Al Amal

War was going on in the city, causing calamities to the people. The streets were blocked, factories and businesses closed, people fled to their villages. I was a victim. I had to close my metal-working business for lack of funds. I stayed in the city, not knowing where to go. There seemed to be no options for the future. The horizon was gloomy. One morning, I was standing by my machines, which would soon be rusty and useless, when two people, whom I had never seen before, knocked at the door. They greeted me; one of them gave me a brochure and said, 'We are from Al Amal Bank.' He then began to explain to me some of the services the bank offers, saying I could get a loan from them. That changed my mind and made me happy for the first time for many weeks. So, I told them that I needed YR 1 million, about US$5,000, to restart my workshop. They soon completed the formalities and the loan was approved; it restored life to my workshop and hope to my 10 workers and me.

---

by the ongoing instability. Nevertheless, AMB has done its best to satisfy its clients' needs and was able to disburse several hundred loans in the months immediately following the start of the conflict in March 2015. This transcript of a statement by a client, Jameel, shows how Al Amal has tried to help its clients (Box 8.4).

By the end of 2014, Al Amal had over a third of the Yemen microfinance market, as measured by the number of active clients. This diversified the bank's market, so that it covered all its target groups of men, women, and even children. Al Amal maintains its leadership position by providing a diverse range of financial services, to a wide range of clients. The bank has also entered into a number of partnerships and has expanded its outreach throughout the main and secondary cities and rural areas through the establishment of a broad branch and agency network, in order to achieve its aim to be 'the bank of the unbanked'.

Al Amal has a 100 per cent eventual repayment record for all its loans so far, and in mid-2015 the PAR30 ratio was 6.15 per cent. This performance can be attributed to its emphasis on regular follow-up after loan disbursal, and on a strong culture of on-time payment. This message is communicated to its clients in a number of ways, and is enforced all the way up to the leadership of the AMB, who feel that the right payment culture among its clients is vital. Clients should feel that they are dealing with a serious yet socially oriented financial institution and not a grant-making body.

Despite the war, Al Amal has been able to continue to offer its services; in the 14 months between April 2015 and the end of May 2016, the bank disbursed some 4,000 loans, with a total value of US$3.4 m, and PAR30 ratio had increased to 8.35 per cent.

Al Amal goes to great lengths to follow up on payments and to maintain a professional relationship with the client. On the day when payment is due, either monthly or quarterly depending on the product, the client is given a 15-minute slot at a particular hour when he or she is expected to come into the branch. If local or family customs make it difficult for a woman client to leave her home, she can send a male family member to the branch on her behalf, or she can pay a field officer when she makes a home visit. Female clients are usually served by one of Al Amal's 90 female field staff.

If there is any delay, the client's name is entered into a daily arrears list, and this is followed up between 9 a.m. and 10 a.m. the next day by a loan officer. If there are no good reasons for non-payment, the officer will then make a client visit, and if the money is not received by 10 a.m., it is followed up by a group visit to the client to press for payment. Loan guarantors or other social groups are contacted as necessary, and senior management is involved in visits and communication on the same day.

Any overdue payments are captured by the management information system in real time and are escalated to the branch manager and area manager on the same day, and then to head office and to the executive director, who sees lists of all payments due on a particular day and their updated status as and when payment reports come in from the branches. This system functions successfully even during active hostilities. Payments are not as yet made by phone, but mobile phone coverage is almost universal in Yemen and mobile phones and SMS messages are used for routine and one-off communications by clients and by staff at all levels.

Arrears are kept at a minimum level by restricting clients' flexibility on changing payment dates, and by keeping the number of clients serviced by one loan officer to between 150 and 200. The branch managers regularly review all overdue repayments, all branches are kept informed of overdue cases, and clients in arrears are blacklisted from further services. Management places the highest importance on on-time repayments, and this culture feeds through to clients; prospective clients who may default are unlikely to apply to Al Amal. The high rate of recoveries also contributes to the financial sustainability of AMB.

Since repayment dates are evenly distributed through the month, a loan officer oversees between seven and 10 client repayments per day. The officers usually have to follow up only one of these at most, because the others are on time. This is possible in most urban areas, but this high level of client contact will be harder to achieve in more remote rural areas as AMB expands. In time it may become necessary to adopt a different model, working through a village bank or council of elders.

Under the concept of 'there are no bad clients, only bad loans', Al Amal has developed an advanced methodology for client screening and selection. AMB also ensures that its funds are going towards economic activities and enterprise development; most loans use the *murabaha* system, whereby Al Amal buys whatever the client requires and then resells it to the client, and this in itself makes it easier for AMB to be fully aware of how its loans are used. Because of this, it is not possible for Al Amal to flourish unless its clients are also doing well. Al Amal also offers partnership and other loans that can be used to finance non-business purposes, such as healthcare, school fees, and so on.

Al Amal is regulated by the Central Bank of Yemen, and like other banks, is required to fulfil the same requirements as any commercial bank, including write-off policy. A loan account can be written off only when it is genuinely uncollectible and worthless. Only if no recoveries have been made for three months after the due date, and there appears to be no chance of recoveries in the foreseeable future, can a loan be written off.

Al Amal has thus far avoided write-offs, through the practices described in this case study, and in general the bank follows the Islamic finance principle: 'If in hardship, then deferment until a time of ease.' It remains to be seen how this policy plays out in the current turmoil that is affecting the country.

Note

1.   The exchange rate of the Yemeni rial to the US$ varied quite widely during the period covered by this chapter. In order to convey the general order of magnitude, I have used an approximate rate of YR 200 to US$1.

About the author

Abdullah Al-Kassim (aaalkassim@alamalbank.org) is the founder of the Partnerships and International Co-operation Department of Al Amal Microfinance Bank.

CHAPTER 9

The experience of Kompanion-Invest in the Kyrgyz Republic

Zamir Pusurov

Kompanion-Invest started its microfinance business in Kyrgyzstan in late 2012. It is a subsidiary of Kompanion Bank (successor to Kompanion Financial Group NBFI), which was set up in 2004 by the USA-based Mercy Corps. Kompanion-Invest is based in the city of Osh. It is one of the smaller microfinance institutions in the country, and has some 500 clients; its growth is limited by its shortage of funds. The majority of its loans are murabaha *based, but it also offers profit- and loss-sharing products and, for particularly needy clients,* qard hasan *loans.*

Keywords: Kyrgyzstan, Mercy Corps, *musharaka, mudaraba, murabaha, qard hasan*

Kompanion-Invest MCC LLC (K-I, or the company) was established by Kompanion Financial Group MFC CJSC (Kompanion), which was registered with the National Bank of the Kyrgyz Republic (NBKR) in November 2011 and transformed into Kompanion Bank in February 2016. K-I became operational in November 2012. Kompanion was founded in 2004 by Mercy Corps, an international NGO headquartered in the USA and Scotland. Mercy Corps was the sole shareholder of Kompanion until February 2015, when a capital increase brought in FMO, the Dutch development bank, and Triodos as shareholders, but Mercy Corps retains majority ownership.

K-I is located in Osh, which has a population of 232,000 and is the second largest city in Kyrgyzstan, located in the Fergana Valley in the south-western part of the country. About 75 per cent of the population of Kyrgyzstan are Muslims. Osh is an ancient city often referred to as 'the capital of the south' and has an ethnically mixed population of Kyrgyz, Uzbeks, and Tajiks. Osh was also the site of ethnic violence between Kyrgyz and Uzbeks in June 2010 that resulted in the deaths of approximately 420 people, with some 80,000 displaced as well as many homes and businesses damaged and destroyed. In response to the violence and in recognition of the gap in access to finance among the Muslim population, Kompanion, with support from Mercy Corps, designed Kompanion-Invest as a way to provide *Shari'ah*-compliant finance to help members of the local community get back on their feet. K-I was capitalized with US$500,000 from Kompanion and was launched in 2012 with

http://dx.doi.org/10.3362/9781780449555.009

the mission to be a contemporary microfinance organization consistent with Islamic norms and to be the company of first choice for its clients.

The leading provider of *Shari'ah*-compliant services in Kyrgyzstan is the Eko-Islamic Bank, which was formed through a predecessor institution in 1998 and began providing Islamic financing products in 2006. It is the only bank in the Kyrgyz Republic that is licensed to use Islamic financing products. At end of 2014, the bank had assets of KGS (Kyrgyzstani som) 3.4 bn (US$57.6 m), loans of KGS 1.21 bn (US$20.5 m), and shareholders' equity of KGS 427 m (US$7.24 m). The bank earned a profit in 2014 of KGS 14 m (US$237,000). Eko-Islamic Bank has approximately 120 offices throughout the country, serving over 100,000 customers with a variety of financial services. These include Islamic deposits and financing, bank cards, and *halal* transfers, among others. The remainder of the Islamic financing market is serviced by around six non-bank institutions, which have total assets of about KGS 55 m, or just over US$9 m. The non-Islamic micro-finance market in Kyrgyzstan is dominated by three microfinance institu-tions (MFIs): FINCA and K-I's parent, both of which are registered banks, and Mol Bulak. In June 2015, they had a combined US$272 m in loans outstanding and 345,000 clients.

K-I disbursed its first loans in 2012 and concluded its first year in business with a portfolio of KGS 2.5 m or US$55,000, which quickly grew to about KGS 20 m or US$333,000,[1] which is where it remained in June 2015 (Table 9.1). Due to a lack of fresh capital, portfolio growth has been stagnant, resulting in ongoing losses since the launch of the business. Client numbers have declined over the period 2013–15 due to the decline in working capital. At present, 70 per cent of K-I's clients live below the poverty line and more than 50 per cent

Table 9.1 Kompanion-Invest's key financial indicators

Year	2012	2013	2014	2015
Loan portfolio	2,511 US$55,000	19,557 US$326,000	20,742 US$345,000	20,097 US$335,000
Number of clients	98	629	466	445
Net income (loss)	(3,021) (US$700)	(1,355) (US$23,000)	(828) (US$13,800)	(810) (US$13,500)
Average loan size	25.6 US$510	31.1 US$518	47.2 US$790	45.2 US$750
Number of write-offs	0	0	444	0
Number of staff	8	17	13	9
Number of loan officers	3	7	7	7
Number of offices		5	5	5
Women borrowers (%)	47%	54%	49%	53%
Disbursed loan amount as a percentage of GNI per capita	52%	52%	64%	64%

Note: All monetary figures are in thousands of Kyrgyz soms unless otherwise stated.

are women. K-I offers four main products, although most of its business is on the basis of *murabaha*.

K-I has been managed by its executive director Zamir Pusurov since its formation in 2011. His background includes work for Eko-Islamic Bank and also for the Islamic microcredit organization Ak-Tilek Finance, of which he was the founder, as well as five years as a lecturer in Islamic finance and business at Osh State University. The board of directors is comprised of four individuals, two of whom also serve on the board of Kompanion. They are as follows:

- Mr Marlis Duishegulov, Chairman, Director of Branch Operations, Kompanion Bank;
- Mr Ulanbek Termechikov, Member, Chief Executive Officer, Kompanion Bank;
- Dr Robin Currey, PhD, Member, Associate Professor, Green Mountain College, Vermont, USA;
- Mr Steve Mitchell, Member, Vice President Financial Services, Mercy Corps.

In addition, K-I has a *Shari'ah* advisory board consisting of three members: two researchers from the Department of Theology at Osh State University and one local practitioner. These individuals advise K-I on issues relating to *Shari'ah* compliance in its business practices. The role of the *Shari'ah* board is as follows:

- approve the conditions of all K-I products and model agreements and approve material amendments and additions that change the status of model agreements;
- ensure monitoring of K-I's compliance with *Shari'ah* standards;
- provide reports on compliance with *Shari'ah* standards to the general meeting of shareholders and the executive board;
- take decisions that are understood by both clients and the public and that are published and announced through other means. K-I should, when required, provide explanations on any decision of the *Shari'ah* board and such explanations should be agreed in advance with the *Shari'ah* board.

In addition to its own in-house board, K-I also uses the board of the Association for Islamic Economics and Finance Development. Together, these two boards assess K-I's compliance with *Shari'ah* principles every year. This might have caused problems, but when K-I launched its business, the director, an expert on Islamic economics, began collaborating with the theological faculty at Osh State University, which has an excellent reputation in Kyrgyzstan. Initially there were some differences of opinion in the interpretation of *qard hasan* and *murabaha* but these have been resolved.

K-I has not had any negative reactions from religious authorities at its launch or since that time, but it needs capital to expand and is considering raising additional external debt financing from institutional lenders. These lenders expect a return and K-I will seek the consent of the *Shari'ah* Advisory Council to borrow funds at interest to be used to grow the company's portfolio. K-I has been informally advised by the council that, in the absence of any alternative sources, it may borrow interest-bearing funds to finance its growth. The situation will be assessed annually to ensure its continued compliance with Islamic principles.

Like its parent, Kompanion Bank, K-I emphasizes good corporate governance. As a result, K-I has a strong company board which strictly applies its corporate governance principles set out in governance documents including a charter and by-laws, as well as *Shari'ah* provisions that govern the institution. The financial statements are audited by Deloitte, an internationally recognized firm, as part of the annual audit of Kompanion Bank. In addition, Kompanion's internal audit team performs the internal audit function at K-I.

K-I currently offers four financing products for income-generating purposes, both for group and individual borrowers. The products available to K-I borrowers are as follows:

- *Murabaha*. Purchasing goods for borrowers and reselling them to the clients with an added mark-up.
- *Mudaraba/musharaka*. The two parties share the profits or losses according to a predetermined agreement. This is typically used to finance assets or working capital. Under *mudaraba*, one party usually provides the finance while the other provides the management expertise, while *musharaka* usually includes some joint equity participation in the business.
- *Qard hasan*. Short-term, interest-free loans, with no conditions built into repayment. These are usually disbursed to very poor people or to students.
- *Bai salam*. An advance payment against future delivery of goods, most often used in agricultural transactions.

In accordance with the *murabaha* agreement, K-I buys the goods being financed and resells them to the client. The client chooses the supplier of the goods, but if the proposed products do not comply with the client's requirements, then K-I offers an alternative supplier with the goods, hopefully, of higher quality. Very few wholesalers or other suppliers in Kyrgyzstan are willing to sell on credit because of the country's economic problems, so K-I's services are very useful for small businesses with limited resources.

Potential clients submit a completed loan application, an identity card, a statement of residence, and some evidence of their sources of income and their credit history. In Kyrgyzstan, everyone has a national identity card and there is a high level of literacy, so nearly everybody has all the necessary documentation, which is required even if they need to borrow only K-I's minimum credit of US$50. Clients or their guarantors can submit salary verification documents, and there is a functioning credit bureau. Clients who have not borrowed before may not have a credit history, but this requirement can be waived when necessary.

Borrowers can choose to be in a group whose members agree to assist each other in case of repayment problems. The group has to have at least three members. Most groups are all men or all women, but mixed groups are possible. In such cases, members must be close relatives to each other. Men and women who are unknown to each other are forbidden from being members of the same group. Individual borrowers who are not in a group are required to obtain guarantors who have to provide at least the same documents as the individuals. The guarantors are assessed in a similar manner as direct borrowers. Individual borrowers must also provide collateral; this can be in the form of movable or immovable assets, and the required coverage ratio is 130 per cent. The collateral may include vehicles, real estate, livestock, or cash.

Kompanion follows the view of Islamic scholars in Central Asia, and buys the required goods on its own account and then resells them to the clients. It may use agents for this purpose, but these agents must not be connected to the clients. Many Islamic financial institutions allow clients to arrange the purchases themselves, theoretically as agents of the institution but actually on their own account, which means that they are not strictly compliant with Islamic principles. K-I adheres more strictly to *Shari'ah*, and the sale of goods by the supplier to K-I and from K-I to the client are documented separately using delivery notes and receipts. The payments by clients to K-I under *murabaha* are made on a weekly, monthly, or quarterly basis, according to the receipts from the clients. As of 30 June 2015, K-I had 407 *murabaha* (see Box 9.1 for an example) and three *bai salam* agreements in progress.

K-I has financed several clients under *mudaraba* profit-sharing agreements, and works satisfactorily on a long-term basis with various small trading companies. If their turnover and profits decrease, K-I's income also goes down. This does not usually result in losses on the principal, as K-I usually has liquid collateral from its clients. As the following case study demonstrates (Box 9.2), KI's policy is first to get to know its clients through *murabaha*. If a client appears to have the potential to be a partner in a *mudaraba* agreement, then K-I prepares him or her for this. It offers its clients training and mentoring, both in farming and business, including elementary financial management and marketing. The cost of this is included in the profits charged for *mudaraba* contracts.

K-I provides non-interest-bearing or *qard hasan* loans, with no fee or margin; these are used for medical treatment, education, refinancing of an old debt, house purchase, livestock, or clothing for vulnerable people. Repayments are also made weekly, monthly, or quarterly in equal shares. As of June 2015, K-I had 27 active *qard hasan* loans in its portfolio, and about a quarter of the credit was for consumer goods. Some items for household use may also be utilized for business, such as a washing machine that is used for a client's own family's clothing but also for outside customers.

Under *mudaraba* or *musharaka* contracts, the two parties divide the profits (if any) from the business transaction. If the business earns a profit, 70 per cent of it is retained by the client and 30 per cent is paid to K-I. If there are losses,

---

Box 9.1 Buying materials with *murabaha* financing

Client A is an active client of K-I. He started a confectionary business in 2013 with KGS 30,000 (US$500) from K-I. K-I purchased confectionery raw materials for the client with *murabaha* financing. The business has been successful and now employs five people. In two years the turnover has risen to KGS 500,000 (about US$8,300). Client A paid a margin of KGS 9,000 or US$150 for the total amount financed of KGS 30,000, making a total of KGS 39,000. He later took a further loan of KGS 100,000 or US$1,700 at a 20 per cent margin and repaid a total of KGS 120,000 or US$2,000.

Box 9.2 Expanding a kindergarten on a profit-sharing *mudaraba* basis

Client B runs a kindergarten. After receiving *murabaha* financing of KGS 500,000 (US$8,300), the kindergarten lost the lease on its premises. K-I helped the client to find a suitable new building, to introduce better accounting procedures and personnel records, and to establish relationships with the pedagogical faculties of local universities. The school now educates 100 children. This project encountered many problems after disbursement of the first loan, but, with support from K-I, the outcome was successful. The client has taken four loans from K-I since 2013. The first was to buy furniture, the second to buy a vehicle to transport the children, the third to finance equipment for the school, and the fourth for building materials to expand the school. Client B's most recent credit was for KGS 400,000 (about US$6,500) on a profit-sharing *mudaraba* basis. The profit is to be shared 70:30 between the client and K-I. For the first three months she could not make her payments to K-I on the profits, but she started to do so in the fourth month. She still has to repay the loan itself of KGS 400,000. This obligation will continue for as long as the original credit is outstanding, and she has the right to repay the capital amount whenever she wishes and then she will have no further obligation to pay K-I its share of the profits.

K-I receives no return but is still entitled to recover its original investment. In all these arrangements, K-I also acts as a mentor and business adviser for its clients. In mid-2015 there were only eight active profit-sharing contracts because of K-I's shortage of funds. As more funding becomes available, K-I intends to increase its profit-sharing portfolio.

As the case in Box 9.3 demonstrates, there have been cases when K-I's clients have had to delay their repayments because of business problems but have then paid in full because their businesses have recovered. Thus far, none of K-I's clients have declared bankruptcy. Almost all the projects that K-I has financed have been successful, and client failure has not been an issue. Clients are not discouraged by the need to keep detailed accounts, because K-I assists them with this as part of its service; the relationship is between partners, rather than between a client and a supplier. Clients appear to always attempt to repay what they owe. They also share the traditional Muslim belief that if someone dies in debt, his or her relatives should take on the commitment to repay.

There are many different types of *mudaraba* or profit-sharing loans, and K-I tries to adhere to the strictest standards. The organization's management has designed one approach that it refers to as 'limited *mudaraba*', which

---

Box 9.3 A client's approach to the losses incurred by an unsuccessful business

Client C received KGS 200,000 (US$3,300) on the basis of *mudaraba* to buy cattle for the production of *halal* sausages. However, he had no experience in this business and did not follow the proper methods for sausage making. As a result, the product was unsellable and the shop was forced to close, resulting in losses for the business. These losses of KGS 10,000 (about US$170) were shared by the client (KGS 7,000) and K-I (KGS 3,000). K-I had initially tried to assist the client to find a consultant to help him run his sausage business, but the client was no longer interested in it. After a six-month delay, the client returned the money and repaid the debt, not by selling equipment but from the family's other income. He recognized that, as a Muslim, he was obliged to repay a debt, even if it had been forgiven. Eventually, he restored the sausage shop and today is making traditional Kyrgyz sausages. The business is now sustainable on its own and does not require any external finance.

---

is financing for a specific project. Each month, on the basis of the client's financial statements, the profits or losses of the project are shared between the client and K-I on a 70:30 basis. K-I's share of any losses is usually deducted from the client's obligation to repay the initial capital. *Mudaraba* is only used for investments in tangible assets, which the client cannot easily remove. The client's obligation also includes an element of mutual insurance, or *takaful*, which in part covers any losses.

When problems do arise with clients who have *mudaraba* financing, K-I monitors the situation on a monthly basis and steps in with advice and other assistance. Since K-I offers *mudaraba* finance only to clients who have successfully completed and paid off *murabaha* credits, including K-I's margin, the partners will already have a close working relationship and are able to collaborate closely in remedying the situation. In the future, K-I hopes to be able to offer *mudaraba* profit- and loss-sharing finance to more of its mature clients who have shown their ability to manage the simpler *murabaha* finance, but they cannot yet do so because of a lack of funds.

Most of the projects in 2012, K-I's first year of operation, were not successful, leading to substantial write-offs and losses as shown in Table 9.1. This was because many customers had limited information about Islamic financing principles, and in their haste to launch the organization successfully, mistakes were made by both K-I and its clients. However, beginning in 2013, K-I conducted client training sessions on 'Financial literacy in Islamic micro-finance', which raised their level of understanding. Following this training, K-I's performance improved.

K-I has never received any grant funding and operates on commercial terms within *Shari'ah* principles. It has continued to operate only with the US$500,000 initial capital contribution from Kompanion that was invested in 2012. This has been used for on-lending to clients as well as to supplement K-I's income to cover operating expenses. Because of its limited capital, K-I is currently not sustainable, but it is raising additional capital, which it hopes will come from a combination of debt and an additional equity infusion. Any new debt funding will be subject to approval by the *Shari'ah* Advisory Council, and the conditions will also have to satisfy any existing creditors.

Note

1. The exchange rate has varied substantially, but the rate used in this analysis is US$1 to 60 Kyrgyz soms.

About the author

Zamir Pusurov (pusurov@k-invest.kg) is Chief Executive Officer of Kompanion Invest.

CHAPTER 10

Ebdaa Microfinance Bank: *musharaka* for small-scale farmers in Sudan

Nawal Magzoub Abdallah

Ebdaa Microfinance Bank is a not-for-profit microfinance institution, which was promoted by the Arab Gulf Program for Development. It is a joint stock company, but its shareholders are committed to reinvesting any profits in the business in order to extend its services to more people. Ebdaa was started in 2013, and has a portfolio of about US$1.7 m and some 6,000 active borrowers with an average loan of US$500, and approximately 9,000 savers. The vast majority of its clients, 90 per cent, are women, and they are organized into groups and served by 49 field staff, operating from seven branches. Most of the bank's clients use murabaha *finance, but Ebdaa also offers* bai salam *or advance purchase and profit- and loss-sharing partnership finance to smallholder farmers.*

Keywords: Sudan, savings, *mudaraba, murabaha, bai salam, ijarah,* AGFUND

Ebdaa Microfinance Bank in Sudan is a private joint stock company which was established with a paid-up capital of US$5 m[1] and received an operating licence in December 2013 in accordance with the Central Bank of Sudan's regulatory framework for microfinance. It was set up as a non-profit institution to provide financial services to owners of small businesses; its legal form is that of a regular for-profit bank, but the institutional and individual shareholders have invested in Ebdaa Bank to achieve social rather than financial gains, and any profits it makes will be invested in its future growth and development, and not distributed to the investors. The bank started its activities in January 2014 with an ambitious three-year plan; it has a target to open 15 branches and reach 43,000 clients over the next three years. This case study briefly describes Ebdaa's activities in promoting Islamic financial products, with particular emphasis on *bai salam* contracts.

Ebdaa's institutional shareholders are the Arab Gulf Program for Development (AGFUND), the Islamic Development Bank, the Farmers Commercial Bank of Sudan, the Sudanese Microfinance Development Company, and the Export Development Bank of Sudan. There is also a small number of individual private sector investors. In addition to its initial capital, Ebdaa Bank is mainly financed by commercial banks using *mudaraba* profit-sharing contracts. The cumulative amount of these credits was US$4,152,000 in May 2015.

http://dx.doi.org/10.3362/9781780449555.010

Ebdaa Bank's objectives are to provide financial and non-financial services to increase economic, investment, and operational opportunities for economically active poor people, to achieve wide outreach in urban and in rural areas by opening a network of branches to increase financial inclusion for the target group, and to promote positive and responsible use of microfinance services.

About 90 per cent of the portfolio is based on solidarity group lending, using a variant of the Grameen model. Loans are disbursed through a group of five to 10 self-selected members. This approach has many advantages: the members are jointly liable and responsible for each other's loans and they therefore use peer pressure to ensure that loans are repaid properly. The members also encourage one another in their voluntary savings, and the groups facilitate training and loan appraisal, cash handling, and recovery. They also learn from each other through the exchange of their experiences.

Field officers play a vital role in the achievement of the bank's lending objectives, and they make up more than 70 per cent of Ebdaa Bank's employees. Fifty-five per cent of them are women. They are carefully selected, and Ebdaa Bank's top management places great emphasis on their training. The field officers work to reach their target clients in urban neighbourhoods and rural villages. They are responsible for promoting the bank's services and making direct contact with customers, helping them to form and join groups, encouraging and assisting them to prepare loan applications, and then evaluating them. They undertake field visits to the customers' homes, families, and businesses, and analyse their findings and data in order to determine the customer's ability and willingness to manage the project and repay the loans. They continue to make follow-up visits to maintain good portfolio quality.

Table 10.1 highlights key financial indicators as of the end of May 2015.

Table 10.1 Ebdaa's key financial indicators

Items	Amount
Number of loans disbursed since inception	7,921
Value of loans disbursed since inception	US$3,959,284
Average loan	US$500
Total number of active clients at the end of May 2015	6,072
Value of outstanding portfolio at the end of May 2015	US$2,261,501
Number of savings accounts opened since inception	9,084
Total number of branches and sub-branches	7
Total number of branches and sub-branches in rural areas	4
Number of solidarity groups	990
Percentage of women borrowers	90%
Percentage of youth borrowers	32%
Total number of staff	70
Total number of loan officers	49
Average clients per loan officer	124

Note: Figures as of 31 May 2015.

Ebdaa does not pay its regular savers anything for their deposits, since the costs of administering these small savings amounts would make this unviable. The only people who Ebdaa pays are the investment depositors, whose deposits are remunerated on the basis of a *mudaraba* contract. The proportion of the profit that arises from their deposits is calculated according to the percentage of the total funds employed which they have contributed. Eighty per cent of this amount is paid to the investment depositors and 20 per cent is retained by the bank.

About 1,200 of the 1,849 clients who have repaid their loans have borrowed for a second time, while about 600 did not want to borrow again immediately. Unlike some microfinance institutions, Ebdaa Bank does not require them to take further loans as a condition of remaining in good standing. Twenty-one clients were dropped from the client list. The reasons vary, but Osama is a typical case (Box 10.1).

Ebdaa Bank provides four basic types of financial products for its clients, using different Islamic methods. They are *murabaha, mogawala, bai salam,* and *ijarah* or leasing. Table 10.2 shows the number and value of contracts under each method.

As Table 10.2 clearly shows, *murabaha*, with 61.6 per cent of all loans provided, is Ebdaa Bank's most popular financial product. Under a *murabaha* contract, the client chooses the items he or she wishes to finance. The bank then purchases these items from the wholesaler or other supplier, and resells and delivers them to the client at an agreed mark-up and according to an agreed payment schedule.

Box 10.1 Ebdaa uses a guarantor's collateral

Osama has a metal workshop and earns a net monthly income of US$365. He borrowed US$1,150 for equipment and materials on the basis of *murabaha* from Ebdaa Bank's main branch. This was on the basis of a 30 per cent profit margin, with repayment over 15 months with equal monthly instalments. He was not in a group and borrowed on an individual basis; he provided a guarantor's cheque as collateral. Osama repaid regularly until the seventh instalment and then stopped his payments. Ebdaa Bank informed the guarantor, who refused to pay. The bank then presented the guarantor's cheque and was paid in full.

Table 10.2 Types of financing techniques and number and value of loans

Product	Number of clients	Value of loans (US$)
Murabaha	10,225	4,500,000
Ijarah	1,785	900,000
Bai salam	1,985	590,000
Mogawala	2,630	1,300,000
Musharaka	2	5,000
Total	16,600	7,300,000

Note: Figures as of 23 March 2016.

Leasing or *ijarah* is most often used to finance the purchase of machinery or equipment. The client selects the item he or she wants to acquire. The bank then buys it and effectively rents it out to the client over a pre-agreed period; the amounts paid, the schedule, and the bank's profit are agreed with the client before the item is purchased. The bank retains title to the item during the rental period, and at the end of this period, the bank transfers ownership of the item to the client for an agreed price, or possibly as a gift.

Ebdaa Bank has increasingly financed clients under *Mogawala* contracts; this is also more commonly known as *istisna*. This is effectively a means whereby a construction business, or a business which manufactures machinery or other large items that take a long time to be completed, can obtain the necessary finance. It allows payments to be made in stages for large projects, and it makes it possible for small businesses with limited funds to finance the production of high-value goods in separate stages when the customer has not been identified or is unable or unwilling to finance the production process itself. In general, it is most often used for buildings, and the customer for the product may be a public sector or other government entity that is not permitted to provide advance finance for its purchases.

About 88 per cent of Ebdaa Bank's clients use one or other of these three Islamic financing techniques, and they make up almost 92 per cent of the bank's contracts by value. Almost 2,000 clients use *bai salam*, which is a less well-known financial product that protects the client from some of the effects of loss. The rest of this case study focuses on this approach.

Bai salam is a form of forward sale and allows advance payment to be made for goods that are to be delivered at a later date. The seller undertakes to supply the customer with a specific product at a future date, and the seller receives the total of the agreed price in advance at the time of contract. The quality of the commodity to be purchased has to be clearly specified, without any ambiguity that could lead to future disagreement.

Bai salam can be used to finance any form of working capital for which a client needs finance before payment will be received from the final customers, but it is particularly suitable for agricultural crops or other commodities, whose quality can be specified by reference to familiar and generally accepted standards, and whose market prices may vary. All Ebdaa Bank's *bai salam* clients are farmers, and the average value of their contracts is about US$250, around half the average for Ebdaa's clients as a whole. *Bai salam* is particularly suitable for smallholders, who tend to be among the poorest people in Sudan; *bai salam* thus reflects Ebdaa Bank's commitment and responsibility to assist the more needy members of society.

Ebdaa Bank started to offer *bai salam* contracts only in late 2014, and it is envisaged that this form of finance will become an increasingly important part of the bank's portfolio. The average profit margin earned by Ebdaa Bank on *bai salam* contracts is about 14 per cent, and the average repayment period is about six months; this product can therefore be profitable for the bank as well as being very beneficial for the bank's clients.

Under a *bai salam* contract, the seller undertakes to supply specific goods or commodities to the buyer at a specified future date in exchange for an advance price that is fully paid at the time of contract. The seller is thus protected from possible future declines in the market price, and the buyer is also able to know the cost of the commodity well in advance. In order to comply with *Shari'ah*, a *bai salam* contract must specify the quality of the goods to be delivered, and full payment must be made to the client at the time when the contract is entered into.

If a client wishes to acquire finance through a *bai salam* contract, he or she must first decide how much money he or she needs, and for what type of crop. The bank's field officer then assesses the proposal and informs the client of the price he or she will receive, based on the figures provided by the Agricultural Bank of Sudan for all commonly cultivated crops. These prices are determined regularly by the Agricultural Bank, taking into account all of the relevant global and local factors. The officer will specify the quality and quantity of the goods to be delivered. After the contract has been approved, issued, and signed by the client, the bank pays the full amount of the agreed price to the client.

Immediately after the harvest of the individual crop, the farmer delivers the agreed amount of the crop, as directed by the bank, to a customer to whom the bank has sold the goods at the prevailing market price. As can be seen, the bank bears the risk that the market price might have decreased between the date when it paid the farmer and the date when the crop is harvested and brought to the bank. If the market price is far above the expectations of the farmer and the bank, such that the farmer appears to be suffering a severe injustice, the bank follows not the letter but the spirit of *Shari'ah*, and pays a proportion of its excessive profit to the client, even though the contract did not stipulate that this was necessary. If, on the other hand, the market price obtained by the bank is lower than the price the bank paid to the farmer according to the initial contract, Ebdaa Bank takes the loss. The farmer is in no way liable for it; the bank's management considers this to be a moral obligation under *Shari'ah*, as well as being important to ensure a long-term sustainable business relationship with its clients.

Kordofan in West Sudan is a traditionally drought-prone area, and the main economic activity is rain-fed farming. Typically, farmers cultivate sesame, groundnuts, and sorghum, as well as gum arabic, which is considered to be Sudan's most important cash crop. Gum arabic is a very widely used natural substance that is harvested from acacia trees in Sudan and other dry or even semi-desert areas; it is an important ingredient of many cosmetics, processed foodstuffs, and other products.

Farmers in the Kordofan often depend for their day-to-day expenses on borrowing from local moneylenders who also buy their crops. These merchants lend only small amounts, however, and they impose very high costs on their loans. The transactions are similar to Ebdaa Bank's *bai salam* contracts, in that they buy the farmers' crops in advance and then sell them at a profit after the harvest, but the profits are usually very high. These transactions are commonly known as '*shail* finance'. For example, in the 2005 season, traders paid farmers the equivalent of US$35 for one *gontar* of gum arabic, which is roughly equivalent to a twentieth of a metric tonne, but when the product was delivered the traders were able to sell it for US$85 per *gontar*. The traders did not attempt in any way to compensate the farmers for the difference.

Ebdaa Bank provides *bai salam* finance for farmers who produce gum arabic and other crops, but on a much fairer basis. The following examples (Tables 10.3, 10.4, and 10.5) show the prices that the bank paid to three typical farmers for their production of sorghum, sesame, and gum arabic in Abu Safifa village during the 2014–15 season, along with the price that the bank received when it sold the commodities after harvest, and the subsequent profit (or loss) made by the bank. The examples demonstrate that, while the bank was repaid in full in that it received the numbers of bags of each crop that had been stipulated in its *bai salam* contracts, the bank made a loss on the sesame transactions because the price fell unexpectedly between the date when the contracts were agreed and the time when the bank received and was able to sell the commodities.

Table 10.3 Example of a typical farmer for gum arabic receiving *bai salam*

Farmer's expense on the crop	US$350
Advanced to farmer by Ebdaa	US$350
Farmer delivered to Ebdaa and sale proceeds received by Ebdaa	3 bags @ US$135 (US$405)
Period of advance	4 months
Profit Ebdaa received from the sale	US$55

Table 10.4 Example of a typical farmer for sesame receiving *bai salam*

Farmer's expense on the crop	US$335
Advanced to farmer by Ebdaa	US$335
Farmer delivered to Ebdaa and sales proceeds received by Ebdaa	4 bags @ US$67.50 (US$270)
Period of advance	7 months
Loss Ebdaa made on the sale	US$65

Table 10.5 Example of a typical farmer for sorghum receiving *bai salam*

Farmer's expense on the crop	US$85
Advanced to farmer by Ebdaa	US$85
Farmer delivered to Ebdaa and sales proceeds received by Ebdaa	2 bags @US$50 (US$100)
Period of advance	8 months
Profit Ebdaa received from the sale	US$15

Table 10.6 Ebdaa's balance sheets

Items	2014 (US$)	2013 (US$)
Assets		
Cash and equivalents	988,000	3,282,000
Investments	2,789,000	–
Outstanding portfolio	1,744,000	113,000
Receivables	323,000	75,000
Stocks	111,000	–
Fixed assets	553,000	176,000
Intangible assets	90,000	–
Establishment expenses	35,000	44,000
Total assets	**6,633,000**	**3,690,000**
Liabilities		
Demand deposits	177,000	2,000
Loans from banks	2,042,000	–
Trade payables and other payables	470,000	177,000
Accrued expenses	8,000	–
Total liabilities	**2,697,000**	**179,000**
Equity		
Paid-up capital	3,896,000	3,500,000
Profit and loss carried forward	10,000	–
Profit and losses for the year	(106,000)	10,000
Total equity	**3,800,000**	**3,510,000**
Total equity and liabilities	**6,497,000**	**3,689,000**

Note: Figures as of 31 December 2014 and 31 December 2013.

Table 10.7 Ebdaa's income for 2014 and 2013

Items	2014 (US$)	2013 (US$)
Income from financing portfolio	253,000	–
Income from investments	53,000	–
Application fee	14,000	1,000
Surplus on revaluation of foreign currencies	158,000	27,000
Surplus on revaluation of stocks	26,000	–
Total income	**504,000**	**28,000**
Less: Expenses		
General and administrative expenses	539,000	17,000
Depreciation of assets	67,000	–
Total expenses	**606,000**	**17,000**
Profit/loss before tax and *zakat*	**(102,000)**	**11,000**

Fortunately, the volume of sesame transactions was relatively low, and the profits made on gum arabic and sorghum were sufficient to cover the losses on sesame. This demonstrates the way in which the *Shari'ah*-compliant transaction enabled the risk to be shared between Ebdaa Bank and its clients, and between the clients who cultivated different crops and thus made losses or profits. This is a distinguishing feature of genuine Islamic banking.

Tables 10.6 and 10.7 show the approximate balance sheet and income statement for Ebdaa Bank in the financial year 2014 compared with 2013. The bank hopes in the future to finance most of its loans from client deposits, but Sudan has a history of high and erratic rates of inflation. Ebdaa Bank therefore considers it necessary to maintain its financial position by holding large cash reserves in US$.

Note

1. Monetary amounts are expressed in US$. Sudanese pound (SDG) amounts have been converted to US$ at an approximate rate of 6 SDG to US$1, which was the rate at the time of the case study.

About the author

Nawal Magzoub Abdallah (nawar7098@gmail.com) is a Senior Manager at Ebdaa Microfinance Bank.

CHAPTER 11

The Port Sudan Association for Small Enterprise Development in Sudan: an NGO 'project' and now a profitable business

Layla Omer Bashir

Port Sudan Association for Small Enterprise Development (PASED) is based in Port Sudan, the main seaport and second largest city in Sudan. PASED was originally started in the 1980s by the UK-based non-governmental organization ACORD, and in 2010 it was reconstituted as a Shari'ah-*compliant microfinance institution serving low-income people in the city. It has five branches in Port Sudan and one in Suakin, a smaller nearby town, and it employs a total of 31 loan officers to service approximately 8,500 clients. In 2015, PASED's loan portfolio was US$2.3 m.*

Keywords: Sudan, ACORD, refugees, *murabaha, mudaraba, ijarah, qard hasan, musharaka*, NGO transformation

Port Sudan is the main seaport and the second largest city in Sudan. It is the capital of Red Sea State, and according to the last census in 2008 the population of Port Sudan was around 1.4 million. It accounts for over 90 per cent of the Red Sea State's urban population and dominates the state in many ways. Although it used to have a high number of refugees, due to the improved political status in neighbouring countries refugees make up a negligible proportion of the city compared with numbers in the mid-1980s. Port Sudan has gone through a process of urbanization resulting from 'push' factors that made people leave rural areas, such as rural decay and drought, and 'pull' factors that attracted people, such as better employment opportunities, improved standards of living, services, and security. This has resulted in an expansion of shanty towns and residential areas that are characterized by poor housing and poor access to basic services.

The Red Sea State has a land-based economy. The main occupations in the rural areas are animal husbandry and agro-pastoral activities. Port Sudan has an active small business sector engaged in various economic activities such as trading and retail services, transportation, and fishing. During the 1980s, many international non-governmental organizations (NGOs) worked in Port Sudan, including ACORD International from the United Kingdom. ACORD's main activities revolved around supporting small-scale craftsmen

http://dx.doi.org/10.3362/9781780449555.011

and apprenticeships through support for the provision of training and microfinance.

Donors supported ACORD International's activities in Port Sudan for more than 15 years, but it was felt that after such a long period of time, the activities in Port Sudan should become self-sustainable and, particularly since the number of refugees had fallen substantially, ACORD decided to gradually phase out its work in Port Sudan. The ACORD Sudan team had succeeded in promoting and building a strong local team, and this meant that the external support, in terms of finance and expertise, could be gradually withdrawn.

After reviewing various options, ACORD was converted into a local NGO with the understanding that the new organization could reach institutional and financial self-sufficiency while at the same time maintaining its commitment to serve the poor. In 2000, an independent poverty-focused local NGO was established, called the Port Sudan Association for Small Enterprise Development, commonly known by its acronym PASED. It continued to deliver financial and non-financial services to poor people, and ACORD gradually phased out its assistance and handed over the programmes to PASED through a three-year twinning agreement. PASED is considered to be a very successful case of transformation from an international NGO to a local NGO.

PASED designed its microcredit programme to be *Shari'ah* compliant. The main objective of PASED is to alleviate poverty among the population of Port Sudan. In 2010, PASED acquired a licence from the Central Bank of Sudan to operate as a non-deposit-taking microfinance institution (MFI), and it continues to operate and expand within this mandate. The high number of financed clients and an increasing turnover indicate that the services of PASED are well accepted among the communities where it works, and that demand from clients is growing.

PASED serves the economically active poor, whether they are women or men. It targets those who have the skills, motivation, and desire to run their own enterprise. Priority is given to the lowest-income entrepreneurs who are financially excluded from the formal financial sector. PASED aims to reach as many poor clients as possible by establishing branches in or near to their communities, and by sending loan officers to the field. There are six branches: five of them are located within the main residential areas of Port Sudan, and the sixth is in Suakin, a town 70 kilometres south of Port Sudan. Women make up more than 65 per cent of PASED's total clients.

In addition to its core programme of providing microcredit, PASED provides a non-financial service called 'Learning for Empowerment Against Poverty' (LEAP). This is a programme exclusively for women and is entirely donor funded. The main donor and strategic partner of the programme is Oxfam-Novib. The programme creates community-based associations for women and these are then used as a channel through which women acquire the necessary skills to start their own small businesses and to manage them with simple accounts and bookkeeping. As the businesses are usually family affairs, illiterate clients can seek the help of their close relatives to keep the books for their businesses, or they attend literacy classes. The programme has created about 30 associations and helps women who have been trained in the groups to access microcredit. Most of the women who have been trained in LEAP apply for finance, and experience has shown that they are invariably the best clients. LEAP includes a women's development centre, capacity-building programmes for the community, and a special poverty loans fund.

PASED operates in a competitive market. In addition to PASED, there are three significant competitive MFIs in Red Sea State, all with offices in Port Sudan. All three use *Shari'ah*-compliant financing methods, with *murabaha* making up the majority of their advances. They provide finance for all kinds of productive and service activities, and they also supply some finance for consumption needs such as healthcare and education fees.

Red Sea Microfinance Institution is a state-owned organization that was licensed by the Central Bank in 2013. Its activities cover all modes of finance including *ijarah* or hire purchase. The Port Sudan branch of Al Osra Bank is part of a specialized national microfinance bank that was established as a public enterprise. It has a wide range of shareholders including the Central Bank of Sudan, the Ministry of Finance, the Sudan Pension Fund, the Social Security Fund, the *Zakat* Fund, the Businessmen's Union, the Business Women's Union, Khartoum State, and some private individuals. It started its activities in 2014. The Port Sudan branch of the Saving and Social Development Bank is part of one of the oldest government banks. It started as a specialist micro-finance bank, but due to its continuing losses it was transformed into a commercial bank with a microfinance window. The bank started its branch activities in Red Sea State in 1993. Table 11.1 summarizes the main features of these banks, along with those of PASED.

In order to compete effectively with these institutions, to promote its lending services to its clients, and to facilitate smooth, efficient, and quick delivery by its branches, PASED's loan products are simply designed with clear procedures described in its operations manual. The manual specifies the loan amounts and duration for each type of loan, and gives simple conditions for clients to move from one step to another. PASED's loans cover productive activities, crafts, home improvements, and services, but PASED does not finance social consumption needs such as school fees and medical expenses, although some banks do provide finance for such expenses. Table 11.2 describes PASED's main loan products.

All PASED's loans are *Shari'ah* compliant. The main methods of Islamic lending used are *murabaha*, whereby PASED buys the products required by the client and then resells them to the client with a mark-up; and *ijarah*, or hire purchase, where PASED buys items of equipment requested by clients and then leases them to the clients, who have the opportunity to purchase them at the end of the lease period. For some larger businesses, PASED offers *musharaka* and *mudaraba* modes of finance in which the risks are shared between the clients and PASED. *Qard hasan* or interest-free loans are also provided when

Table 11.1 The microfinance landscape in Red Sea State

Institution	PASED	Red Sea MFI	Al Osra Bank	Saving and Social Development Bank
Sectors	Income-generating activities and housing loans	Income-generating activities	Income-generating activities	Income-generating activities and housing loans
Loan size (US$)	165–2,500	165–1,650	165–3,300	165–3,300
Term or repayment period	3–14 months	12–36 months	12–24 months	12–24 months
Lending systems	Islamic	Islamic	Islamic	Islamic
Murabaha mark-up rate	2% per month	15% per year	18% per year	15% per year
Documentation requirements	Reasonable	Reasonable	Excessive	Excessive
Grace period	1 month	1 month	1 month	1 month
Loan processing period	5–7 days	15 days	1 month	2 months
Opening balance required (US$)	None	None	85	50
Operation sites	City slum areas	Town centre	Town centre	Town centre
No. of branches	6 branches	Headquarters only	1 branch	1 branch
Target groups	Poor clients	Government employees and poor clients	Poor and non-poor	Poor and non-poor
Non-financial services	Women's empowerment programme and bookkeeping training	None	None	None
Legal entity	NGO	State government	Public enterprise	Central government
Repayment incentives	Larger loans and faster service	Larger loans	Larger loans	Larger loans
Promotional methods	Mouth to mouth, community meetings, and training activities	Local radio and TV stations	National and local media	National media

Table 11.2 PASED's main loan products

Products	Purpose	Type of loan	Period	Collateral
Business loans	Small business start-up or expansion	Individual or group lending	14 months	Personal guarantee for loans Personal guarantee plus post-dated cheques Group guarantee Formal job letter of guarantee
Home improvement loans	Shelter, pit latrines, rooms, fences	Individual or group lending	12 months	Personal guarantee for loans Personal guarantee plus post-dated cheques Group guarantee Formal job letter of guarantee
Community projects	Electricity, drinking water, and other items	Group lending	14 months	Personal guarantee for loans Personal guarantee plus post-dated cheques Group guarantee Employer letter of guarantee

clients are considered to be particularly needy. Brief details of these products are given below:

- *Murabaha* or capital plus mark-up is an agreement between the institution and the client whereby PASED purchases the required goods on behalf of the client and resells the same goods to the client after adding a mark-up of 2 per cent per month. There are fixed, regular repayments.
- *Ijarah* or hire purchase is similar to *murabaha* in that the client buys the required asset from PASED, but *ijarah* is usually used for acquiring durable assets such as equipment, whereas *murabaha* is used for consumable items. PASED uses the same mark-up of 2 per cent per month for both types of loan.
- *Musharaka* is a financial partnership whereby the client and PASED agree to share the initial capital investment and to share the subsequent profits or losses in proportion to their initial contribution to the capital, after 25 per cent of the profit has been allocated to the client to compensate him or her for managing the business.
- *Mudaraba* is similar to *musharaka* except that PASED provides all the capital rather than a share of it, and the client contributes only her or his time and skill. The profits are shared between the two partners according to an agreed percentage, and if the business fails PASED loses its capital and the client gets no returns for her or his effort.

The following case studies (Boxes 11.1, 11.2, and 11.3) describe the experience of three clients.

PASED's loan repayment policy depends either on the type of activity financed and expected cash flow or on the mode of finance, or on both.

Box 11.1 Graduating from small *murabaha* loans to a larger loan

Insaf is a married women aged 45 with five children. In her efforts to improve the family income, she started a small business selling used household furniture to people within her own neighbourhood. Insaf lacked capital and received a small *murabaha* loan from PASED for about US$400. She took similar loans several times, and was then able to get a further *murabaha* loan for about US$2,100, with a 2 per cent monthly mark-up and repayment over 12 months. This enabled her to expand her business and to start to sell new furniture and electrical appliances. Her business has enabled her to earn a good income and to transform her whole livelihood. She can now provide her family with all their daily needs of food and water, and can also quite easily manage to pay the school and college fees for her children in their various stages of education.

Box 11.2 A successful business pioneer started with a PASED loan

Mohammed Hassan is 40, married with three children, and lives in Port Sudan. He comes from a poor background, and, encouraged by his family, when he was young he used to take jobs in his school holidays. After completing school he decided that he would start his own small business. He contacted PASED and applied for a *murabaha* loan for about US$400 to buy a small cement block-making machine. His business grew and he took seven more loans, all on the basis of *murabaha*, with a 2 per cent monthly mark-up and repayment over 12 months, until he reached the stage where his small business had grown into a much larger enterprise. With PASED's encouragement and support he managed to access finance from the Industrial Bank and purchased a full-scale cement products factory. In 2015, his business employed 32 workers, and he has been able to build a house for his family. His children are now all doing well at school and he has also been able to support his extended family. He has also managed to fully repay his bank loan. In 2011, at the Sanabel annual conference in Khartoum, Mohammed Hassan was awarded a prize by Grameen-Jameel as a successful business pioneer.

Box 11.3 A loss due to severe flooding

Alrayah is 58 years old and is married with five children. He is a teacher by profession, but his small salary did not cover his needs. He contacted PASED in 2005 and received a *murabaha* loan to purchase teaching materials so that he could establish a small evening class for students. Alrayah then decided to start a new activity in order to earn a higher income, and chose to start trading in dates. He applied to PASED for a new short-term *mudaraba* loan for four months and contacted his relatives in his home village to arrange for the purchase and transport of the dates to Port Sudan. The operation was successful. He repeated this three times, and then got a fourth loan for about US$2,000 to expand the business. As before, he contracted the farmers and paid the cost in advance. However, that season the Nile flooded far more than usual and destroyed all the houses, farms, and date trees in North State. Alrayah got no dates for his money and PASED also lost the *mudaraba* money that they had lent to him.

The financing contracts usually specify the principal, the profit margin, and the repayment schedule. A grace period is usually allowed in accordance with the type of activity financed. Repayments can be made in monthly or periodic instalments, or by a lump sum payment at the end of the contract, depending on the expected cash flows from the business and the reputation of the client.

PASED requires different forms of security depending on the type of loan. Personal guarantees are the easiest and most affordable for individual loans, and clients are not required to have a bank account. They may be asked to submit a cheque from a third party, and all individual clients must have an official identity card and personal guarantee or social identification from their community leader. In the case of group loans, the loan officer's assessment of the homogeneity and strength of the group is the main guarantee, and the group must also be officially registered and have a legitimate productive activity.

Shari'ah requires that the client should not bear the risk alone. *Murabaha* contracts are the least risky type of finance for PASED in that they are purchase contracts where the client is obliged to repay a fixed amount, which includes a profit margin. In *musharaka*, if there is an unavoidable complete loss, both parties lose all their contributions; if there is a partial loss, it is shared according to their contributions to the initial capital. Under *mudaraba*, the client gets nothing for his or her work and PASED loses all or part of the principal. In all cases, if the operation is insured, the insurance company bears the cost of the loss on condition that the loss was not due to negligence.

As of 2014, PASED had disbursed around 9,000 loans in total with a value of about US$4.5 m,[1] while the loan portfolio during the year was about US$2.3 m. Women constituted about 68 per cent of the total number of clients, and each loan officer handled on average 288 clients. Table 11.3 summarizes PASED's operations.

PASED has certain procedures for approving a loan; these are adhered to strictly in order to ensure that the organization reaches its target group and keeps the risk of default low, but also in order to conform to *Shari'ah*. These procedures cover all the necessary steps for loan processing and recovery,

Table 11.3 PASED's key organizational indicators as of 2014

Total number of loans disbursed	8,905
Total amount disbursed	US$4.3 m
Number of active clients	8,494
Proportion of women clients	68%
Size of loan portfolio at year end	US$2.3 m
Cumulative repayment rate	99%
Portfolio at risk greater than 30 days (PAR30)	1.47%
Proportion written off	0.63%
Number of branches	6
Number of loan officers	31
Total number of staff	49

starting from the initial contact by the client up to settlement of the total loan amount. These procedures can be summarized as follows:

1. The applicant comes to the branch office and the loan officer undertakes initial discussions with him or her in order to determine whether he or she fits the eligibility criteria, and which mode of Islamic finance is most appropriate. If the applicant does not fit the criteria, the application is usually rejected at this stage.

2. Loan officers visit the client's home and place of business to cross-check the information provided earlier at the branch office interview, and to be familiar with the client's home and business for the purpose of future follow-up and monitoring. In the case of community projects or group lending, the leader of the community or the group is visited, as well as the business places of all the members of the group.

3. The loan officer passes the client's application to the branch manager, who studies the case, discusses it with the loan officer, and requests further information if needed.

4. If the branch manager is convinced about the case, then he makes a written recommendation to the operations manager for final approval.

5. PASED and the client sign the contract according to the lending mode of finance, which may be *murabaha*, *ijarah*, *musharaka*, or *mudaraba*. The contract specifies the loan terms and repayment dates. In case of *murabaha*, the cost of the purchased item and the amount of mark-up are clearly stated.

6. For all modes of finance, the guarantors, the clients, and two independent witnesses present their identity cards and sign the contract.

7. The PASED accounts department delivers the approved amount of cash to the loan officer as an advance payment against purchase. This is cleared on provision of the original invoices and receipts. The loan amount is recorded in the branch office cashbook.

8. In the case of *murabaha* and *musharaka*, the loan officer and the client go together to make the required purchases. These are invoiced by the dealer to PASED. The goods are then passed to the client and the client acknowledges their receipt – cash never passes through the client's hands.

9. The loan officer submits the invoices and receipts for the purchased items together with a copy of the signed contract to the accounts section directly after completing the purchase. The contract is checked and signed by the branch manager on behalf of PASED.

10. Based on the original purchase invoices, the accounts section prepares the loan payment voucher and enters the details into the computerized loan-tracking system.

11. In the case of *mudaraba* contracts, the client receives the approved loan amount in cash and is directly responsible for the money. He or she must be able to prove that it is entirely utilized in the business and must keep simple accounts to record the expenses and income of the operation.

PASED strictly applies *Shari'ah*-compliant methods and follows the manual of instructions that has been issued by the Central Bank of Sudan. This ensures that all the procedures are *halal* and are in conformity with the directives of the religious authorities.

The figures in Table 11.4 and Table 11.5 summarize the financial position of PASED at the end of 2014, and its operations during the year.

PASED has accessed finance from five different sources, both for on-lending and for its non-financial programmes. These are briefly summarized in Table 11.6.

Table 11.4 PASED's balance sheet

	Amount in US$
Cash in bank	227,000
Gross portfolio	2,295,000
Less loan loss provision	16,000
Net fixed assets	313,000
Short-term financial investments and other assets	136,000
Total assets	**2,987,000**
Long- and short-term debt	1,550,000
Total liabilities	**1,550,000**
Paid-in capital	365,000
Other reserves	238,000
Accumulated profit	813,000
Total equity	**1,416,000**
Liabilities and equity	**2,966,000**

Note: Figures as of 31 December 2014.

Table 11.5 PASED's income statement for 2014

	Amount in US$
Mark-up and profit on portfolio	863,000
Grants, investment fund returns, rent	57,000
Total income	**920,000**
Financial costs, profit and loss sharing, and costs of *mudaraba* contracts	141,000
Salaries and benefits	343,000
Administrative expenses	153,000
Result before grants and taxation	658,000
Non-cash expenses (depreciation)	18,000
Net income	**244,000**

Table 11.6 PASED's sources of finance

Source of finance	Type of finance	Project purpose
The microfinance unit of the Islamic Development Bank	Loan	Microfinance
Sudan Microfinance Development Company	Loan	Microfinance
Blue Nile Mashreq Bank/ Grameen-Jameel Guarantee	Loan	Microfinance
Oxfam-Novib (UK and Netherlands)	Grant	LEAP women's empowerment programme
European Union	Grant	Enhancing the capacities of civil society organizations

Note

1. Monetary amounts are expressed in US$. Sudanese pound (SDG) amounts have been converted to dollars at an approximate rate of 6 SDG to US$1, which was the rate at the time of the case study.

About the author

Layla Omer Bashir (laylaomerbashir@gmail.com) is General Manager of Sudan Microfinance Development Company, which provides technical and financial support to microfinance institutions.

PART IV

Institutions that also promote (some) profit and loss sharing

This final section contains five cases that are in some ways very different from the 10 preceding examples. BASIX and ACCSL are in India, which has one of the largest Muslim populations in the world but is in no way an Islamic country, and Vasham and BMT Daarul Qur'an operate in Indonesia. This is the world's largest Muslim country by a large margin, but religion is generally interpreted in a more relaxed and liberal way than elsewhere.

The other case is MicroDahab; Somalia and Somaliland, where it is based, are certainly 'mainstream' Islamic places, but MicroDahab is unusual in that it is a newly established subsidiary of a large group whose main activity is international remittances. The Dahabshiil group is wholly commercial, and it has its own very substantial programme of charitable activities, but it also provides a lifeline for the Somali diaspora in Europe and North America to assist their families at home. MicroDahab aims in the future to achieve the same 'double bottom line', and its performance in its first year suggests that it will be able to do this.

BASIX's single branch, *Shari'ah*-compliant operation in Mewat, a predominantly Muslim area south of New Delhi, is also part of a for-profit group, which includes a wide range of finance-related and other types of institution. BASIX was one of the pioneers in Indian microfinance, and was at one time one of the four or five leaders in the field. The business was seriously damaged during the so-called 'Andhra Pradesh crisis' in 2010 but the Mewat operation is one of several parts of the group that have survived the crisis and continue to innovate in a variety of different activities.

BASIX's original motto was 'equity for equity', to demonstrate that mainstream investment capital could also promote equitable distribution of wealth, and the Mewat branch was set up in 2012 in part as an experiment to see whether Islamic financial products could achieve this overarching objective more effectively than traditional interest-based finance. The early results are encouraging, but its expansion is constrained by the parent company's lack of the funds it needs in order to reach break-even.

ACCSL is one of the two examples we have of co-operative institutions. This seems odd, in that Islamic microfinance is in a sense about sharing with others, as opposed to a traditional finance business that makes profits from its clients, but there are large numbers of community-run Islamic microfinance institution (IMFIs), particularly in Indonesia. BMT Daarul Qur'an is one of these. It was founded for religious rather than commercial reasons, and distributes a large proportion of its profits to its members in payment for their savings deposits. It appears to be one of the most successful institutions in our collection; it has not grown dramatically, but it pays for its finance and sustains its operations from its earnings, and seems likely to continue to do so.

ACCSL and BMT Daarul Qur'an are unusual in that their clients' and members' savings balances are sufficient to fund all their outstanding loans; their overall financial position is quite strong, and, unlike most MFIs of all kinds, they do not depend on external funds for their financing. Conventional retail commercial banks usually raise far more from their clients' deposits than they advance to them in loans. ACCSL's and BMT Daarul Qur'an's clients are the owners of the institutions, and thus have a closer link to them than most clients of externally funded institutions; this may also have an effect on their repayment behaviour.

One aim of this collection of case studies was to find *Shari'ah*-compliant institutions that use profit- and loss-sharing products as opposed to *murabaha* or *ijarah* trade and leasing methods, which are in some sense 'cosmetic' in that they avoid the forms of fixed interest but are actually little different in their operations and impact on their clients.

It is thus appropriate to include the case study about Vasham, the only institution in the collection that operates wholly on a profit- and loss-sharing basis. Vasham does not use Islamic terminology, and it obtains its funds from sources that are not wholly *Shari'ah* compliant, but all its transactions with its clients include some element of risk sharing. Vasham might be considered as a crop-trading business, not as an IMFI, but it can be argued that it is more genuinely Islamic in spirit than most of the other cases.

BMT Daarul Qur'an, the subject of the final case study, also provides *mudaraba* profit- and loss-sharing finance. This is mainly used for substantially larger amounts, presumably by better-off clients. Several of the other case studies describe institutions that are experimenting with such products, presumably with the intention of using them more widely in the future, but it may be significant that the one institution that has several years' substantial experience with such products is moving away from them.

CHAPTER 12

BASIX in Mewat, India: an Islamic experiment by a major Indian microfinance institution

Syed Zahid Ahmad, Anoop Kaul, and S.N. Rahaman[1]

This case study describes the pioneering operations of the Nuh branch of Bhartiya Samruddhi Finance Ltd, the microfinance arm of the BASIX group in India. The branch serves the predominantly Muslim population of Mewat, an area some 50 kilometres south of Delhi, although some 15 per cent of its clients are Hindus. The main financial product is murabaha *trade finance, but the branch is also experimenting with other* Shari'ah-*compliant financial products.*

Keywords: BASIX, Mewat, *murabaha*, *musharaka*, participatory finance, India

Bhartiya Samruddhi Finance Ltd

The BASIX Social Enterprise Group in India started its microfinance activities in 1996 under the name of Bhartiya Samruddhi Finance Ltd (BSFL), which was registered as a non-banking finance company (NBFC) by the Reserve Bank of India (RBI). The aim was to provide microcredit to low-income households. Over time, BSFL also started providing them with micro-insurance for life, health, crops, and livestock, as well as technical assistance to support agriculture, livestock, enterprise, and institutional development. By October 2010, BSFL had over 10,300 staff in 220 branches, across 18 states in India, and was serving 1.8 million customers with loans outstanding of US$400 m. In 2009–10, BSFL was rated among the top 10 global microfinance institutions (MFIs) in the MIX Global 100 Composite Rankings.

During the period 2008–10, several MFIs increased significantly in size and four in the state of Andhra Pradesh grew very aggressively. One of them, SKS, decided to go for an initial public offering (IPO) of its shares and had a very successful IPO in August 2010. This attracted the adverse attention of politicians, who were already averse to MFIs because of the perceived 'high' rates of interest they were charging – 24 to 30 per cent per annum – which was construed as profiteering from the poor. MFIs were also experiencing high repayment rates of 99 per cent plus, which was hard

http://dx.doi.org/10.3362/9781780449555.012

for government-subsidized bankers to accept as their recovery rates never exceeded 60 to 70 per cent. In 2010, some MFIs were alleged to have driven a small number of their borrowers who could not afford to repay to suicide. The media accused MFIs of employing coercive recovery practices.

Politicians reacted by making efforts to appear 'pro-poor' and garner votes from this section of voters. The ruling Congress Party felt obliged to come down heavily on MFIs and the Andhra Pradesh state government promulgated an ordinance in October 2010 that effectively prevented MFIs in the state from either collecting remaining instalments of their outstanding loans or giving new loans. This legislation led to a considerable fall in repayments but opposition parties, in their quest to appear more 'pro-poor', demanded the waiving of loans or debt forgiveness, and this in turn triggered mass default. MFIs in Andhra Pradesh lost over US$1.2 bn, while BSFL lost US$120 m.

In spite of this, BSFL continued to operate in states other than Andhra Pradesh, though on a much diminished scale. In 2015, its outstanding loan portfolio was about US$10 m, all outside Andhra Pradesh. BSFL's founder and chief executive officer, Vijay Mahajan, came to believe that *Shari'ah*-compliant finance was more just and equitable as the financier shared the prosperity as well as the adversity of those financed. India is home to the world's second largest Muslim population of nearly 180 million yet it is a secular country, and many non-Muslims are willing to try out this method of financing. So Mahajan chose to call it 'participatory finance' and nurtured a pilot project.

BSFL was built on innovation – in products, channels, market segments, and diversity of services it offered, always with an aim to extend its outreach to those excluded from the mainstream financial sector. As BSFL had about 15 per cent of its clients from the Muslim community, it began to explore working with them in 2007 after publication of the report of the Prime Minister's High Level Committee (2006) – better known as the Sachar Report after the lead author Justice Rajindar Sachar. This report showed that Muslims in India were deeply financially excluded. Many Muslims were not using banks because in Islam, according to *Shari'ah*, giving and taking of money by charging fixed interest (*riba*) is prohibited.

Vijay Mahajan initiated dialogue with several Muslim organizations and he, along with Rahman and Raja Khan, two colleagues with an interest in Islamic finance, visited and studied the work of several Muslim financial institutions around the country – the Roshan Vikas Mutually Aided Cooperative Society in Hyderabad; the All India Council for Muslim Economic Upliftment, which ran Baitulmal Cooperative Credit Society in Mumbai; the 3M Trust, which funded women's self-help groups at no interest in Chennai; the Muslim Fund in Najibabad; and the Al-Khair Cooperative in Patna. Mahajan also attended several conferences on Islamic finance and met scholars and activists in the field of Islamic finance.

Considering the huge untapped potential for participatory finance in India, BSFL decided to initiate a pilot project in July 2011 in the Parbhani district of Maharashtra, where the Muslim population was around 30 per cent and BSFL's

Muslim customer base was around 50 per cent. In the wake of the Andhra Pradesh microfinance crisis, borrowers in Parbhani were also encouraged by local leaders not to repay MFI loans. When BSFL explained the concept of participatory finance to these leaders, they approved the recommencement of business and not only was BSFL able to offer new financing under the participatory method but the recovery of earlier loans also slowly resumed.

While the project showed positive results in Parbhani, the team felt that the past was haunting the future and BSFL should experiment with participatory finance in a location where it had not worked earlier. Therefore, in June 2012, the pilot was brought to the Mewat district of Haryana, about 70 kilometres south of Delhi, where a particular group of Muslims, known as Meos, constituted over 70 per cent of the population. Their main source of livelihood was agriculture; this was dependent on rain as canal and bore well irrigation covered less than a quarter of the land. Many depended on animal husbandry – buffaloes for milk and goats for meat. Non-farm activities included stone quarrying and small trading.

Before BSFL entered this market in June 2012, its staff carried out a number of exploratory visits, which were greatly facilitated by Mehmood Khan, who had decided to return to his native Mewat after a successful career that had culminated in his position as Global Director for Innovation at Unilever in London. Khan had already taken several initiatives to uplift this backward area, including setting up demonstrations in organic farming, dairy, vermicomposting, biogas, and a village factory for stitching uniforms and clothes.

BSFL transferred its experienced executive S.N. Rahaman from Parbhani to establish the first ever exclusive participatory microfinance unit of BSFL in Nuh, a small town 70 kilometres from Delhi that is the district headquarters of Mewat. He appointed a fresh team of five livelihood service representatives, two field executives, and one accountant to promote operations. A Mumbai-based consultant, Syed Zahid Ahmad, was taken on board to guide, train, and counsel the team as well as to involve local religious leaders and organizations. This team was given the task of promoting the new participatory finance business in five blocks of Mewat district spread out over an area of 1,860 square kilometres and inhabited by 1.1 million people.

As is common in India, there are many branches of government-owned banks in Mewat. These banks had lending targets that they tried to meet reluctantly, as their loan recovery rates were as low as 20 per cent. The state government agencies and some NGOs had also started a campaign to form women's groups for savings and credit, and these 'self-help groups' were then linked to banks for the purpose of giving bulk loans to the group for on-lending to its members. There were no MFIs in this district; SKS Micro Finance had worked in the area for two years but had had to close its operations because of a high default rate.

Initially, it was a challenging task to convince people that BSFL was there to provide *Shari'ah*-compliant microfinance. The team needed to educate people and create awareness about this type of finance, addressing questions such as how were its products *Shari'ah* compliant. And how would BSFL go about participating in their micro-enterprises and sharing their risk? The population had never seen a company providing *Shari'ah*-compliant finance and was not sure of its intentions. BSFL decided to meet local religious leaders to brief them about its model and to receive their support. After three months of field surveys, customer education, and awareness campaigns, BSFL started identifying potential activities and customers and finally started extending microfinance in September 2012.

BSFL has lent to a wide variety of businesses, including agriculture and animal husbandry, clothes, footwear and other retail outlets, transport and garages, workshops making items and offering repairs, construction, and even medical laboratories.

India has yet to introduce any regulatory provisions specifically for Islamic banking. Therefore BSFL, being a registered NBFC under the RBI, had to undertake the participatory finance pilot in line with the existing guidelines of the RBI. For example, the repayment instalments of loans, including principal and interest, expressed in monetary amounts or as a proportion of the principal, must be fixed and mentioned in the repayment schedule that is handed to the customer at disbursement. Any delay beyond 90 days, irrespective of the cause, means that the loan has to be treated as non-performing. Even if the reason was genuine and BSFL were willing to reschedule the loan, it would not be allowed to do so. Further, the annual effective percentage profit rate must not exceed 26 per cent.

BSFL designed and introduced four *Shari'ah*-compliant financial products:

- *Murabaha (cost plus mark-up).* BSFL purchases the materials from the supplier, adds a certain profit margin, and resells the materials to customers on credit for between 12 and 24 months. The value added taxes are duly collected from the customers at the time of financing and paid to the authorities concerned. The profit percentage is adjusted so that the effective rate of interest on the transaction does not exceed the RBI limits.
- *Diminishing musharaka (diminishing equity finance).* BSFL enters into a partnership with the customer to purchase an asset, such as a buffalo. The customer and BSFL jointly purchase the buffalo and then BSFL allows the customer to use the buffalo by paying monthly rent to BSFL against the use of BSFL's outstanding share in that asset and also to buy part of BSFL's share every month. The rent amount decreases in accordance with BSFL's diminishing share in the asset. After buying back all BSFL's share in the asset, the customer becomes complete owner of the asset and does not have to pay anything further to BSFL. In the event of any loss in the asset, BSFL, along with the customer, is liable to share the risk.
- *Bai salam (advance purchase).* BSFL signs a forward sale agreement with farmers at the time of sowing wheat or barley. BSFL specifies the quality, quantity, and price at the time of agreement and makes full

payment in advance for the crop; the date of supply is deferred until harvest. After receiving the crop, BSFL sells it at the prevailing price, including tax (VAT), in the open market.

• *Qard hasan (benevolent loan without interest).* So far, BSFL has extended just one *qard hasan* loan of Rs (rupees) 15,000 (about US$225) to help one patient obtain medical treatment. BSFL did not charge anything over the actual loan amount and recovered the principal in 12 months. As this is a non-commercial product, BSFL has decided that it will be given only sparingly.

Operational procedures

Unlike conventional interest-based microfinance, under participatory finance BSFL's focus is on increasing customers' income levels through livelihood promotion rather than merely extending loans and recovering debts. BSFL encourages individuals to undertake additional livelihood activities, especially those who are already working and have sufficient knowledge, skills, and experience to expand their activities. For example, a farmer with one buffalo can continue agricultural activities but increase the number of buffalos to enhance his dairy production, or a grocery merchant can expand his business by building a larger shopfront.

Under the participatory finance model, the customer has to have a minimum of two years of experience in a particular livelihood activity. Along with the application form, the customer also needs to provide proof of identity, which states her or his age; this can be, in order of preference, a secondary school certificate, an election identity card, a government ration card, a driving licence, a certificate from the village government department or '*gram panchayat*', or a self-declaration from the customer. BSFL, of course, makes no distinction between Muslims and non-Muslims in its loans; the terms and conditions are the same for everyone, and the Nuh branch has a number of non-Muslim clients.

Self-declaration of age is accepted only in selected cases, and so far only 10 per cent of proposals with this form of identification have been assisted, and it is not acceptable for customers over 50 years of age. A recent photograph is also required from borrowers and the following additional documents are required for the different loan products (Table 12.1).

Performance so far

Up until 30 April 2015, the project had cumulatively financed 589 people, spread over 92 villages of Mewat district, in 34 months. The cumulative financing was Rs 13.5 m (US$225,000), with an average investment by BSFL of Rs 19,904 (US$330). By the end of November 2015, there were 76 per cent Muslim and 24 per cent non-Muslim customers, and 81 per cent were male and 19 per cent female. More could have been done had more funds been

Table 12.1 Documentation required for *murabaha*, diminishing *musharaka*, and *bai salam* loans

Documents	Murabaha	Diminishing musharaka	Bai salam
Registration (applicable for 5 years)	Essential	Essential	Essential
Recent photograph	Essential	Essential	Essential
Application and sanction	Essential	Essential	Essential
Agreement with the customer	Essential	Essential	Essential
Letter of undertaking (for amount above Rs 20,000 or US$330)	Essential	Essential	Essential
Simple mortgage deposit of title deeds			Essential
Co-obligation or guarantee	Essential	Essential	Essential
Statement of continuity of partnership (for repeat customers)		Essential	
Proof of identity for borrower and guarantor	Essential	Essential	Essential
No overdue letter (from bank)	Essential	Essential	Essential

Table 12.2 The financial performance of BSFL in Mewat

	2012–13	2013–14	2014–15	2015–16
Income	3,400	12,100	12,800	10,200
Salaries	12,100	24,800	25,000	24,700
Travel	600	600	300	3,500
Rent	700	1,600	1,800	2,000
Administration	1,600	1,900	2,400	14,700
Total expenses	15,000	28,900	25,900	44,900
Loss	(11,600)	(16,800)	(16,700)	(34,700)

Note: All figures are given in US$. Indian rupee amounts have been converted to approximate US$ amounts at the rate of Rs 60 to US$1.

made available for the experiment from BSFL, but by March 2016 considerable progress had been made, as is shown in Table 12.2.

Due to rigorous follow-up by field staff and the network of outlets where clients can repay their instalment to BSFL locally, it was able to maintain nearly 100 per cent recovery. There were 17 borrowers in default out of 396 current clients, with a total overdue amount of US$800; this was about 1.2 per cent of the total outstanding. In the majority of these cases, the business activities had closed and in some cases the borrowers had left the area.

This project is still at pilot stage. BSFL was constrained for funds and so the project has not yet achieved break-even, but once the lending levels increase it is expected that the cumulative losses will be wiped out. The figures in Table 12.2 summarize the financial performance of the BSFL Mewat operation for the four years since its inception.

Actual operations started in October 2012, halfway through the 2012–13 financial year, so these figures represent results for three and a half years. The cumulative disbursements up to 31 March 2016 amounted to US$250,000. This is only a small proportion of BSFL's total portfolio, as might be expected from a single branch experimental project. The cost of funds is not included in the expenses, since the funds were not specifically borrowed for this operation from an investor or depositor; they were allocated for the pilot project by BASIX head office.

The cost plus *murabaha* product, whereby BSFL buys and resells materials to its clients, accounts for 93 per cent of the total portfolio, but, as is shown below (Table 12.3), it is hoped that the value of other financial products will increase when further funds become available. The transaction costs involved in buying the required assets from the market and then reselling them to clients are not shown separately, since these transactions go through the local market and BSFL does not take physical delivery.

Although *murabaha* dominates the initial portfolio, it is anticipated that as and when the operation expands its financing, partnerships will be spread over a wider range of methods, as shown in Table 12.3.

It was decided not to allocate funds to increase the scale of the operations and to reach break-even point, because this was a pilot project whose objective was to test the concept of participative *Shari'ah*-compliant financing. The administrative costs are overstated by perhaps 25 per cent because the staff at the Nuh branch also work on other BSFL activities.

Table 12.3 The characteristics of BSFL's finance products

Product	Anticipated share of portfolio (%)	Average amount (US$)	Used to finance	Profit margin (%)	Repayment period
Seasonal *murabaha*	25	250	Perishable items such as milk, eggs, baked items, vegetables, and fruit.	5	12 weeks
Annual *murabaha*	25	350	Non-perishable items such as cloth, garments, crockery, cosmetics, and furniture.	15	12 months
Diminishing *musharaka*	25	750	Capital items such as buffalos, copying machines, printers, and computers.	20	24 months
Bai salam	15	750	Advance purchase of food grains.	20	6 months
Musharaka	10	8,000	Participation through equity to help existing enterprises to grow, such as dairy cattle, poultry, beekeeping, horticulture, and fish farming.	25	30 months

BASIX has projected that the operation will reach break-even and will cover all its costs, including the cost of funds, once the portfolio reaches an outstanding value of Rs 50 m, or around US$850,000. It would be substantially profitable beyond that point, and it could earn its investors an annual return of around 10 per cent once the portfolio reached US$1.2 m. The experience of the Nuh branch in Mewat demonstrates that this is achievable. The success that the pilot has achieved can be attributed to the determination and confidence of the BSFL team and its leader, and the guidance, co-operation, and support that was provided by Mehmood Khan and other local leaders. The local Muslim community fully accepted and approved of the intervention.

The pilot operation in Nuh demonstrated that *Shari'ah*-compliant financing has a market and that it is potentially profitable. In spite of its unfamiliarity, and the apparent complexity of the various types of financial products, the experiment has shown that it does have some advantages over conventional fixed-interest financing.

The customers appear sincerely to appreciate that BSFL is joining their micro-enterprises as a partner, and will share in both the profits and the losses. BSFL is not regarded as yet another lender that burdens people with debt, but as a partner that trusts them and is willing to bet on their capacity to earn a living for themselves and a return for their financial partner. The system also ensures that finance is properly used; BSFL pays the money directly to the supplier and not to the micro-entrepreneur.

All the money is used for business, and none is spent on meeting consumption needs. The *murabaha* buying and reselling system also helps build the local economy, since BSFL first purchases the livestock, raw materials, or whatever other equipment or assets are required and then gives them to the client; this promotes trade in the local area, and creates an income multiplier that enhances the purchasing power of local citizens.

The *bai salam* forward sale system helps farmers to receive an assured fair price for their harvest; they can sell their agricultural produce in advance and meet their financial needs without resorting to high-interest loans from local moneylenders. This also protects them from price uncertainty at the time of harvest.

BASIX is considering a number of possible steps through which it might build on the pilot in Nuh. It may choose to hive off the participatory finance portfolio from BSFL and to raise funds to scale up the project, or to explore opportunities for BSFL itself to extend the model to other states or locations in India. BASIX has already completed a business potential survey for this. Regardless of which option is chosen, it will be necessary to persuade the government of India or the Reserve Bank to grant full policy support to the participatory finance model.

During the four-year period from 2012 to 2016, there were no client failures or dropouts. A small number of clients were in arrears, but BSFL anticipated that all its investments would ultimately be recovered. The following short case studies describe four of BSFL's participatory finance partners, were finance was given using *murabaha*, and show how their businesses benefited from the partnerships (Boxes 12.1, 12.2, 12.3, and 12.4).

Table 12.4 summarizes these four customers' transactions.

Box 12.1 Using a *murabaha* loan to purchase ayurvedic medicine

Haroon is 60 years old and has been practising traditional '*unani*' or ayurvedic medicine for 35 years in Khodbasi, a village near Nuh. While he was studying medicine at Allahabad University, a poor person approached him with a severe stomach complaint. Young Haroon looked in a medical textbook and prepared some medicine for just 75 *paise* (three-quarters of a rupee or about one US cent). It cured the patient completely. Since then, Haroon has been making his own ayurvedic medicines and providing them at low prices to treat poor people. He also sometimes prescribes regular allopathic medicines. He has earned a good reputation and has about 300 patients. However, he often has to sell medicine on credit, and he has always been short of finance; he never has enough money to hold sufficient stocks of the materials he needs to make his medicines. He approached BSFL and has taken two *murabaha* loans, for US$225 and US$300; these have enabled him to increase his stocks from US$250 to US$420. BSFL not only provided the finance for this, they also identified the suppliers. He estimates that his earnings have gone up by about US$1,000 a year, and he is also able to offer a better service to his patients. Haroon has paid back his loans in full and as a result BSFL received a profit of US$80 from this investment. He is grateful to BSFL for the assistance; he has eight children and would otherwise not be able to afford to take care of his family.

Box 12.2 Buying rickshaws to expand a business

Sadi earned about US$150 a month pedalling his cycle rickshaw in Nuh. He has taken two loans from BSFL, for US$140 and US$225, and these have enabled him to buy three more rickshaws. He still pedals himself from time to time, and rents out the other three; this has increased his monthly earnings from US$150 to US$200. His old rickshaw is worth about US$40 but his assets now amount to almost US$550. He, too, has completely repaid his loans and BSFL has in turn earned US$60 from him.

Box 12.3 Two *murabaha* loans from BSFL allowed for an increase in stock

Hafijan has been selling cosmetics, costume jewellery, and shoes in Ghasera, a small town about 10 kilometres from Nuh, for about five years. This enables her to supplement her husband's income and to educate their six children. She has taken two *murabaha* loans from BSFL, for US$300 and US$345. The extra finance has enabled her to increase her stocks of bangles, and the loans, along with the additional profits she has earned, have allowed her to double the value of her stock from US$2,500 to US$5,000. To accommodate the stock, she had to rent a larger shop in 2014 and she is now looking at still more spacious premises. She estimates that her annual income has increased by about US$750. She has been able to repay BSFL the loans as well as enabling BSFL to earn about US$100. Her husband, who owns a small farm and had also been working as a driver, has given up the driver's job. He plans to join his wife's enterprise and they are planning to start selling ready-made garments, starting with suits for women.

Box 12.4 A Hindu entrepreneur benefits from BSFL's *murabaha* loans

Mukesh is from the minority Hindu community in Tauru, a small town some 20 kilometres from Nuh. He does not own any land, so when he left school he started a business selling cosmetics and bangles. When he got married, his wife, Santosh, joined him in running the business and they keep their shop open for 12 hours a day. During the wedding season they keep their shop open even longer, until 11 p.m., and their sales can reach as much as US$350 per day. They have now been married for 17 years and have four children. They took their first loan of US$300 from BSFL in 2013 and followed it up with another loan of US$375. This has enabled them to increase their stock from around US$650 to US$2,500. They estimate that their profits have gone up by about US$750 a year, and their loans have enabled BSFL to earn about US$100. The loans are on the same interest-free basis as all the loans from BSFL's branch in Nuh; most of the people in the Mewat area are Muslims, but non-Muslims also find the terms attractive. Mukesh has repaid his loans on time and he is now looking for another loan from BSFL, as he and his wife have decided to get into the business of selling costume jewellery.

Table 12.4 The four customers' transactions

	Enterprise	Purchase cost (Rs)	Added profit (Rs)	Total recovered (Rs)	Repayment period	Months
Haroon	Doctor	15,000	2,250	17,250	Nov. 2013 to Nov. 2014	13
		20,000	3,000	23,000	Feb. 2015 to Feb. 2016	13
Sadi	Rickshaw	9,300	1,395	10,695	Jan. 2014 to Dec. 2014	12
		15,000	2,250	17,250	Apr. 2015 to Apr. 2016	13
Hafijan	Shoes and cosmetics	20,000	3,000	23,000	July 2013 to June 2014	12
		25,000	3,750	28,750	Aug. 2014 to June 2015	11
Mukesh	Bangles and cosmetics	20,000	3,000	23,000	May 2013 to Apr. 2014	12
		25,000	3,750	28,750	July 2014 to Aug. 2015	14

Note

1. The three co-authors work with the BASIX Social Enterprise Group and its NBFC MFI Bhartiya Samruddhi Finance Ltd. They have received guidance and inputs from Vijay Mahajan, Mehmood Khan, Mohammed Riaz, Raja Khan, and field support from Mohmmed Sajid, Waseem Akram, Arshad Hussain and Ms Zarin. The programme was headed by S.N. Rahaman.

Reference

Prime Minister's High Level Committee (2006) *Social, Economic and Educational Status of the Muslim Community of India*, New Delhi: Government of India.

About the authors

Anoop Kaul (anoop.k@basixindia.com) is National Head, Inclusive Growth, Basix Social Enterprise Group.

Syed Zahid Ahmad (economicinitiatives@gmail.com) is the Founder of Economic Initiatives and BASIX's consultant for its participatory finance initiatives.

S.N. Rahaman was Head of BASIX's Social Enterprise Group's participatory finance initiatives. He died in a road accident in Mewat on 9 February 2016. The editors and his colleagues wish to pay tribute to his invaluable contribution to the pioneering work of BASIX's project in Mewat.

CHAPTER 13

MicroDahab in Somalia: a subsidiary of Africa's largest remittance company

Mohamed Ahmed Liban

MicroDahab was set up in Somaliland in 2014 by Dahabshiil Bank International, a subsidiary of Africa's largest remittance company, in order to enable unbanked people throughout Somalia to access financial services. MicroDahab offers a full range of Shari'ah-*compliant financial products, and the majority of its around 3,000 clients are using* murabaha *finance. MicroDahab has seven branches in all parts of Somalia, and is expanding rapidly.*

Keywords: Somalia, Somaliland, ex-conflict, Puntland, Dahabshiil, *murabaha, musharaka, mudaraba, qard hasan, ijarah*

Introduction

MicroDahab is a microfinance institution (MFI) based in Somalia, with a presence in all three regions of South Central, Somaliland, and Puntland. It started operations in October 2014, after spending several months researching the market and demand for Islamic microfinance and conducting a detailed feasibility study. MicroDahab is a subsidiary of Dahabshiil Bank International, the largest Islamic bank in Somalia by both deposits and outstanding loans portfolio, and the bank itself is a subsidiary of the Dahabshiil Group, which owns and manages the largest remittance company in Africa, Dahabshiil Money Transfer.

The various regions of Somalia are emerging from a period of internal conflict and strife, and, as the country grows, the demand for different types of financial services is increasing. The majority of the population has no access to the formal banking sector, and the demand for microfinance has always been substantial.

In order to address this demand and to reach the large number of people who had no access to formal financial services, MicroDahab was launched and has seen tremendous growth in its short lifespan. In October 2014, it had just 35 clients; a little over one year later, in December 2015, it had 2,758 active customers. This rapid growth is illustrated in Figure 13.1

The few clients who have dropped out have done so for various reasons: some have closed their businesses or left the area; some have been pushed

http://dx.doi.org/10.3362/9781780449555.013

	Oct 14	Nov 14	Dec 14	Jan 15	Feb 15	Mar 15	Apr 15	May 15	Jun 15	Jul 15	Aug 15	Sep 15	Oct 15	Nov 15	Dec 15
■ Total customers	35	142	351	541	607	744	987	1,240	1,368	1,589	1,921	2,047	2,584	2,684	2,902
☐ Active customers	35	142	351	541	605	742	974	1,216	1,336	1,538	1,854	1,978	2,484	2,570	2,758

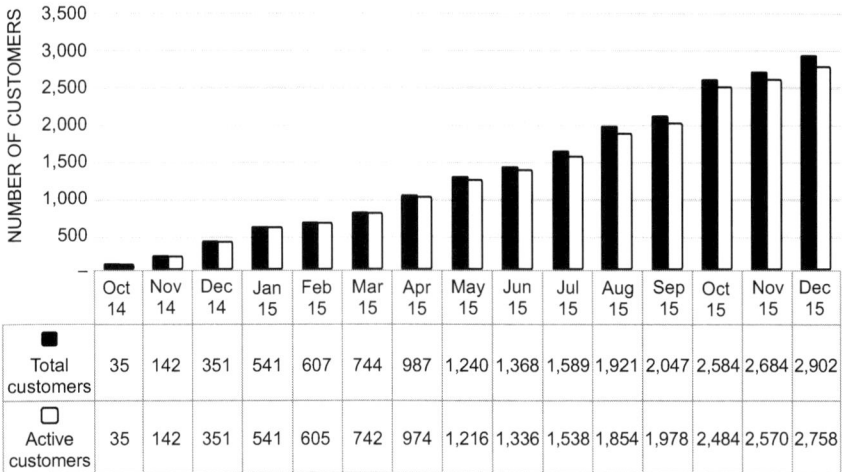

Figure 13.1 The growth in MicroDahab's customer numbers from October 2014 to December 2015

out by their groups because of internal conflicts or repayment difficulties; some do not need more finance; and others have been discouraged by the formalities that MicroDahab necessarily requires. Nevertheless, the dropout rate of about 0.5 per cent is very low by regional standards.

Having served almost 3,000 clients across Somalia, MicroDahab considers that it has only scratched the surface of the demand for microfinance services and plans to increase its number of active customers to 10,000 by the end of 2016 and to increase its presence in the country from seven to 11 fully fledged branches.

As a microfinance business that serves customers in various economic sectors with different financing requirements, MicroDahab has developed *Shari'ah*-compliant financing products that meet the many different needs of its customers. The most important products are *qard hasan, murabaha, mudaraba, musharaka,* and *ijarah*.

Qard hasan loans are loans that are provided by MicroDahab with no profit. These loans are usually provided to students or to very poor people, given that one of MicroDahab's main objectives is to alleviate poverty and to help people who are in absolute need. *Qard hasan* loans are provided at zero mark-up, with no fees for administrative charges, in order to help bridge the financing gap for the many people who have no other options. These loans are typically provided to pay for university costs or school fees for students who are working part-time and are unable to raise the necessary finance for the fees that have to be paid when their studies start, or for health expenses and other non-traded goods and for people considered as living in absolute poverty.

Murabaha loans are made to enable borrowers to receive goods now and to pay later. MicroDahab buys whatever the client wants, and then resells it to the client at an agreed fee or mark-up. The cost of the product, and the mark-up, have to be paid for over time according to an agreed schedule, so in effect this is like a regular credit sale. *Murabaha* financing accounts for the vast majority of MicroDahab's portfolio. Small business owners have diverse needs, and they seek financing for all sorts of items such as small fishing vessels, farm equipment, fuel, fertilizers, and other goods, either for their own use or, if they are small shopkeepers, for resale.

The usual procedure is for the client to identify a supplier and find the right product and then negotiate a price. The client then approaches MicroDahab, which directs its agent to purchase the specified goods at a pre-negotiated price. This avoids suppliers overcharging the agents or purchasing goods with slightly or even completely different specifications. After MicroDahab has bought and paid for the goods as per the request of the client, MicroDahab's agent takes possession of the goods and then transfers their ownership to the client by obtaining his or her signature on the delivery note and on the *murabaha* contract, which lays out the timing and amounts to be paid. The case study in Box 13.1 describes a client who has taken out several *murabaha* loans.

A *mudaraba* contract is based on a partnership in which one partner is the financier and investor, or silent partner, and the other partner is the manager of the funds, or working partner, who manages the financier's investment in an economic activity. MicroDahab considers that there are many people in Somalia who have the technical skills to operate a small farm or open a small fishing business but who lack the finances to do so. It provides finance to such people so that they can apply their skills, knowledge, and experience to a business and can receive the capital they need from MicroDahab.

In more formal small- and medium-sized businesses, such as many of those based in the larger cities in the region, MicroDahab uses standard accounting procedures to determine the profits of the businesses in which it

---

Box 13.1 One of MicroDahab's first *murabaha* clients

Muna Ahmed was one of MicroDahab's first *murabaha* clients. She is a 35-year-old female entrepreneur who has a small home-based catering business in Ahmed Dhagax district of Hargeisa. Through her business earnings she was able to cover the day-to-day needs of her family, but no more. In 2014, she bought US$500 worth of goods on credit from MicroDahab under a *murabaha* contract. MicroDahab bought the goods from a supplier according to the price and specification that Muna had agreed. She repaid the debt on schedule in five months. This demonstrated the potential of her business and Muna then received a second loan for US$1,000 to be repaid over seven months. She completed the repayment of this second loan ahead of schedule in October 2015. Muna then identified a guarantor who was acceptable to MicroDahab and, because of her good credit history, MicroDahab provided Muna with her third loan worth US$3,000, with which she bought more supplies and opened a new catering shop 500 metres from her home. Muna's business flourished and enabled her to provide for her family's living expenses and also cover their education fees. Her 20-year-old daughter is now enrolled in university and her two sons are currently studying in school. Muna also has further ambitions and definite future plans for her business. She aims to apply for a further loan of US$6,000 to enable her to open a second branch in another neighbourhood in order to reach more customers.

has invested through a *mudaraba* contract. These procedures are transparent and acceptable and can be closely monitored by both parties. When financing so-called 'informal sector' businesses, such as the livestock trading enterprises that many Somali women run, or home-based micro-businesses, a MicroDahab staff member and the client discuss and agree on an assessment of the likely future profits using past figures or rough estimates. They then agree on an estimate of the profits that will be earned in a certain number of months. These rough figures can, of course, turn out to be wrong. If this happens, the client has to produce credible reasons to show that the reduced profits or losses were not caused by her or his negligence, but MicroDahab does not charge any extra fees or levy any penalties whatever the circumstances, as this is considered to be against *Shari'ah*. The following case study (Box 13.2) describes the case of a client who graduated from *murabaha* to *mudaraba* loans.

Musharaka is designed to finance joint ventures on a profit- and loss-sharing basis, and is similar to *mudaraba* in that it is designed to provide funding to

---

Box 13.2 Graduating from *murabaha* to *mudaraba* finance

Maryam Nasir Jaamah was one of MicroDahab's first clients, and she has taken both *murabaha* finance and, after this was successfully completed, a *mudaraba* profit- and loss-sharing loan. Maryam is a 49-year-old fruit and vegetable retailer who had been selling in the city market since 1998. In that time, Maryam had built her business from being a small retailer who purchased goods from various wholesale suppliers for resale to become the leader of a whole group of importers who bring bananas from neighbouring Ethiopia and either resell the fruit themselves directly or sell it through other retailers. Maryam received her first *murabaha* loan of US$500 from MicroDahab in December 2014. She repaid this ahead of schedule in March 2015, and then she and a group of four other women requested that their financing be converted to *mudaraba*. They found that *murabaha* was too restrictive, in that it could only be used to purchase items for resale from one or a small number of nearby suppliers. This limited the number and variety of goods that the women could buy with the loan. After assessing the overall risks involved, MicroDahab agreed to provide funding to the group of five women at US$750 each, a total financing of US$3,750. This money was to be repaid after six months, and they agreed that the expected profit during the period would be about 14 per cent or a total of US$525. It was agreed that this would be shared on a 60:40 basis, with 60 per cent of the profit allocated to MicroDahab for providing the finance and 40 per cent to the five women for their management and labour. The group used the money to procure nine shipments of bananas from Ethiopia and made a profit of US$324 in the period, about US$200 less than expected. The profit was below their expectations because of fluctuations in the exchange rate between the Somaliland shilling in which they were selling their goods and the Ethiopian birr in which they had to pay their suppliers. This was further complicated by the fact that the loan they had taken out from MicroDahab was denominated in US$, as the women had requested. The profit was shared between them and MicroDahab on the agreed basis, and the five women received a new *mudaraba* loan in early October 2015 for US$1,000 each, or a total of US$5,000, on the same basis as before, so that they could continue expanding their business. MicroDahab made a smaller margin on the transaction than it had anticipated, but the staff recognized that the reduction in the profit was no fault of Maryam's; they extended the larger loan without any hesitation.

people who have the ability and skills to start a business but who have insufficient capital. *Musharaka* differs from *mudaraba* in that it provides part-funding to individuals who already have some capital but need more financing.

As with *mudaraba*, the profits and losses are distributed between MicroDahab and the client according to a predetermined ratio. The active partner – that is, the client – gets a larger share than would be allocated only on the basis of her or his monetary investment, to take account of the time, skill, and effort involved in management. The active member is also entitled to some fixed remuneration irrespective of the profits or losses, but this cannot exceed the amount of the entitlement based only on the investment.

MicroDahab also offers *ijarah* financing, which is a *Shari'ah*-compliant form of asset leasing. This includes an option whereby the client agrees to purchase the assets at the end of a lease period. It is especially useful for farming and fishing. Equipment such as water pumps for farms, fishing vessels, and other farm equipment are too expensive to purchase outright for most small business owners. *Ijarah* provides farmers and fishermen with the opportunity to rent or lease these assets over a period of time, with an option to purchase. This enables clients to use the assets to develop and expand their businesses without the need to pay for the assets in full at the outset. The case study in Box 13.3 describes a typical *ijarah* arrangement.

MicroDahab was set up as a for-profit business but also as an impact investment with the ultimate goal of alleviating poverty, increasing financial inclusion, and creating jobs and employment opportunities for entrepreneurs and blue-collar workers. Therefore, MicroDahab's prices are lower than those of most other MFIs in the region. For the majority of debt-financing products, such as *murabaha* and *ijarah*, the annual rates charged vary from an equivalent of between 5 and 8 per cent 'flat' per year, or an annual rate of around 10 or 15 per cent on a declining balance basis. Large loans are charged at rather higher rates; small loans for poorer individuals are charged at 5 per cent per annum, and *qard hasan* loans for the very poorest people and students are without any cost.

The majority of MicroDahab's loans are made in US$. Initially, some loans were made in Somaliland shillings, but as this currency lost almost 13 per cent of its value against the US$ in 2015, it was decided to make all loans in US$; the exchange rate recovered slightly in early 2016, but management decided

---

Box 13.3 An *ijarah* loan helps with irrigation

Abdirashid Ahmed Ibrahim is a typical *ijarah* customer. He is 35 years old and lives in Arabsiyo district, a farming area about 35 kilometres west of Hargeisa in Somaliland. He negotiated an arrangement with MicroDahab whereby the organization bought a set of solar-powered water pumps, which he needed to irrigate his land, for around US$6,000. MicroDahab then leased the pumps to Abdirashid under an arrangement whereby he pays small monthly instalments for three years. After that period, and on condition that all the monthly payments have been made in full, the ownership of the equipment will be transferred from MicroDahab to Abdirashid.

that MicroDahab's profits were too low to allow for any coverage of foreign exchange risks.

Equity products and other profit-sharing finance, such as *mudaraba* and *musharaka*, carry a higher risk and the profits are generally split on a 60:40 basis, as in the example of Maryam Jaamah described above (Box 13.2). MicroDahab receives a larger share of the profits as it bears the majority of the risk. Very few of MicroDahab's clients have the necessary education or financial management skills to manage the reporting and recording requirements of equity investments, so these products make up only a very small part of the portfolio.

Tables 13.1 and 13.2 provide a simplified and approximate statement of the financial condition of MicroDahab at the end of December 2015, and its income and expenditure during the preceding 12 months. The 'other income'

Table 13.1 MicroDahab's financial position

Uses of funds/assets	US$	Sources of funds/liabilities	US$
Cash and bank balances	496,000	Client savings	3,000
Murabaha accounts outstanding	973,000	Accounts payable	37,000
Musharaka/*mudaraba* accounts outstanding	38,000		
IT, equipment, vehicles, etc.	23,000	Deferred income	199,000
		Reserve for employee obligations	11,000
		Other liabilities	172,000
		Equity investment	945,000
		Accumulated profits	163,000
Total	1,530,000	Total	1,530,000

Note: Figures as of 31 December 2015.

Table 13.2 MicroDahab's income and expenditure in 2015

Income	US$	Expenditure	US$
Murabaha sales	1,565,000	Wages and salaries	92,000
Murabaha costs	(1,480,000)	Services from parent company	24,000
Murabaha gross profit	85,000	Advertising and promotion	12,000
Musharaka and *mudaraba* income	11,000	Transport and travel	14,000
Other income	403,000	Administration and depreciation	35,000
Total income	499,000	Total expenses	177,000
		Profit	322,000
		Less loss from previous period	159,000
		Profit carried forward	163,000

includes grants received from partner institutions, and the 'deferred income' relates to grants that have been approved by donors but have not yet been disbursed because, at the time of the accounts, MicroDahab had not reached the milestones at which the grant funds would be released.

MicroDahab's management envisions that by 2017 the institution will be self-sufficient and will generate a modest profit. It is hoped that by the end of that year they will have successfully built a quality portfolio that will use all their existing financial products; they expect that 50 per cent of the portfolio will consist of *murabaha* finance, 20 per cent *ijarah* leases, 15 per cent *musharaka* and 10 per cent *mudaraba* investments, and 5 per cent *qard hasan* cost-free loans. It is planned that the portfolio should be invested over a full range of activities, including agriculture, small-scale retailers, small- and medium-scale manufacturing businesses, schools, livestock farming, and solar energy, and that the urban poor will not be excluded.

About the author

Mohamed Ahmed Liban (mohamed.ahmed@dahabshilbank.com) is Chief of Operations at MicroDahab, Somaliland.

CHAPTER 14

The Al Khair Co-operative Credit Society: a co-operative Islamic microfinance institution

Najmul Hoda

The Al Khair Co-operative Credit Society Limited (ACCSL) is a Shari'ah*-compliant multi-state co-operative savings and credit society in Patna in Bihar, one of India's poorest states, which has expanded to 13 branches in Delhi and in the neighbouring states of Uttar Pradesh and Jharkhand. It started functioning as a trust in 1997 and converted to a co-operative in 2002 in order to expand its operations. There are about 11,000 members, and their savings deposit balances with ACCSL amount to around US$8 m; about 3,000 of the members are currently borrowing from the society and their outstanding loans amount to a similar sum.*

Keywords: India, Bihar, co-operative, *murabaha, mudaraba, musharaka,* Patna

Muslim clients need microfinance that is culturally and religiously appropriate. Many Muslims consider interest-based transactions to be against their religion; according to Obaidullah (2007), this has contributed to their large-scale financial exclusion. A number of market studies suggest a strong demand for Islamic microfinance products (PlaNet Finance, 2007; IFC and FINCA, 2006; Frankfurt School of Finance and Management, 2006; IFC, 2007).

Helms (2006) states:

> diverse approaches are needed – a one-size-fits-all solution will not work. Diverse channels are needed to get diverse financial services into the hands of the many people who are currently excluded. Making this vision a reality entails breaking down the walls – real and imaginary – that currently separate microfinance from the much broader world of financial systems.

An appraisal of poverty across northern India (Kozel and Parker, 1999) found that people of many castes and religions were deprived of the benefits of institutional finance and government services. Muslims form a significant part of this disadvantaged population. They tend to live and work in urban areas, and not in agriculture. Micro-enterprise is vital for their survival.

http://dx.doi.org/10.3362/9781780449555.014

They need easier options for getting credit. Dominant groups tend to discriminate subtly against them, directly or through the control they exercise over financial institutions of the state. Microfinance that complies with the Islamic faith can be tremendously important for these clients. Segrado (2005) and Akhtar (1996, 1997) have proposed microfinance models based on Islamic principles that can sustainably reach many clients, especially Muslims.

The Al Khair Co-operative Credit Society Limited (ACCSL) of Patna, the capital of the state of Bihar in India, is a Muslim faith-based microfinance institution (MFI). The organization targets the Muslim community and was started by individuals who have a strong allegiance to their faith, and actively promote the institution in their places of religious worship.

ACCSL had a modest beginning. It started in early 1997 as a social organization and registered as a charitable trust on 22 August 1997 in Patna. The society's founders adopted 14 semi-urban villages in one area near Patna as the focus for its operations. In its first two years, the society reached about 1,400 families in slums and villages in its chosen area, and at the same time ACCSL's promoters also identified six more affluent colonies nearby where they enrolled 289 well-off families who committed themselves to help ACCSL's work on a long-term basis. ACCSL's principal concern from the very beginning has been to provide 'livelihood opportunities for the poor or economic measures that could generate employment'.

Its first programme package included direct financial help, interest-free loans, finance for landless labourers to rent cultivable land so that they could do their own farming, cattle and poultry, and assistance with official formalities such as obtaining forms, filling them in, and submitting them to appropriate authorities in order to acquire financial help from government agencies or to access various development programmes.

The scale of assistance needed with small loans turned out to be so enormous that ACCSL's promoters began to think of starting a specific programme to provide such loans. They organized a workshop in August 1999 to investigate various institutional options, and finally decided to start an interest-free co-operative, as proposed by Mr M.H. Khatkhatay, an Islamic finance specialist. A core group of promoters or co-operators was organized to be the apex body with responsibility for working out the details of the co-operative society's set-up. It was registered as a multi-state co-operative in 2002 so that it could function in many states, including Bihar, Uttar Pradesh, and Delhi.

The broad objective of ACCSL is to help poor people by creating a sustainable support system that integrates more affluent people with poorer groups. The founders of ACCSL share the belief that affluent people have intellect, contacts, and wealth, but that if they do not use their strength to uplift poorer communities, society as a whole will suffer and eventually rich people may suffer even more than the poor. The linkage can thus be mutually beneficial. ACCSL therefore has two programme objectives. It undertakes motivational campaigns and mobilizes resources from the rich, and it reaches out to poorer people in the spheres of education, health, and employment.

ACCSL makes use of local mosques in order to promote its activities. It also aims to create awareness about co-operative principles, and, in order to increase its membership, to encourage members to save with the society. It plans to promote self-help groups of poorer people, particularly women, to lend money to members, to buy items and to sell them on to members at a profit, and generally to provide financial and other services to members.

ACCSL started its operations in south-west Patna and in particular in the old settlement of Phulwari Sharif, which is an area inhabited predominantly by Muslims. ACCSL works along the main road leading from the city to the area. The population of Phulwari Sharif is about 350,000. The main road area is dotted with residential zones housing colonies, and market settlements, such as an open grain market, two in-house market complexes, small-scale industry units, and hardware stores. There are roadside shops, workshops, grocery and poultry shops, timber traders, transport businesses, and low-cost restaurants.

A survey of credit availability was conducted in the area when ACCSL started its operations (Bhushan, 2001) in order to assess the population's domestic and business credit needs. 'Household small business' was the single largest occupation, and there were very few medium-sized business, large retailers, or even large service workshops. One important finding was that many of the people did not feel a need for large, formal loans. There were also clear differences in perceptions about credit size. Poorer people considered Rs (rupees) 5,000 to 10,000[1] (about US$500 to US$1,000) to be a 'large loan', while those who wanted to borrow larger amounts considered such loans to be a 'small credit'. It was clear that many households needed and could benefit from small loans of as little as Rs 2,000 or US$30. Another finding was that the majority of people's existing informal loans had been taken for four main purposes: festivals, marriages, legal services, and healthcare.

Since Patna has a population of over 2 million people, and many of them who live in the newly emerging settlements around the city are excluded from the city's services, ACCSL decided to extend its reach beyond the poorer backward settlements to include small and household businesses in markets and in residential areas. It also decided that the operations of ACCSL should not be confined only to Bihar but should reach migrants from Bihar, especially Muslims, wherever they might be in sizeable numbers. ACCSL has grown to have 13 branches: four in the city of Patna, four in other cities in Bihar state, two in the steel town of Jamshedpur in Jharkhand, two in Lucknow, and one in Delhi. The society employs about 30 staff in total.

ACCSL provides *Shari'ah*-compliant loans and savings, and it plans to introduce new financial products and services in the future. Short-term loans are for up to 12 months, medium-term loans are for between 12 months and three years, and long-term loans are for over three years. Loans of up to Rs 5,000 (about US$75) are classified as small, Rs 5,001 to 10,000 (US$75 to US$150) are categorized as medium-sized loans, and loans above Rs 10,001 are considered large loans.

There are three major types of loan, all of which have been derived from the Islamic financial system and are widely used in mainstream Islamic banks, but they have been designed to suit low-income clients. However, ACCSL's financial products are not based on the usual product classifications that are used in Islamic finance. The existing profit- and loss-sharing product specifically is regarded as an experimental entry point into profit- and loss-sharing finance, and its details are expected to evolve over time. This is a partnership, or *musharaka*, by its nature, as ACCSL provides it only on a profit- or loss-sharing basis, but more specific details are settled depending on experience. ACCSL's relationship with its clients, who are also its members, is such that this unconventional approach to product design is expected to be successful. The financial products are designed for small and micro-businesses in manufacturing, trading, or services.

Initial experience suggests that exact profit calculation is not possible, since many clients do not record their costs or their profits in a methodical way. The entrepreneur estimates his or her profit on the basis of past experience and this is recorded in the loan agreement. At the time of repayment, the borrower declares his or her estimate of the profits earned on the asset that was obtained with the loan, and this is shared with ACCSL on a 70:30 basis; the entrepreneur receives 70 per cent and ACCSL receives 30 per cent. This is the highest proportion of the profits that the society can take, and lower rates can be agreed on a case-by-case basis.

These profit-sharing *musharaka* loans make up 85 per cent of the total of ACCSL's loans, but there are still some inherent deficiencies in the product. Very few of the borrowers have so far reported losses; this may be because they do not want to lose the chance of receiving a further loan, but this issue needs to be assessed. There is also a tendency for borrowers to claim excessively high profits, even though this means that they have to pay a higher amount to ACCSL. They may do this in order to impress ACCSL's staff, to secure a subsequent loan, to support the society, out of ignorance, or for some combination of these reasons. Whatever the reasons, it does confirm that ACCSL's members are loyal to their society and that they wish to keep their credit line open, even at some cost to themselves. ACCSL's *musharaka* product still requires further development and improvement.

Short-term business loans are provided on a profit- or loss-sharing basis when the loan is required for only a short and predictable period. These loans are given for hotels and restaurants, to pay for fish, chicken meat, vegetables, and other perishables, and to retailers to cover stock purchases during festivals. The maximum loan is Rs 20,000 (about US$300), and it cannot exceed 10 times the member's share value. ACCSL shares a pre-agreed ratio of the anticipated profit to be made from the item that is purchased. The member's records are not checked and there is no way of ascertaining the accuracy of the declared profit. ACCSL is attempting to find a way of checking borrowers' statements of the profit they have made, although thus far none of the borrowers who have taken out these loans have reported losses.

ACCSL provides consumption loans under *murabaha*. The society purchases the required product at the lowest price possible and then resells it to the member with a mark-up of between 10 per cent and 15 per cent. The member has to pay 25 per cent of the total amount on the spot before taking possession of the product, and the balance has to be repaid in mutually agreed instalments over one year. This is roughly equivalent to a fixed-interest loan at an annual rate of between 20 per cent and 30 per cent. The borrowers usually arrange for the products they need to be delivered to their premises direct from the suppliers; the items do not have to physically pass through the ACCSL's hands. These loans make up only a very small proportion of the total.

ACCSL also offers what are called 'demand loans' for business, education, health, social, and family needs, and for property construction and maintenance. The member pays a one-off service charge for the loan, calculated as a percentage of the loan amount. The percentage varies according to the amount of the loan and is higher for smaller loans since it is charged to cover administrative costs and these do not vary directly with loan amounts; smaller loans are more costly to administer than larger ones, as a proportion of the loan amount. The maximum loan amount available to a member is 10 times his or her share value. The repayment schedule is designed to suit the pattern of the member's income and expenditure; these 'demand loans' constitute about 14 per cent of the total.

ASSCL's loan processing, sanctioning, and monitoring is done by the Loan and Admittance of Members Committee (LAMC). The members of the LAMC are all members of the society, and every branch has its own LAMC. The committee sits weekly and examines all the applications and the records of disbursement and recovery of loans in that week. The committee also tries to resolve bad debts, and, importantly, it aims to find ways to spread the lending in a socially just manner.

Loans are sanctioned depending upon the funds available. After the application forms have been completed and approved, the amounts are disbursed in cash or by cheque. A client survey (Ahmad, 2009) found that clients find the process of loan application, disbursement, and recovery easy and simple.

No security is required for loans below Rs 5,000 (US$75), but two personal guarantors are needed. For loans above Rs 5,000, post-dated cheques or valuables as well as two guarantors are required. Most guarantors are members of ACCSL, and it is not usually a problem for borrowers to identify guarantors. Very few members have bank accounts and the guarantees are usually personal valuables such as jewellery.

Loans are only approved for legitimate purposes, and extravagant or speculative proposals are declined. The ACCSL's board of directors has the right to recover loans at any time prior to the final date if loans are misused, although this has never happened, and its decision is final. Generally, loans are taken out for the purchase of livestock, farming tools, and equipment, for catering and food preparation, trade, manufacturing, and the repair and maintenance of equipment and vehicles. The majority of loans are for trading and business.

The following case study (Box 14.1) describes a *murabaha* loan provided to a shopkeeper in Patna.

ACCSL typically uses a 30 per cent profit margin on its profit- and loss-sharing loans. For example, a cosmetics and beauty goods retailer has taken out a number of Rs 5,000 (US$75) loans, on which he paid Rs 700 (US$12) each as ACCSL's 30 per cent share of the profits, and a ready-made garment

---

Box 14.1 *Mudaraba* finance for a retail business

Mohamed Jamaluddin is 55 years old and has taken out a number of medium-term *mudaraba* loans from ACCSL over several years. He runs a general grocery store in the Phulwari Sharif area of Patna. He used to have great difficulty in financing the purchases of goods for his shop; as a result, sales suffered and his income was insufficient to meet the day-to-day expenses of his family. His first loan was for Rs 10,000 (US$150) and he used it to buy additional stock for his shop. He was encouraged by the outcome, and repaid the loan on time over eight months. He estimated that his profit on the goods he bought with the loan would be about 47 per cent, or Rs 4,700 (US$70); this was shared with ACCSL on a 70:30 basis, so he paid ACCSL an additional Rs 1,400 (US$21) on top of the capital amount of Rs 10,000. His most recent loan was for Rs 50,000 (US$750), for which he paid ACCSL Rs 7,000 (US$106) on the same profit-sharing basis. He is very satisfied, and is now able to better provide for his family's needs.

Box 14.2 Repayments are delayed when a business has difficulties

Mohammed Ajaj Sagir is a tailor who joined ACCSL in September 2012. He borrowed and satisfactorily repaid three medium-term business loans on schedule; in fact, he was among the most regular and punctual members of the society. He took out a fourth loan of Rs 20,000 (US$300) in April 2014, which was to be repaid in eight months, together with Rs 2,400 (US$35), which he had earlier agreed would be a reasonable share of his estimated profits. He had repaid only Rs 3,900 (US$60) when his situation changed dramatically because two assistants he employed left their jobs. He hired others, but none of them stayed. He was unable to fulfil his customers' orders, and his income fell quickly. He could not keep up with the needs of his business or his family, his rent and electricity bills went unpaid, and his electricity connection was disconnected by the landlord. Ajaj Sagir tried without success to revive his business and even hired new staff, but again they left. He sold two sewing machines to meet his daily expenses and to secure an electrical connection in his own name, and he stopped repaying his loan. ACCSL's staff contacted Sagir several times but he informed them that he was unable to repay the loan. He even asked for a further loan of Rs 100,000 (US$1,500) to buy a new machine with which he estimated that he could earn Rs 2,000 or US$30 a day, but this was declined. His neighbours and the guarantor of his loan are also concerned with his situation. He says that his present earnings are about Rs 9,000 (US$135) per month, out of which he has to pay Rs 2,000 (US$30) for rent and electricity. ACCSL's staff recognize that Sagir's position is difficult. He failed to make any repayments after February 2015, and in February 2016 he still owed Rs 18,500 or US$280 on his most recent loan, or Rs 16,100 (US$240) if ACCSL's share of the profit is waived because he has been losing money. The staff have suggested to him that he should put aside Rs 10 a day to start to pay off his loan. This would have the advantage of keeping his name off the wilful defaulter's list and preserving his goodwill with ACCSL, so that he can – if possible – restore his position in the future.

shopkeeper has twice borrowed Rs 100,000 (US$1,500), for which he paid Rs 14,000 (US$210) to ACCSL on the same basis.

However, not every borrower is successful; the case study (Box 14.2) describes one of the few unsuccessful borrowers.

The maximum period within which a loan must be repaid is five years. A daily collector collects the money from borrowers at their homes or their work places, as is convenient for them. If a borrower makes no repayments for a whole year, in spite of reminders, a legal notice is sent to him or her, but in general ACCSL attempts to be liberal to defaulters.

ACCSL also offers savings facilities to its clients. There are several types of deposit account, but no interest is currently paid on any ACCSL deposit account; this is in accordance with Islamic principles, and ACCSL does not as yet offer any profit-sharing deposit accounts. There are daily savings schemes for members who earn on a daily basis, which suit small traders, rickshaw pullers, auto drivers, hawkers, and daily labourers. The total deposits outstanding on 31 March 2015 were Rs 55 m, or just over US$800,000, most of which was held in one of the two types of account described below. ACCSL also offers monthly deposit accounts, co-operation accounts, accounts that are earmarked for special purposes, children's accounts, *Hajj* pilgrimage accounts, social welfare funds, and growth funds to meet the various needs of its members.

The daily deposit account is designed for daily wage earners. The account can be opened for an entry fee of Rs 25 (about 40 US cents) and a minimum donation to ACCSL of Rs 5 (about 7 cents). The client can decide on the daily deposit amount, with a minimum of Rs 10, and deposits cannot be withdrawn for 15 days. Savings can be withdrawn at any time after one month. A minimum balance of Rs 20 must be maintained, and regular depositors are eligible to take out loans; they can also obtain cheques or demand drafts if they need them. The outstanding balance on daily deposit accounts was about Rs 50 m or US$750,000 at the end of March 2015. Some clients prefer an Amanat account. They can deposit any amount in this account, and it can be opened for a fee of Rs 50 (about 70 cents). Cash can be withdrawn as needed and account holders are also eligible to be considered for loans. They can obtain demand drafts and cheques and they can also pay electricity and telephone bills through the account. The outstanding balance on the Amanat accounts was about Rs 63 m or US$950,000 at the end of March 2015.

ACCSL has been providing financial services to the poor for more than a decade. Like any MFI, it has to sustain its activity as well as reach and assist a large number of clients. The number of members increased from 6,489 in 2012–13 to 10,993 in 2015–16. The outstanding value of members' shares also increased significantly in the period, from Rs 43 m to Rs 92 m, or almost US$1.4 m.

On the deposit side, ACCSL has grown consistently. The deposit balance rose from Rs 306 m to Rs 554 m (US$8.4 m) between 2012 and 2015. Some 60 per cent of the borrowers were men and 40 per cent women, and the majority of the loan portfolio was made up of business loans based on *murabaha* or *musharaka*.

Table 14.1 shows income and expenditure over the past three years. ACCSL made losses in 2013–14 and in 2014–15, largely because new branches were opened. These losses may continue in the short term as ACCSL continues to grow. However, its management does not consider this to be a problem so long as the basic financial position remains strong.

Donations remain an important part of ACCSL's income, and amounted to Rs 145,000 (US$2,200) in 2014–15. These were all from the local Muslim community, and were generally voluntary donations. The approximate balance sheet as at the end of March 2015 was as shown in Table 14.2.

As ACCSL grows and increases its scale and outreach, it must address a number of important existing and future issues. Arshad Ajmal, the founder and former chair of ACCSL, believes that ACCSL not only has a responsibility to service the financial needs of its members, but as a pioneer it must also undertake research and development into the possible future of Islamic financial co-operatives. The model gained a wider acceptance for replication at a national level. ACCSL leads the efforts of establishing interest-free MFIs across the country under the aegis of Sahulat Microfinance Society.

The increasing scale of operations brings new challenges and opportunities for ACCSL. The need for funds is a major challenge, since new technology, research and development, and staff training all require substantial cash reserves that are currently unavailable. On the other hand, with increased scale, its products may be diversified and become more attractive to people who require genuine Islamic finance.

Table 14.1 ACCSL's approximate profits and losses

Year	Income		Expenditure		Profit and (loss)	
	Rs million	*US$*	*Rs million*	*US$*	*Rs million*	*US$*
2012–13	5.0	76,000	4.8	73,000	0.2	3,000
2013–14	6.7	101,000	6.8	103,000	(0.1)	(2,000)
2014–15	9.5	144,000	9.6	146,000	(0.1)	(2,000)

Table 14.2 ACCSL's approximate balance sheet

Uses of funds/assets			Sources of funds/liabilities		
	Rs million	*US$*		*Rs million*	*US$*
Cash and bank balances	93	1,410,000	Member deposits	554	8,400,000
Loan accounts outstanding	552	8,360,000	Other current liabilities	1	15,000
Fixed assets and IT	1	15,000	Members' shares	91	1,370,000
Total	646	9,785,000	Total	646	9,785,000

Note: Figures as of 31 March 2015.

One feature of ACCSL is that it serves people of all faiths. It is hoped that, as it expands, it will provide an alternative to conventional microfinance in India and will address poor people's need for financial services irrespective of their religion.

Note

1.   The rate of exchange used throughout this analysis is US$1 to Rs 66.

References

Ahmad, A. (2009) *A Study on Working of Interest-free Co-operative Society*, Patna: ACCSL Archive.

Akhtar, M.R. (1996) 'Practice and prospects of *musharaka* financing for small enterprises in Pakistan', *Journal of Islamic Banking and Finance* 13 (3): 7–27.

Akhtar, M.R. (1997) 'Partnership financing of microenterprises', *International Journal of Social Economics* 24 (12): 1470–80.

Bhushan, S. (2001) *Small Credits and Institutional Financing Gap: A Survey Report on a Micro Region*, Patna: ACCSL Archive.

Frankfurt School of Finance and Management (2006) *Access to Finance Study in Algeria: Final Report*, Frankfurt: Frankfurt School of Finance and Management.

Helms, B. (2006) *Access to All: Building Inclusive Financial Systems*, Washington, DC: World Bank.

IFC (2007) *Syria Microfinance Market Assessment*, Draft Report, Washington, DC: IFC/World Bank.

IFC and FINCA (2006) *Business Plan for a Microfinance Institution in Jordan*, commissioned by IFC and FINCA, Washington, DC: FINCA (Table C.16).

Kozel, V. and Parker, B. (1999) *Poverty in Rural India: The Contribution of Qualitative Research in Poverty Analysis*, Washington, DC: Stiglitz Summer Research Workshop on Poverty. <http://siteresources.worldbank.org/INTPOVERTY/Resources/WDR/stiglitz/Kozel2.pdf> [accessed 14 November 2016].

Obaidullah, M. (2007) 'Islam, poverty and microfinance: "best practices"', *Islamic Finance Today: The Pulse of Ethical Business* <http://instituteofhalalinvesting.org/content/Islam_and_poverty.pdf> [accessed 14 November 2016].

PlaNet Finance (2007) *Microfinance Market Survey in the West Bank and Gaza Strip*, Washington, DC: PlaNet Finance.

Segrado, C. (2005) *Islamic Microfinance and Socially Responsible Investment*, Turin: MEDA Project, University of Turin.

About the author

Najmul Hoda (najmulhoda19@gmail.com) is Assistant Professor at the College of Business, Umm Al-Qura University, Mecca, Saudi Arabia.

CHAPTER 15

Profit and loss sharing with smallholder farmers in Indonesia: the experience of PT Vasham Kosa Sejahtera

Irvan Kolonas and Timothy E. Rann

PT Vasham Kosa Sejahtera provides several services to smallholder farmers growing staple crops such as maize. This includes input and working capital loans, ongoing agricultural extension, and guaranteed market linkages at an above-market price premium, by selling to its partner Japfa, which is willing to pay a premium price for good-quality and assured deliveries. Vasham takes a 10 per cent share of the farmers' profits on their sales of maize, when prices allow a profit, while farmers keep the remaining 90 per cent.

Keywords: Indonesia, Sumatra, smallholder farmers, profit and loss sharing

PT Vasham Kosa Sejahtera, commonly shortened to Vasham, was established and fully registered as a venture capital company in Indonesia in late 2011, but was not fully operational until 2014. Vasham was initially funded from private family sources; Mercy Corps of the USA and Unitus have since invested a further US$2.5 m of social impact investment funds. Vasham has not received any operating grants.

Vasham's unique approach to working with smallholder farmers was developed after diligent analysis of the maize commodity market in Indonesia. The founder, Irvan Kolonas, previously worked for Japfa Comfeed, which is one of Indonesia's largest animal feed manufacturing, chicken breeding, poultry processing, and aquaculture farming companies, with US$2.9 bn in sales in 2014. It is now Vasham's preferred purchaser for its customers and its most important partner. Kolonas also worked for his family's investment firm and an Indonesian commodities trader. Collectively, these experiences gave him useful access and insights into the maize market in Indonesia.

Kolonas noted three major trends in the maize industry. The two primary maize-buying feed mills in Indonesia were increasingly looking to secure their supply chains, rather than buying at random, and this required them to work with smallholder farmers. The government of Indonesia was acutely interested in food security and in improving the livelihood of smallholder farmers and had started to establish regulations and policies to encourage

http://dx.doi.org/10.3362/9781780449555.015

the domestic production and consumption of staple crops. At the same time, smallholder farmers were being negatively affected by numerous factors, including price instability, unfair pricing, lack of access to finance, lack of access to quality inputs, usurious interest rates from local traders, and general gaps in their knowledge.

In Indonesia, there are over 50 million farmers, of whom 30 million qualify as smallholders with less than 2 hectares of land. Around 18 million Indonesian smallholder farmers live below the poverty line and are trapped in a cycle of poverty due to the current market dynamics. Based on Vasham's experience, Indonesian smallholders face several major hurdles.

Established financial institutions cannot disburse loans to farmers who work rented land or do not own clear land titles. Staple crops, unlike cash crops, are sold by smallholders mainly to local buyers and organizations that do not have the resources to provide finance to smallholder farmers. Rural moneylenders who charge high interest rates are often their only source of credit, and the farmers are trapped in a cycle of poverty and debt.

The government of Indonesia provides fertilizers at a subsidized rate to smallholder farmers. However, due to corruption and weak governance, these subsidized fertilizers are rarely available. The quantity and quality of inputs used on farm land are not ideal due to the inability of farmers to pay the high prices of good-quality seeds and other inputs. As a consequence, farmers have difficulty acquiring the inputs they need at optimal planting times. Furthermore, the majority of smallholder farmers lack access to new low-cost farming technologies and methods for farm improvement that would significantly improve their farming yields. Many farmers still use traditional methods that have been handed down for many generations. Moreover, the relatively small plots of land they cultivate hamper the use of modern mechanization. The result is low yields, below average quality of produce, and low incomes for the farmers.

Farmers who are already indebted to local moneylenders are frequently forced to sell their harvests to them at below-market prices. Moneylenders typically control the machinery and trucks required for harvesting as well. When they purchase smallholders' crops, these traders sometimes use a variety of means such as faulty weighing machines, or paying below-market prices for wet maize while also charging for drying, to reduce further the profitability of the smallholders' crops.

Using these insights and leveraging his connections in the maize industry, Kolonas launched Vasham in 2014. Vasham aggregates and provides a bundle of services to smallholder farmers growing staple crops such as maize. This includes input and working capital loans, continuous operational assistance through technology and advisory staff, and guaranteed market linkages at an above-market price premium. Vasham does the latter by selling to its off-take partner Japfa, which is willing to pay a premium price for good-quality and assured deliveries. Japfa can buy at premium prices because of the improved quality, assured delivery, and large quantities that are available from the farmers with which it co-operates, and because it buys direct from farmers rather than from small local traders.

Vasham aligns its value, risks, and profitability with the smallholder farmer through its innovative profit-sharing model. This closed-loop business model provides smallholder farmers with the financing, expertise, income security, and market linkages they need to significantly improve their standard of living.

Kolonas aimed to create a genuine social enterprise, in that Vasham would be sustainable and would earn a return on the capital invested in it, but it would also work hand in hand with its suppliers and make a positive difference to the livelihoods of smallholder farmers. He realized that this would require some element of profit sharing between Vasham and its suppliers; they could not be expected to bear the total risk of cultivation, without any assistance, but Vasham could not afford to lose money either.

This philosophy of risk sharing led to what is essentially a *Shari'ah*-compliant financing arrangement. The farmers pay a small 'administrative fee' for the service they receive, which is not increased if the payments to Vasham are delayed beyond the expected date, so is not 'interest'. Vasham also takes a 10 per cent share of the farmers' profits on their sales of maize, when prices allow a profit.

The total earnings that accrue from these sources of income are at present insufficient to cover Vasham's costs, but it is hoped that when the company grows beyond Sumatra into Central and East Java and can start to diversify its business with other crops instead of relying wholly on maize, the results will improve.

Since its first planting season in 2014, Vasham has seen impressive growth. In addition to securing multiple major partnerships with input suppliers, major banks, and the government of Indonesia, it has disbursed over US$2 m in loans to over 2,000 farmers. In the financial year 2015, Vasham received approximately US$1.5 m in revenue, which was three and a half times the previous year's figure. Vasham's farmers have seen a 15 per cent increase in their yields and an increase of up to 106 per cent in their income. As of January 2016, Vasham had one field office in Lampung, Sumatra that serves 3,500 farmers in two farmer groups; 352 of these farmers are women.

The following cases (Boxes 15.1 and 15.2) describe two typical clients of Vasham.

In 2016, Vasham planned to expand beyond its initial two farmer groups in Lampung, as well as to open additional field offices in Central Java and East Java. By the end of 2020, it plans to have developed its product line to cover more of the maize value chain, to adapt its approach to other crops, and to serve over 200,000 farmers across Indonesia.

At present, Vasham's clients are all smallholder farmers, with less than 2 hectares of land. Their average age is 39, and their average income per harvest, before they started to work with Vasham, was between US$185 and

---

Box 15.1 Using a loan to buy good-quality farm inputs

Masiran is a member of a Vasham-promoted 'group', a farmer group leader, and a construction labourer. He is 50 years old and has been growing maize since he was 18. He has always found it difficult to finance his smallholder farm, since he needs all his earnings from the farm and his construction labour to maintain his family. Masiran joined Vasham because he did not have enough money to pay for farm inputs and to take care of his farm. Vasham gives him low-cost loans without charging high interest, and it operates on a profit-sharing basis that allows him to buy good-quality inputs. He can now use all his construction labour wages for his household expenditure and can work on his farm without having to worry about obtaining loans – the programme provides him with loans for his operations and for farm inputs. The profit-sharing system also helps him to become independent and to improve his family's livelihood.

Box 15.2 Vasham helps farmers increase their income

Dalimin farms in Jaya Sari village in East Lampung in Sumatra. He grows maize, and used to borrow from the traders to buy farm inputs. As a smallholder farmer he had no other source of credit. The traders who gave him credit charged very high prices for farm inputs, and they sometimes also compelled farmers such as Dalimin to sell their maize to them, at low prices, as well as buying inputs from them at high prices. Because of this, Dalimin and other farmers like him could never earn a proper income despite all their hard work. Since he has joined one of Vasham's groups, he no longer has to borrow from the traders, or to sell through them. All he has to worry about is planting and maintaining his field. He and his fellow farmers have increased their incomes and they also suffer less stress than they used to.

US$260, or around twice that figure for a complete year. Table 15.1 summarizes Vasham's performance in 2014 and 2015.

Vasham's board of directors is comprised of three directors, one of whom is from the Unitus Impact Fund, and one non-voting observer, who represents Mercy Corps. Vasham emphasizes good corporate governance. As a result, the company has a strong board that strictly applies its corporate governance principles, including social impact measurement and reporting. The governance documents include a detailed charter and by-laws, as well as specific social mission measurement requirements to ensure that the institution maintains its core values.

In particular, after each season, Vasham conducts impact reporting using a random sample of its own farmers and non-Vasham farmers in the same locations, in order to measure the difference that Vasham makes to its smallholder clients. This not only allows all stakeholders to understand the social impact of its services, but also represents an important opportunity for Vasham to gain valuable insights into its customers and how the market is changing.

Vasham's business model and products include a number of components. Vasham organizes its supplier farmers into business units that consist of around 1,000 farmers, the total of whose holdings must be below 3,000 hectares. These are self-sufficient units with their own administration, finance, logistics, and field operations teams. At full capacity, the operations

Table 15.1 Vasham's financial and operational performance

Year	2014	2015
Gross loan portfolio	US$223,653	US$2,796,253
Number of clients (wet and dry seasons combined)	347	3,382
Hectares	879	3,506
Average disbursed loan size	US$351–US$575	US$351–US$575
Write-offs	0.1%	<2%
Number of staff	60	82
Number of loan officers	18	43
Offices	2	2
Farmer groups	88	351

team of each group will include 30 field officers, each of whom will cover about 100 hectares, six field supervisors, who will cover 500 hectares each, and one field manager and head of unit.

Vasham also provides loans for farm inputs and working capital: these include collateral-free production loans, in kind and in cash, worth a total of US$566, including an input loan for seeds and organic fertilizer of US$316 that costs the farmer a 1.25 per cent a month administrative fee. This amount is a 'pass through' advance from a bank and does not include any margin for Vasham. A small number of farmers also take optional working capital loans of up to US$240 for expenses that arise during the growing season; for these, they pay an administrative charge of 2.25 per cent a month. These fees are lower than those available from local traders and moneylenders, and they are not increased if the farmers' crops are delivered later than expected.

Through its partnerships, Vasham also ensures that its farmers have access to the optimal amount of high-quality seeds, manure, and fertilizer. Lack of access to fertilizer at a competitive price is often a major burden for smallholder farmers, as the government-subsidized fertilizer distribution system is highly corrupt and often results in traders amassing cheap fertilizer to resell illegally at a high premium.

Once the inputs and cash have been disbursed, Vasham provides ongoing training and support on improved agricultural techniques. This includes access to low-cost technologies, soil testing, and regular checks via SMS messages and field staff visits. Vasham has one such field staff member for every 100 farmers. Vasham has thus far not focused on increasing yields, but intended to make this a priority in 2016.

Vasham has also started on an experimental basis to provide weather-based crop insurance in partnership with Syngenta Foundation and Mercy Corps: if a farmer's crops fail due to adverse weather, Vasham will be able to write off his or her total debt. This ensures that farmers do not become stuck in a cycle of debt.

Vasham's own profitability is based on a unique profit-sharing scheme whereby 90 per cent of the profits on crop sales go to the farmers, and 10 per cent to Vasham. This model ensures that risks and incentives are aligned between Vasham and the farmers. Vasham is incentivized to help farmers increase their yields, product quality, and on-site storage, as well as to connect farmers to the buyers when and where prices are highest.

During the twice yearly harvesting seasons, Vasham facilitates the transport of the harvest directly to the feed mills, which are owned by Japfa. By aggregating farmers' outputs and cutting out middlemen, Vasham is able to offer a guaranteed price premium of US$0.008 per kilogram above the market price. This amounts to a 3.3 per cent premium over the current market price of US$0.24. Vasham collects the crop, facilitates its sale to Japfa, and receives the full sale price from Japfa. Vasham then pays the farmer after subtracting administrative fees, loan repayment, and its 10 per cent share of the profit. This system reduces the cost of delivering and servicing financial products to smallholder farmers, because Vasham does not have to employ a force of loan officers to collect farmers' repayments on a monthly basis. Table 15.2 compares Vasham's service with the average trader's offering.

The administrative charges that Vasham imposes on working capital and input loans may seem similar to fixed interest, and therefore not to conform to *Shari'ah*, but although these charges are levied on a monthly basis, they do not continue once the due date for delivery of the crop has passed, and are thus, strictly speaking, not considered to be fixed-interest charges by Vasham.

Vasham is dependent on fixed-interest loans, for which it pays an annual interest rate of 15 per cent; this is therefore passed on to its smallholder clients at the same rate on a monthly basis – that is, 1.25 per cent a month. This does not conform to *Shari'ah*, but other sources of finance are not available and informed observers have said that Vasham's *Shari'ah* compliance is not compromised by its use of the only funds available. Vasham's profit on its financing business is thus limited to its 10 per cent share of the profits.

Most Islamic banks in Indonesia use a similar system, except that their administrative charges are usually levied on a monthly basis, and they increase if the loans are overdue. The banks say that this is necessary because their sources of funds – depositors' savings – are not profit sharing, so they have to pass on their costs to their customers on the same basis.

Like many so-called *Shari'ah*-compliant arrangements, these systems are *halal* only in name. Vasham did not intend at the outset to create a *Shari'ah*-compliant system; its aim was to develop an approach that genuinely shares the risks and profits with the farmers, and to help the farmers reduce their risks and increase their earnings. Vasham does not promote itself as a *Shari'ah*-compliant institution but it is regarded by its clients and by informed observers as being closer to the spirit of Islamic finance than other institutions in Indonesia that conform only to the letter of *Shari'ah* compliance. Smallholder farmers use Vasham's services because they offer a much better deal than traditional moneylenders; the lack of fixed interest is an added bonus.

Table 15.2 Key characteristics of Vasham's and the average trader's offering

	Vasham	Traders	Note
Direct access to inputs on demand	Yes		Vasham provides direct access to high-quality inputs when required by farmers and at a lower price, which is the official government subsidized price. Farmers often struggle to acquire inputs that meet their needs in time for optimal planting schedules. This is sometimes due to corruption and poor management of the subsidized fertilizer system, leading to traders illegally amassing cheap fertilizer and reselling it at a premium.
Monthly administrative charge on inputs	1.25%	2% to 8.3%	Vasham has designed this loan and the charge to cover its own borrowing expense from banks, which charge 15 per cent per annum.
Working capital loan	Yes		Typically not provided by traders. Approximately 40 per cent of Vasham's farmers request this working capital loan to smooth out their cash flows during the growing season. Vasham hopes that these funds will be invested in productive activities that enable higher returns for the farmer.
Monthly administrative charge on working capital loan	2.25%	n/a	
Training and extension services	Yes		This is central to Vasham's model, and is provided by extension workers and, eventually, through mobile channels.
Direct and guaranteed market access	Yes		Vasham eliminates layers of middlemen by facilitating direct access to the feed mills. Due to the profit-sharing agreement, Vasham's core financial driver is to increase yields, increase quality, and facilitate the sale of farmers' produce when prices are highest. Traders act as off-takers, but are incentivized to purchase at a price that is as low as possible.
Post-harvest service (shelling, drying, storage, and transport)	To be added in 2016	Yes	Traders purchase wet maize at the farm gate. Farmers are often charged a very high rate for this or receive a large reduction in the sales price from traders. Vasham previously helped farmers to arrange their own shelling, drying, storage, and transport to improve their ability to be independent market actors. Farmers now want Vasham to provide the full service. Vasham intends to provide shelling, transport, and drying at cost, and to help farmers find ways of drying and storing their maize on the farm.
Insurance	Piloted in 2015, still in development		With Mercy Corps and Syngenta Foundation, Vasham is developing a crop insurance product to ensure that farmers do not become stuck in a cycle of debt or poverty. This will also help limit Vasham's losses in the event of a widespread crop failure. It was tested by Vasham on a self-insured basis in 2015. A total of 858 farmers were insured and claims were paid to five farmers. Farmers whose crops fail and are unable to repay traders are often forced to sell their next crop to the traders at a low price.

Bankers in Indonesia who have observed the Vasham system say that it is in fact more *Shari'ah* compliant in spirit than their own systems, because of the way in which the profits and risks are shared. Vasham does not use the normal terminology of Islamic banking, but it is very much in line with the genuine intentions of *Shari'ah*-compliant financing.

About the authors

Irvan Kolonas (irvan.kolonas@vasham.co.id) is the Founder and Chief Executive Officer of PT Vasham Kosa Sejahtera.

Timothy Rann (trann@mercycorps.org) is a Senior Adviser at Mercy Corps Social Venture Fund.

CHAPTER 16
Co-operative Islamic microfinance: Daarul Qur'an BMT from Jakarta, Indonesia

Rio Sandi and Ajaz Ahmed Khan

Daarul Qur'an Baitul Maal Wat Tamwil is an Islamic savings and loans co-operative that was established in 2005 in Jakarta, Indonesia. It offers a range of Shari'ah-*compliant savings accounts and financing arrangements to its almost 3,000 members. It has savings deposits of US$665,000 and an outstanding loans portfolio of more than US$1.2 m. The organization manages to cover operating costs from the income it generates. Daarul Qur'an is continuing to develop new services, particularly savings accounts, in response to demand from members.*

Keywords: Indonesia, Islamic co-operatives, Baitul Maal Wat Tamwil, *murabaha, mudaraba, ijarah, wadiah*

Introduction

With a population of approximately 237 million people, almost 90 per cent of whom are Muslims, Indonesia is the largest Muslim majority country in the world. It is also one of the leading countries in the world for microfinance, and has a long history: for example, the leading microfinance bank – Bank Rakyat Indonesia – was founded in 1895. Indonesia also possesses the greatest diversity of both conventional and Islamic microfinance institutions (MFIs), comprising some 6,000 formal and 57,000 semi-formal registered microfinance units serving about 45 million depositors and 32 million borrowers. A majority of MFIs in Indonesia are found in rural and semi-urban areas. Indonesia accounts for approximately 60 per cent of all Islamic microfinance loans in terms of amount disbursed worldwide. Despite this, the Islamic microfinance sector is a relatively small proportion of the overall microfinance sector in Indonesia, accounting for less than 5 per cent of loans. Almost two-thirds – 60 per cent – of clients of microfinance in Indonesia are female.

Since 1990, Indonesia has maintained a dual conventional/Islamic micro-banking system (officially sanctioned by the central bank, Bank Indonesia, through legislation in 1998). There are three types of institution that provide Islamic microfinance services in Indonesia: Islamic commercial banks (*Bank Umum Syariah*), Islamic rural banks (*Bank Perkreditan Rakyat Syariah* or BPRSs), and Islamic savings and loans co-operatives (referred to as *Baitul Maal Wat*

http://dx.doi.org/10.3362/9781780449555.016

Tamwil or BMTs, although a small number are called *Koperasi Jasa Keuangan Syariah*). It is worth adding that the largely government-owned Bank Rakyat Indonesia Syariah (BRI Syariah) is also an important actor, with approximately 30 per cent of its portfolio directed towards Islamic microfinance. It is a subsidiary of Indonesia's largest MFI, Bank Rakyat Indonesia. Despite the preference of many people to seek Islamic finance, the development of Islamic financial institutions lags behind interest-based commercial and rural banks and co-operatives in Indonesia. This can be partly explained by the fact that their service has, in the past at least, been poorer, more complicated, and more expensive (Masyita and Ahmed, 2013). Nevertheless, there is demand for Islamic microfinance and it continues to grow.

There are 12 *Shari'ah*-compliant commercial banks in Indonesia – this includes Bank Muamalat, Bank Syariah Mandiri, and Bank Mega Syariah – and 22 *Shari'ah* business units that are also known as 'Islamic windows' operated by non-Islamic banks (Shodiq, 2015). However, the largest providers of Islamic microfinance are the 163 Islamic rural banks and the more than 3,000 Islamic savings and loans co-operatives. The Islamic rural banks are much smaller than commercial banks and offer only basic products. They have a dual mandate that is both commercial and social: that is, 'to assist the enterprising poor'. They are allowed to accept deposits but are limited in terms of location, function, and portfolio composition. They are locally based and mostly privately owned institutions.

The Islamic savings and loans co-operatives or BMTs are grassroots organizations that are funded, owned, and managed by their members. As with Islamic rural banks, the mission of the BMTs is also 'to assist the enterprising poor'. Some co-operatives are quite small organizations with just a few hundred members. However, other BMTs, particularly on the island of Java, are much larger with membership of several thousands. Their success tends to be strongly linked to the skill and commitment of their founders.

BMTs used to operate mostly on the principle of profit and loss sharing, but they have increasingly adopted *murabaha* financing. This is because they consider *murabaha* easier to structure, operate, and monitor, particularly for the purchase of frequently requested items such as motorcycles and other equipment. This reflects a general trend in Indonesian Islamic microfinance: for example, more than 80 per cent of the financing provided by the fully fledged Islamic banks in Indonesia is based on three types of contract – *murabaha* accounts for 54 per cent, while the share of *musharaka* is 18 per cent and *mudaraba* 10 per cent.

Otoritas Jasa Keuangan (OJK), or the Financial Services Authority of Indonesia, formally regulates both the Islamic commercial banks and the Islamic rural banks. Both types of institutions are required to file detailed and frequent reports. In contrast, BMTs voluntarily send reports to the Ministry of Co-operatives and Small and Medium Enterprises, which supervises their activities, but they are not strongly regulated. Indeed, it is estimated that until recently most Islamic co-operatives were not even registered with the Ministry of Co-operatives. In the absence of regular and reliable reporting, information is sporadic. Siebel (2012) considers the performance of Islamic co-operatives to be very uneven. Yet, despite this, most BMTs possess a strong social mission, and in many respects they adhere more strongly than other Islamic micro-finance providers to the spirit of Islamic finance. Juwaini et al. (2010) argue that most BMTs are run by social entrepreneurs with a strong commitment to promoting Islamic values and establishing social justice. This analysis explores the experience of one relatively small BMT, Daarul Qur'an, from Indonesia's capital and largest city, Jakarta.

BMT Daarul Qur'an

With support from the chair of the Daarul Qur'an Foundation, Masyhuri Syahid, and 15 alumni from the School of *Shari'ah* Finance and Economics of the University of Indonesia, the Daarul Qur'an BMT was established in 2005 in Tebet, a sub-district of South Jakarta, one of the administrative cities that form the capital region of Jakarta. It is a densely populated urban area with thousands of small retail and food outlets, workshops, and market stalls. Daarul Qur'an's members are drawn from these neighbourhoods, and as well as small-scale entre-preneurs its members also include salaried civil servants, teachers, and students. It promotes its services at local community gatherings, mosques, and Islamic boarding schools. Although the organization does not keep exact figures, it estimates that there are roughly equal numbers of male and female members. The founders of Daarul Qur'an BMT have a formal background in Islamic education and the organization has also established its own Islamic boarding school. Many members are attracted to the organization by the trustworthy reputation and standing of the founders in the local community.

Savings accounts

Daarul Qur'an is still a relatively small savings and loans co-operative – as of the end of June 2016 it had just one office employing 10 full-time staff, slightly under 3,000 members, savings deposits of US$665,000, and an outstanding loans portfolio of just over US$1.2 m. However, despite its modest size, it offers a range of savings accounts, as shown in Table 16.1. While only a relatively small proportion of members are borrowers – about 1,200 as of the end of June 2016 – all members are savers. Indeed, one of the primary reasons for establishing the co-operative was to provide members with customized savings accounts that were *Shari'ah* compliant and offered a financial return. Despite the number of savers increasing only slightly over the last four years – from 2,634 in 2012 to 2,773 in 2016 – the volume of savings has more than doubled. The types of savings accounts it offers are as follows:

- *Wadiah savings*. These are voluntary savings deposited by members for the organization to invest. Members do not receive a fixed rate of return on their deposits; rather, the rate of return depends on the organization's profits, which are calculated at the end of each month, and takes into

Table 16.1 Daarul Qur'an's types of savings accounts

Type of savings account	2012	2013	2014	2015	2016*
Wadiah (including Eid-al-Fitr and Qurbani)	138,186	256,402	392,302	312,200	400,376
Student	17,703	49,619	81,479	65,168	81,436
Term	147,256	201,982	85,366	169.207	183,689
Total amount of savings	303,145	508,003	559,147	546,575	665,501
Number of savers	2,634	2,715	3,345	3,700	2,773

Notes: All values are US$ equivalent. * Figures as of the end of June 2016.

account the average balance of the account. Daarul Qur'an estimates that because the organization performed relatively well in 2015, members received a return equivalent to around 6 per cent of the value of their *wadiah* savings during the year. In comparison, the same amount of savings in an interest-bearing account offered by other microfinance organizations would have received a return of around 4 per cent. Approximately 60 per cent of the funds deposited with Daarul Qur'an are *wadiah* savings.

- *Eid-al-Fitr mudaraba savings.* Specifically designed for the celebration at the end of the month of *Ramadan*, these savings are only available three weeks before the date of *Eid-al-Fitr*, a time when most Muslims traditionally spend significantly on food, new clothes, and gifts. The minimum first deposit is the equivalent of US$3.70. Once again, members do not receive a fixed rate of return; rather, they are rewarded on a profit-sharing basis – Daarul Qur'an receives 60 per cent of the profits while the member receives 40 per cent.
- *Qurbani mudaraba savings.* This account is also designed specifically for *Qurbani*,[1] the most important celebration during the Islamic calendar, which occurs during the festival of *Eid-al-Adha*. Again, this is a time when most Muslim households incur significant expenditure; in addition to clothes and gifts, the cost of animal slaughter can be considerable, with the price of a goat or sheep around US$260 and a cow or buffalo around US$1,500. The minimum first deposit is the equivalent of US$7.40 and savings can only be withdrawn one week before *Qurbani*. As with the previous accounts, rather than being awarded a predetermined rate of return, members receive 40 per cent of Daarul Qur'an's profits while the institution itself takes 60 per cent.
- *Student savings.* Daarul Qur'an created this account in order to promote a savings culture among students; indeed, students at the organization's own boarding school are obliged to open an account. There are currently around 350 girls and boys aged between seven and 15 who attend the school. The minimum first deposit is the equivalent of just US$1.50. Once again, return is a share of the organization's profits.
- *Term savings.* This type of account offers the opportunity to deposit funds for a fixed term (typically one, three, six, or 12 months) and savers

may receive a profit share of anywhere between 35 and 50 per cent. The minimum deposit is US$75.

In response to demand from its members, Daarul Qur'an is developing another savings account specifically for people intending to undertake the *Umrah*, or lesser, pilgrimage to Mecca. The amount of the initial deposit and the period over which savings are to be made will be decided by members. Any profits generated by the organization from such funds are to be shared equally with the members.

Financing techniques

Daarul Qur'an considers that the vast majority of finance that it provides – approximately 90 per cent – is 'productive' and is used by members to expand existing businesses or establish new enterprises. The remaining 10 per cent of loans are provided for educational purposes, typically paying for course fees and acquiring books and other materials. The organization uses three main financing techniques: *murabaha* or cost plus mark-up; *ijarah* or leasing; and *mudaraba* or profit and loss sharing. All loan contracts are agreed in writing and signed in the presence of two witnesses; one is usually a marketing staff member of the organization and the other a relative of the borrower. Table 16.2 details the amounts provided according to each methodology over the past four years. The total amount of financing that Daarul Qur'an provides has more than doubled over this period, from US$512,272 in 2012 to US$1,208,313 in 2016. Presently, approximately 61 per cent of financing is through *murabaha*, 22 per cent through *ijarah*, and 17 per cent is on the basis of *mudaraba*. While the proportion of *mudaraba* financing has remained approximately the same, the proportion of finance provided through *ijarah* has steadily increased.

The average loan size has increased significantly each year, from US$385 in 2012 to US$575 in 2013, US$750 in 2014, and US$950 the following year. This is mainly because most existing clients request larger repeat loans. The portfolio at risk greater than 30 days ratio has remained relatively stable at around 2.9 per cent during the last five years. Unfortunately, there is no available data on the number of female clients. Table 16.3 describes the range of financing provided. Approximately 42 per cent of loans are below 5 million Indonesian rupiahs or US$382.

Table 16.2 Daarul Qur'an's types of financing

Financing technique	2012	2013	2014	2015	2016*
Murabaha	360,595	393,598	462,119	652,896	740,851
Mudaraba	132,012	149,619	152,439	161,890	195,960
Ijarah	19,665	67,759	109,527	211,814	271,502
Total	**512,272**	**610,976**	**724,085**	**1,026,600**	**1,208,313**

Notes: All values are US$ equivalent. * Figures as of the end of June 2016.

Table 16.3 Daarul Qur'an's range of financing

Amount of financing (US$)	December 2013		December 2014		December 2015		June 2016	
	Borrowers (no.)	Amount	Borrowers (no.)	Amount	Borrowers (no.)	Amount	Borrowers (no.)	Amount
Below 229	596	50,486	657	61,043	278	60,899	334	71,738
230–382	358	75,000	455	83,880	273	112,881	328	132,971
383–763	388	243,602	414	268,501	283	161,052	340	189,716
764–1,145	226	84,601	366	122,350	297	303,201	356	357,164
Above 1,145	59	157,287	65	188,311	196	388,567	235	457,724
Total	**1,627**	**610,976**	**1,957**	**724,085**	**1,327**	**1,026,600**	**1,593**	**1,209,313**

Notes: All values are in US$.

Box 16.1 Buying items for food stalls using *murabaha* loans

Fatah has been a member of Daarul Qur'an for the past eight years. He manages two food stalls selling roast chicken, typically accompanied by steamed rice, vegetable salad, and 'sambal', which is a spicy sauce, and he charges IDR (Indonesian rupiahs) 17,000 (approximately US$1.30). He estimates that he can sell, on average, around 100 meals per day. Over the last eight years or so, Fatah has taken out several *murabaha* loans from Daarul Qur'an. On each occasion, he presents a list of all the items he wishes to buy to Daarul Qur'an for review. Together they select and then visit the best supplier to purchase the items, paying in cash. At present he has an outstanding loan of IDR 15 m (approximately US$1,141). Fatah agreed to repay IDR 1.55 m per month for 12 months, meaning that he will repay a total of IDR 18.6 m to Daarul Qur'an. He employs five people and one of the stalls is managed by his son. With each monthly repayment, Fatah also makes a deposit in his savings account, usually of IDR 200,000 (approximately US$15).

Murabaha

Under this arrangement, members approach Daarul Qur'an to request the purchase of a commodity. Daarul Qur'an purchases and then resells the commodity, after adding a specific profit margin (often referred to as a 'mark-up') to the member who agrees to buy the commodity for the new offered price. The member then pays for the commodity in monthly instalments over an agreed period of time, usually between three and 12 months. *Murabaha* is popular with the organization's members partly because it is easily understood and has a known repayment schedule, but also because they generally demand specific items of equipment, most commonly new or used motorcycles, which are requested by the many members who are taxi drivers and itinerant traders. Daarul Qur'an charges a profit margin which is between 1.8 per cent and 2 per cent per month on the original balance. The case study above (Box 16.1) describes a *murabaha* loan.

Although they can take longer to be disbursed, *murabaha* loans provided by Daarul Qur'an are significantly cheaper for borrowers than loans offered by interest-based MFIs. For a *murabaha* loan of US$1,000 over 12 months, a member will repay Daarul Qur'an US$1,240 in total. In comparison, for a loan for the same amount and term from an interest-based MFI, a borrower will repay between US$1,360 and US$1,480, which is between 50 and 100 per cent more.

Ijarah

Under this arrangement a member approaches Daarul Qur'an to fund the purchase of a productive asset. Daarul Qur'an buys the productive asset and rents it out to the member at a price that enables the organization to recover its investment plus a profit. The asset remains in the ownership of Daarul Qur'an, which is responsible for its maintenance so that it continues to give the service for which it was rented. The *ijarah* contract is terminated

---

Box 16.2 An *ijarah* loan covers the cost of a lease

Together with his brother, Denny runs a barber's shop located near Daarul Qur'an's offices in South Jakarta. Denny has been a member of Daarul Qur'an for the past five years or so and is a regular saver. In 2015, he was asked to vacate the rented premises where he worked as the owner wanted to use the space himself. However, Denny struggled to find a suitable alternative. He asked Daarul Qur'an for assistance and the organization, which is well known locally, helped him to search for new premises. Daarul Qur'an used its knowledge and contacts to find an excellent location and paid the lease of US$2,650 per year up front and in the organization's name. Denny agreed to pay the organization US$274 as monthly rent for 12 months. Denny is extremely pleased with the arrangement as he has been able to attract more customers because of the good location and hopes to renew the arrangement at the end of the lease.

---

as soon as the asset ceases to give the service for which it was rented or the leasing period comes to an end and the physical possession of the asset and the right of use revert to Daarul Qur'an. However, in most cases, since it is impractical or too expensive for the organization to maintain the assets, the member makes regular payments and becomes the owner of the financed equipment once he or she has paid all agreed instalments – in effect, a hire purchase agreement. The case study above (Box 16.2) describes an *ijarah* loan.

Mudaraba

Under this type of partnership financing, Daarul Qur'an provides part or all of the capital required to fund a project, while the member manages the investment using his or her expertise. In a *mudaraba* contract, when a profit is realized, it is shared between Daarul Qur'an and the member according to a predetermined ratio. The proportion and manner in which profits are shared between the parties are negotiated on a case-by-case basis but are usually shared on a 60:40 or 50:50 basis depending on business risk and the track record and expertise of the member.

The organization carefully selects which members it will support through such loans, the length of the agreement, and when and how profits will be divided. After the funds are disbursed, it continues to monitor the financed business through on-site visits and discussions with the member to ascertain profits. So far, Daarul Qur'an has financed 70 *mudaraba* loans, all of which have supported members undertaking building projects such as the construction and sale of shops and the installation of water supply systems. So far, all the projects have realized a profit and Daarul Qur'an always makes efforts to understand the business. The *mudaraba* loans are much larger than the other types of finance that Daarul Qur'an provides – the average size of a *mudaraba* loan is US$3,161, while *murabaha* loans average US$689 and *ijarah* loans US$704. This is because profit- and loss-sharing loans are provided only

---

Box 16.3 Financing a construction project on the basis of *mudaraba*

Gugun is a building contractor from South Jakarta. He has been a member of Daarul Qur'an for the past 10 years or so and is well known to the organization as a trustworthy and enterprising individual. He decided to construct a building and sell the office space. The estimated cost of construction was the equivalent of US$11,400. Gugun already had savings of US$7,600 and approached Daarul Qur'an for finance on a *mudaraba* basis to cover the shortfall. Daarul Qur'an supported his proposal but agreed to provide only US$1,500. However, this was enough for Gugun to begin construction. Employing 10 labourers, he estimated that construction would take around five months to complete and agreed with Daarul Qur'an to meet at the end of each month to assess the progress of the building work. Importantly, both Gugun and Daarul Qur'an agreed to jointly promote the project and advertise the office space to interested parties. As early as the second month, Gugun found a buyer and received a down payment of US$2,300, which covered any remaining construction costs, and he agreed a sale price of US$15,000. Daarul Qur'an received US$1,680 from the eventual sale, generating a profit of US$180, a return of 12 per cent after just five months, while Gugun received US$13,320, after investing US$7,600 of his own funds.

---

to longstanding members who have a good credit history, having received and repaid previous *murabaha* and *ijarah* loans, and who then seek a larger loan. The example above (Box 16.3) describes a *mudaraba* agreement.

Penalties for late repayments

Daarul Qur'an charges penalties for borrowers if, after visits from loan officers, it is established that they have wilfully defaulted on loan repayments despite the success of the business. The late penalty fees are charged each month and are equivalent to 2 per cent of the outstanding loan amount. Daarul Qur'an imposes penalty charges in order to discourage wilful default and uses any funds raised in this manner for charitable purposes. For those members whose business ventures do not succeed for reasons beyond their control or who experience natural disaster, death of a family member, or critical illness, Daarul Qur'an does not impose any financial penalties or demand repayment. Instead, the institution meets with the borrower to restructure, decrease, or even write off the loan.

Sources of funding

Approximately a fifth of loan capital is from the savings of members – Daarul Qur'an keeps the remaining four-fifths of deposits in case of demand from savers. The majority of funds used for loans come from external capital. Over the past three years, Daarul Qur'an has received IDR 9.28 bn (approximately US$714,000) in funding from other financial institutions, both interest-based institutions that have 'Islamic windows' and *Shari'ah*-compliant institutions. At present, Daarul Qur'an has loans outstanding from four

Table 16.4 Daarul Qur'an's summary balance sheet and income statement

Balance sheet	2012	2013	2014	2015
Total assets	559,013	731,277	868,789	1,172,485
Total liabilities	463,402	621,394	735,604	999,314
Total equity	95,611	109,883	133,185	173,171
Income statement				
Total financial income	91,934	84,962	80,827	194,512
Total operating expenses	74,353	66,717	57,525	165,930
Net income	17,581	18,245	23,302	28,582

Note: All figures are in US$.

Shari'ah-compliant institutions, namely BNI Syariah, Bank Bukopin Syariah, Bank Syariah Mandiri, and Induk Koperasi Nusa Makmur. The finance amounts to IDR 6.12 bn (approximately US$466,000) and the length of the loans are between three and five years. All the external loans are on the basis of *mudaraba*, with profits being shared on a 60:40 basis in favour of Daarul Qur'an in three cases, and 30:70 in the fourth, at the end of each year.

Daarul Qur'an considers that the majority of people become members because of their religious beliefs. However, demand for its services might be explained in part because of the fact that the loans that Daarul Qur'an provides are relatively cheaper than those offered by interest-based financial intermediaries, although applications may take longer to process and disburse.

As can be seen in Table 16.4, which presents a summary of the balance sheet and income statements of the past four years, Daarul Qur'an had positive equity of US$171,646 and a net income of US$28,582 in 2015; indeed, both indictors have steadily increased during the past four years.

Note

1. *'Qurbani'* means 'sacrifice' and refers to the ritual slaughter of animals, which can occur at any time of the year, but is a requirement amongst Muslims during the religious festival, *Eid al-Adha.*

References

Juwaini, A., Rambe, M., Mintarti, N. and Febrianto, R. (2010) *BMT (Baitulmaal wa Tamwil) Islamic Microfinancial Services for the Poor.* Paper prepared for the ISO/COPOLCO Workshop, Bali, Indonesia, May.

Masyita, D. and Ahmed, H. (2013) 'Why is the growth of Islamic microfinance lower than conventional counterparts in Indonesia', *Islamic Economic Studies* 21 (1): 35–62.

Shodiq, M. (2015) 'Leadership and human capital development of Islamic finance', *The Jakarta Post*, 9 June <www.thejakartapost.com/

news/2015/06/09/leadership-and-human-capital-development-islamic-finance.html> [accessed 15 November 2016].

Siebel, H.D. (2012) 'Islamic microfinance in Indonesia: the challenge of institutional diversity, regulation and supervision', in Ali, S.N. (ed.), *Shari'a-compliant Microfinance*, Abingdon, Oxfordshire: Routledge.

About the authors

Rio Sandi (riosandi2003@yahoo.com) is a *Shari'ah* Microfinance Investment Specialist. He currently works for Nusa Makmur *Shari'ah* Microfinance Institution in Indonesia.

Ajaz Ahmed Khan (khan@careinternational.org) is Senior Microfinance Adviser at CARE International, United Kingdom.

CHAPTER 17
What do the cases tell us?

Malcolm Harper

This chapter draws some tentative conclusions from the preceding case studies, and suggests some possible ways forward for Islamic microfinance.

Keywords: *murabaha, musharaka, mudaraba, qard hasan, ijarah, Shari'ah compliant*, co-operative, Islamic investment, Islamic savings, *bai salam*

The cases in summary

These 15 case studies in no way describe a random or representative selection of Islamic microfinance institutions (IMFIs); they were chosen from a number of possible examples because they cover a range of different places, different types of institution and clients, and a variety of financial products. Also, of course, their managements were willing to allow what might be considered confidential data to be made public, and it was possible to identify a qualified person who could obtain the data and put together the case study. We had also hoped to find IMFIs that were using some form of profit- or loss-sharing products. Readers who have been through the cases will have seen that this search was not totally successful; this in itself is an interesting conclusion. Table 17.1 summarizes some of the salient features of the cases.

This outline data may not be typical of all IMFIs, but it illustrates the nature of this collection and may also indicate some aspects of IMFIs in general. Some of the terms used may also be contentious or confusing: strictly speaking, the words 'loan' and 'borrower' should not be used to describe a client whose relationship with the IMFI is in theory that of a customer who has bought something on credit from the institution, under a *murabaha* contract. Similarly, a client in whose business an IMFI has invested in a temporary profit- and loss-sharing partnership under a *musharaka* contract is not actually a borrower and the money is not a loan; the terms should be interpreted flexibly.

The 15 institutions are generally young. Only two of them were started before the year 2000. Islamic microfinance thus appears to be a relatively young phenomenon, as might perhaps be expected, given that mainstream microfinance has itself only been operating on a significant scale since the 1990s.

http://dx.doi.org/10.3362/9781780449555.017

Table 17.1 Characteristics of the organizations studied

Institution	Year started	Active borrowers	Percentage of women	'Loan' portfolio (US$)	Average outstanding (US$)	Profits	Savings	Main credit products
Akhuwat, Pakistan	2001	567,000	41	77 m	110	n/a	No	Qard hasan
START, Kosovo	2002	1,200	30	2 m	1,580	Yes	No	Qard hasan, murabaha
Islami, Bangladesh	1995	940,000	79	246 m	260	n/a	Yes	Murabaha, some musharaka
Mutahid, Afghanistan	2011	14,000	24	7 m	500	n/a	No	Murabaha
Reef, Palestine	2007	2,900	15	8.7 m	3,000	Yes	No	Murabaha, some manfa'a, musharaka
KIMS/Kaah, Somalia	2012	3,000	50	n/a	n/a	n/a	Yes	Murabaha
Al Amal, Yemen	2008	40,000	54	17 m	425	No	Yes	Murabaha
Kompanion, Kyrgyzstan	2012	445	53	450,000	1,010	No	No	Murabaha, some musharaka
Ebdaa, Sudan	2014	6,000	90	2.2 m	370	No	Yes	Murabaha
PASED, Sudan	2000	9,000	68	2.2 m	240	Yes	No	Murabaha, some musharaka, bai salam
BASIX, India	2012	400	19	200,000	500	No	No	Murabaha, some declining musharaka
MicroDahab, Somalia	2014	2,750	64	1.1 m	400	Yes	Yes	Murabaha, some musharaka, mudaraba
ACCSL, India	1997	2,300	40	5.5 m	2,390	No	Yes	Murabaha, some musharaka
Vasham, Indonesia	2014	3,400	10	2.8 m	820	No	No	Bai salam
BMT Daarul Qur'an, Indonesia	2005	1,327	n/a	1.2 m	950	Yes	Yes	Murabaha, ijarah, mudaraba

The institutions are also quite small; only two have more than 100,000 active borrowers, and 10 of the remaining 13 have fewer than 10,000 borrowers. The two relatively large institutions are also 'special cases'; one is the Rural Development Scheme of the Islami Bank in Bangladesh, which is not an independent institution and is not particularly large by the standards of Bangladesh microfinance. The other is Akhuwat of Pakistan, which follows a unique and in some sense non-commercial model, but continues to grow and has in its 15 years reached well over a million clients. The microfinance industry is undergoing some concentration, as the pioneers either grow and come to dominate the remainder, or – as in India, and possibly elsewhere – there has been a crisis that has resulted in the disappearance of some smaller institutions. This does not yet appear to have taken place in the Islamic subset of microfinance.

Given the general perception of women's position in Islamic society, it is perhaps surprising that there is such a large number of women clients, but women outnumber men in only six of the 15 cases. This is probably a smaller proportion of female clients than most MFIs would report; the collection does not wholly discredit the general view that Muslim women play a less active role in business and other non-family activities than non-Muslims. Daarul Qur'an does not record the gender of its members; this may seem 'gender insensitive' in these hyper-sensitive times, but it may also reflect the fact that this institution, like Akhuwat, Reef, and others, prefers to be 'gender neutral', to lend to the household rather than to either the husband or the wife. Local convention may mean that the person who is named in the agreement is the husband, but if the finance is genuinely used by and for the benefit of the whole household, this may be much less divisive than lending only to women; experiences in Bangladesh and elsewhere have shown that this can lead to gross exploitation and worse, as described in Morduch (1998) and elsewhere.

The average outstanding 'loan' figures should, of course, be more or less doubled to reflect the actual sums advanced, since the balance sheet figures for the outstanding portfolios include credits at all stages, from initial disbursement to final repayment, although the relative youth and fast growth of many of the IMFIs would mean that this would result in an overestimate of the initial advances. In three cases, the average figure is well over US$1,000, however, and this is well outside the usual 'micro' range except in Eastern Europe and parts of Latin America and Central Asia, where average incomes are well above the figures for incomes in the 'classic' homes of microfinance such as South Asia and Africa. These relatively high figures may arise from the practical difficulty of using *Shari'ah*-compliant methods for the rapid low-cost provision of small sums of money that may be used for consumption or for the purchase of non-traded goods such as medical care or school fees, or for purchases from informal suppliers.

One aim of the collection is to show that it is possible, and that it can also be profitable, to offer *Shari'ah*-compliant microfinance in a wide range of different ways and different conditions. Only five of the sample of 15 IMFIs are profitable; some, such as MicroDahab, Kompanion, and BASIX, appear to have the potential to become profitable if they can access sufficient funds to enable them to reach their break-even volume, whereas others seem likely to continue to lose money indefinitely. This is not so different from microfinance in general, where a small number of generally large MFIs are very profitable, while many others barely cover their operating costs, and continue to rely on subsidized or no-cost finance, and some still operate as NGOs or some other form of not-for-profit institution. BMT Daarul Qur'an, however, is able to sustain itself from the profit it makes on its wide mix of types of loan, and it also pays a major share of its earnings to its depositors, who are also its borrowers and its owners.

Apart from the numerous individual descriptions of client experiences, both good and bad, the cases do not include any formal data on client satisfaction, nor do they make any reference to the long-term impact of the institutions' services on their clients' well-being, however that might be measured. In some situations, as in Bangladesh and elsewhere, the clients have a choice between Islamic and non-Islamic institutions; their choice of the Islamic option presumably indicates that they are more satisfied with it than they would be with a non-Islamic competitor. It is also clear that Islamic microfinance generally involves higher transaction costs for clients as well as for the institutions, such as when a *murabaha* credit requires them to obtain the full details of what they want to buy and to provide this information to the IMFI before they obtain it. Their willingness to put up with this requirement suggests that they are satisfied with the service.

Murabaha financial products are very similar to fixed-interest loans, in that they require the client to repay what he or she has borrowed over a fixed period, with the addition of a 'profit' that is similar to interest but with some important differences. One difference is that, unlike fixed interest, the added profit is not automatically increased if the loan is not repaid on time. Compound interest on unpaid arrears often leads to intolerable levels of indebtedness, and clients of IMFIs are protected from this. This is a major advantage of IMFIs, which is not often mentioned by advocates of *Shari'ah*-compliant finance.

There is more than enough evaluation literature on the impact of microfinance on its clients; in general, the verdict is that it is not a 'silver bullet' that can eliminate poverty, but that it can make a positive difference to poor people's livelihoods. There is no reason to suppose that Islamic microfinance is any worse, or better, for its clients than 'normal' microfinance, apart from its conformity to their religious principles, and it therefore seems reasonable to omit any impact evaluation from these short studies.

Mobile fund transfer systems, which eliminate the need for cash, are also attracting a great deal of attention, and it seems likely that they may in future revolutionize some aspects of microfinance. In particular, they eliminate the main overt function of group meetings, which is to collect savings and repayments; this is already eroding group attendance (Kumar et al., 2010). Such systems are widely used in Somalia and Somaliland, the location of two of our cases. Both these institutions are also engaged in mobile telecommunications, and their clients make extensive use of mobile phones for transferring funds. But here again, there is no reason to suppose that IMFIs will be any more or less influenced by this change than 'normal' MFIs.

Similarly, 'financial literacy training' is much discussed by donors; perhaps because microfinance itself has outgrown its need for their funds and donors must still justify their existence. Several of the IMFIs described in these case studies also run training programmes, but these are separate from their financing activities and do not appear to have any direct relevance to their *Shari'ah* compliance.

Is there a demand for Islamic microfinance?

Some readers may approach the collection with specific questions of their own, to which we hope they will be able to find satisfactory answers. In addition to our search for IMFIs that were using profit- or loss-sharing products, we also had a number of questions which we wished to answer, relating mainly to the types of financial products that can be used and the sources of finance. These cases do not provide definitive answers to any of them, but they do give some useful indications and directions which can be useful for anyone who is concerned with Islamic microfinance, as a student, a teacher, an investor, or a practitioner.

First, is there an unmet demand for Islamic microfinance? The available statistics suggest that Islamic finance as a whole is growing very rapidly. Since 1995, the value of assets in Islamic banking is said to have grown from 'virtually nothing' to US$1.1 tn, and annual growth was 14 per cent, versus around an annual 9 per cent growth for traditional non-Islamic banking assets (Ang, 2013). Islamic microfinance is also a growing field; it has several million customers, mainly in Bangladesh, Pakistan, Indonesia, and Sudan, and these numbers are growing rapidly (El-Zoghbi and Tarazi, 2013).

These numbers, however, are very small in relation to the number of Muslims who might want and could make good use of *Shari'ah*-compliant microfinance. The case studies generally suggest that there is substantial unsatisfied demand. People who may previously have taken loans from formal non-Islamic institutions or from informal moneylenders, or who have not borrowed at all because they perceived the lenders to be un-Islamic, are very happy to be able to borrow from a *Shari'ah*-compliant institution.

Research respondents in Somaliland before MicroDahab or KIMS started operating confirm this; self-employed people, and particularly women, said that they disliked fixed-interest loans, and some even expressed distaste for *murabaha* trading credits, which they felt to be the same as fixed interest under a different label. Several of the case studies show that such reluctance is quite common; potential clients, of course, are also pleased to be able to obtain funds at a low cost, but *Shari'ah* compliance is also a powerful incentive.

The case study about Islami Bank's Rural Development Scheme (RDS) in Bangladesh describes what is the largest microfinance programme in the collection, in terms of numbers of clients and outstanding portfolio, but the RDS is also unusual because it operates in what is generally acknowledged to be the 'homeland' of microfinance, which is also a Muslim majority country. The RDS is the only large-scale Islamic microfinance programme in Bangladesh; it operates throughout the country, but it nevertheless has less than 5 per cent of the total market of some 23 million borrowers. The programme's growth is apparently constrained by the Islami Bank's unwillingness to allocate further funds to it, and perhaps also for political reasons, but it is nevertheless surprising that there is so little Islamic microfinance in Bangladesh. This must inevitably cast some doubt on the growth prospects of Islamic microfinance everywhere.

Akhuwat, the second largest programme in the collection, also poses an issue relating to demand. Its loans are virtually free of cost, requiring no more than the payment of a very small fixed application fee, but the demand is not as overwhelming as might be expected given its low price. Akhuwat has grown steadily and continues to grow, but it coexists and competes with a number of traditional non-Islamic MFIs, which charge 'normal' interest rates of between 20 and 30 per cent a year. This may in part be due to Akhuwat's quite lengthy approval processing times, and to their strict requirement that clients should reside within a specified short distance from branches. It demonstrates what is already becoming clear in microfinance, and, indeed, in consumer finance worldwide: interest rates and the cost of credit are by no means the only or even the most important reason for client choice.

What is stopping Islamic microfinance from growing?

The cases generally show that there is a steady and growing demand for *Shari'ah*-compliant microfinance; the existing suppliers, and newcomers, could almost certainly find clients were they able to grow faster than they currently do. What are the main reasons why Islamic microfinance is not growing more quickly? Why has it not 'taken off' as regular microfinance did in the 1990s?

Is it lack of knowledge, or of staff with the skills to design and deliver Islamic microfinance? Or do religious authorities insist on standards of *Shari'ah* compliance that are unrealistic? Our own field experience, with these institutions and others, and that of our colleagues who wrote some of the case studies, suggests that IMFI staff are at least as well informed as those of most conventional MFIs, perhaps in part because the institutions have not grown at such a breakneck pace; the ingenuity with which products are designed and delivered in order to be *Shari'ah* compliant also suggests that the staff are skilled and well qualified.

The religious authorities do not seem to be a problem. Some IMFIs have their own 'in-house' experts while others appeal to local religious leaders, but it seems clear from the details of the buying and selling systems used in some *murabaha* products that 'cosmetic' solutions are acceptable, even if they are *Shari'ah* compliant only in their form and terminology rather than in their spirit. Clients themselves seem to be rather more demanding, and the staff of the Islami Bank RDS programme in Bangladesh are also apparently dissatisfied with some of their products, although they have been approved by religious authorities. The leadership of some institutions might have been expected to be more critical of the Islamic authenticity of their methods, even if they have been approved by the religious authorities, since this may seem to cast some doubt on the whole concept of Islamic microfinance and indeed Islamic finance in general.

The nature of the available *Shari'ah*-compliant products may in itself be a constraint to the growth of Islamic microfinance. Several of the cases refer to the difficulty of using *murabaha* for very small credits, to buy non-traded goods, or to finance multiple small purchases from informal suppliers. Needs of this kind are of course typically those of poorer people, for whom microfinance is often a tool for cash flow smoothing rather than for the purchase of significant assets. People who are short of cash may not be able to state precisely what they need it for, from whom they will purchase their needs, or for what price or when. Quite clearly, the only form of *Shari'ah*-compliant finance that is suitable for such people is *qard hasan*, through which cash can be made available without strings, and also without any cost – apart, perhaps, from the very small fixed charges such as those levied by Akhuwat.

START in Kosovo offers *qard hasan* loans to its most needy clients, and Akhuwat, uniquely, lends only on the basis of *qard hasan*. The long-term economics of the START approach obviously depend on the majority of its business being sufficiently profitable to cover the losses on a small part of the portfolio. The fixed transaction fee of about US$67, which is charged for all *qard hasan* loans, amounts to an annual charge of about 9 per cent on the lower-value loans, so it is more than a nominal cost but it does not cover all the costs; this may be feasible in the relatively 'developed' environment of the Balkans, but it would not be possible in a market where the majority of potential clients are in extreme poverty, such as a typical low-income urban slum or rural area in South Asia.

Akhuwat is unique; it is obviously financially unsustainable if 'sustain-ability' means covering its operating expenses and the cost of its funds from charges paid by its customers. This type of sustainability is not, of course, the only way in which an institution can survive and grow. Akhuwat shows that it is possible for a business with a strong social mission to be highly successful, in financial as well as welfare terms, through a combination of cash, grants, and in-kind donations, including gifts from its own clients. If sustainability means survival and growth, Akhuwat is certainly more sustainable than many for-profit corporations, including many large international financial institutions.

However, Akhuwat has not expanded beyond Pakistan thus far, and it may be so dependent on its remarkable leadership, on government support, and on the particular circumstances of Pakistan that it is unlikely to do so. It is possible that others will learn from Akhuwat and attempt to follow its example in other countries, as so many have followed the Grameen Bank model. It is to be hoped that this will happen, and Akhuwat's management are keen that it should, but we should also examine the other types of financial product that are described in the case studies to identify any features that may inhibit the growth of the institutions which offer them.

Murabaha

Murabaha is by far the most common financial product, in spite of our efforts to identify IMFIs that offer profit- and loss-sharing methods. We have already seen how *murabaha* is not suitable for many clients, particularly the poorest, but it also has practical weaknesses even for better-off clients who need to finance relatively large purchases of traded goods from formal suppliers. The clients of BASIX in India apparently benefit because BASIX has been able to use the combined purchasing power of its clients to negotiate lower prices, and Reef has done the same for its clients in Palestine. This may compensate for the mark-up, but it is generally unlikely that an IMFI will be familiar with the whole range of products and suppliers with which its clients want to do business. Small-scale businesses are usually specialists in one type of product, and an institution that serves their financial needs cannot possibly be fully informed about all their different requirements.

The clients must therefore identify what they want to buy, and from which supplier and at what cost, and must then inform the IMFI's field staff. The staff member must then buy the product from the nominated supplier and resell it to the client at the agreed mark-up; in order to minimize the time taken and the costs, the transaction must be as rapid as possible, and the IMFI cannot usually take physical possession of the product.

This is inevitably something of a cosmetic operation; some IMFIs, such as Kompanion, appoint an independent agent to buy the product on the IMFI's behalf and then to resell it to the client. The client may suggest a suitable agent, or, as with Al Amal in Yemen and Mutahid in Afghanistan, the IMFI may actually appoint the client him- or herself as a temporary agent. The client buys the items, acting as an agent on behalf of the IMFI, and then resells them to her- or himself. This may simplify the physical nature of the transaction, in that the client and the agent are the same person, and it apparently satisfies the religious authorities, but it complicates the legal position and is obviously cosmetic. It may comply with the letter of *Shari'ah*, but not with its spirit.

One feature of *murabaha* is that the IMFI can clearly control what the client buys with the loan; traditional MFIs can attempt to do this through on-site visits to the client, but this is costly and it is not difficult for clients to deceive the field staff by showing them a neighbour's asset, such as a cow, and pretending that it is theirs. Of course, IMFI clients can resell the assets they have bought with their loans and use the money to pay for assets whose purchase the IMFI might not have approved, but this is likely to be costly; none of the case studies report diversion of this kind.

The usual argument in favour of the IMFI's control over clients' purchases is that it prevents them, or perhaps other family members, from using the money to pay for items that are *haram*, such as liquor or gambling debts. This is clearly a positive form of moral control, but it does run contrary to one argument in favour of microcredit, which is that it 'empowers' its clients to purchase what they know they need. The current debate about the advantages of cash transfers as being preferable to the provision of food, or shelter, or whatever other item the donor thinks is 'right', is informed by the same issue; should a lender wish or be able to control the use to which its money is put, so long as the debt is properly serviced?

A few IMFIs use *ijarah* leasing contracts to finance purchases of capital equipment. As with *murabaha*, this makes little difference to the client's cash flows, but it complicates the process of acquiring the asset, since it must at least nominally be bought by the IMFI before it is leased to the client. The IMFI retains the right to reclaim the asset in case of non-payment, but this is of little practical use unless the asset has a substantial resale value. As with *murabaha*, leasing is less useful or affordable for smaller items, or for second-hand equipment, or for 'home-made' tools, which are more likely to be required by smaller-scale, less well-off clients. The inescapable conclusion is that this mode of financing is also likely to incline IMFIs to support larger businesses, rather than the survival self-employment activities of the poor. This is not in itself a problem, in that such businesses need finance and are likely to provide jobs for poorer people, but it does make *Shari'ah*-compliant microfinance less suitable for poorer people. As with *murabaha*, this method of financing makes it harder for the client to use the money for something other than the declared purposes, and it may also be possible for IMFIs to negotiate better terms for supplies than individual clients could on their own.

Two of the IMFIs, PASED in Sudan and Vasham in Indonesia, use *bai salam*. The cases describe the procedure in some detail, by reference to particular clients. This is essentially a form of forward sale, whereby a client, usually a farmer, sells and is paid for a crop by the institution before it is harvested, and the institution then takes delivery and resells the crop after harvest; the profit, if any, may accrue to the IMFI, or it may be shared between the farmer and the IMFI on a pre-agreed basis. This appears to function quite effectively; the transactions are fully approved by the rather demanding religious authorities in Sudan and in Indonesia; although Vasham makes no particular claim to be *Shari'ah* compliant, it is generally considered to be more genuinely Islamic than the many other IMFIs in the country that use more 'cosmetic' methods.

Bai salam, however, is only applicable to farm crops, and it requires the financing institution also to act as a crop trader. This involves a wide range of specialist skills, and may also require storage and transport facilities; it is not suitable for non-farm businesses or for the mass of micro-trading enterprises that make up the majority of microfinance clients in urban areas, and often in rural areas as well.

Profit- and loss-sharing products

In spite of our effort to identify institutions which use *musharaka* or *mudaraba* profit- and loss-sharing products, only eight of the 15 institutions offer these financial products, and it is generally on an experimental basis, although they may intend to expand this proportion of their portfolio in the future. Only 4 per cent of MicroDahab's portfolio and only eight of Kompanion's 450 clients have this type of loan, and although Islami Bank's staff believe that it is more genuinely fair for the IMFI to share the losses and profits with their clients, they have stopped offering this product except to a few larger clients who have 'graduated' from their earlier micro-*murabaha* loans.

BASIX, like some other IMFIs, offers what is called a 'declining *musharaka*' product for the purchase of substantial assets such as cattle, but this is effectively similar to hire purchase, or *ijarah*. The client pays a rental fee for the asset and its ownership is transferred from BASIX to the client over the agreed period. If the value of the asset is substantially reduced during this period, through no fault of the client, BASIX takes its share of the loss, but this does not include any element of profit sharing. BASIX anticipates that this form of financing will eventually make up 10 per cent of its portfolio, and that the average amount involved will be US$8,000; this is more than 10 times its projected loan size for other products, and suggests that this product will be more suitable for better-off clients.

The share of the profit that is taken by the client and by the IMFI varies substantially; MicroDahab works on a 60:40 basis, with 60 per cent going to MicroDahab, while others use a 70:30 ratio, with 70 per cent for the client. The share going to each party may be calculated after allowing the client to take a certain percentage to remunerate his or her management time, and some IMFIs also use *mudaraba*, which is similar to *musharaka* except that 100 per cent of the investment is covered by the IMFI and the client contributes only her or his management. In this case, the client takes a pre-agreed share of the profit for managing the business.

BMT Daarul Qur'an serves an urban market in Jakarta, and uses a mix of products including *mudaraba*. Almost half of its loans are for less than US$400, which suggests that it is serving very small-scale businesses, but its remaining *mudaraba* loans are for much larger sums.

BMT Daarul Qur'an is also a co-operative – it and ACCSL are the only IMFIs in our collection that are co-operatives, rather than a company or a 'project'; this may affect their relationships with their clients since they are also its members. Like many IMFIs, ACCSL is experimenting with *musharaka*, and it has found, surprisingly, that the members who have been financed on this basis tend to exaggerate their profits, and thus to increase the amount they have to repay to the society. They may do this because they believe that they will not be able to borrow again if they have made losses, or perhaps out of loyalty to the society. Whatever the reason, it shows that the cost of finance, regardless of how it is calculated, is less important to many small clients than its availability.

Islamic microfinance is still young, and it may be that one or more of the IMFIs described in the case studies – or others – will in time learn from their experiments and figure out how to provide profit- and loss-sharing products to very small-scale enterprises, whose owners are often either unable or unwilling to calculate or state their profits. These case studies, however, suggest that this has not yet happened, and the search must continue.

Murabaha financing, on the other hand, is well developed and widely used, and in some cases it may have benefits for IMFIs and for their clients over and above its compliance with *Shari'ah*. Generally, however, it appears to be less adaptable, particularly for poorer clients, and to be more costly to operate. Regardless of that, however, *murabaha* appears to be acceptable to large numbers of Muslim clients, and its modest disadvantages do not appear to discourage the growth of the IMFIs that use it.

ACCSL and some of the other institutions are experimenting with profit- and loss-sharing products that have the potential to be more Islamic in spirit as well as in the letter of their methodologies. However, it is puzzling, and somewhat disappointing, that these experiments are mainly focused on 'down-scaling' existing methodologies that are used in larger-scale non-micro Islamic finance, rather than on designing and testing new methodologies that are specifically designed to suit low-income clients.

Shari'ah does not itself promote particular types of financial arrangements other than *qard hasan* for the poorest people; it merely sets out broad principles. Traditional microfinance can now offer a wide range of financial products, for different types of groups and for individuals. There would appear to be more than adequate potential for new financial products that are *Shari'ah* compliant, suitable for poorer clients, and profitable for the institutions providing them. It is to be hoped that this gap will be filled.

The cost of Islamic finance

Microfinance is widely criticized because it is said to charge poor people excessively high interest rates. Money is no different from many other commodities; the poor pay more. The cost of money is not as important as is sometimes believed, particularly when it is invested in urban petty trading businesses, which are the main users of microfinance (see Harper, 2012), but it does matter. Is Islamic microfinance more or less expensive than 'secular' microfinance?

The credits from Akhuwat in Pakistan are virtually cost free, apart from a small administrative charge, but *murabaha* is the dominant method used by the other institutions covered in this collection; the profit margins that are added by these IMFIs when they buy what their clients need and then resell it to them on credit can be approximately compared with fixed interest rates. The margins sometimes vary from client to client, as does the period allowed for repayment, but it is possible in most cases to make a rough estimate of the effective annual cost of the credit, on a declining balance basis. Some of the case studies include the figure, and in others it is necessary to use the figures given in the client examples, or to work from the gross income and the portfolio data in the annual accounts to assess the return, but the approximate figures are shown in Table 17.2.

Some of these estimates are very rough, and the actual figures will vary depending on the exact timing of repayment instalments; some may also be increased by the requirement for clients to make up-front payments towards welfare funds or for other purposes. Most *murabaha* contracts also allow the client some redress in case the goods are faulty, and the margins are not increased if clients fall into arrears. The clients may also benefit from the lower prices that the greater purchasing power of the IMFI allows, which may in part compensate for the profit margin.

Overall, the above figures show that the cost of credit from these IMFIs is not excessive. The effective rates are not dissimilar to those charged by non-Islamic MFIs in the same regions, and are certainly lower in some cases, particularly when other factors are taken into account. The credits are less flexible, and they may cost more because clients have to spend more time on

Table 17.2 The annual cost of credit

Institution	Effective annual cost of finance (%)
START, Kosovo	11
Islami RDS, Bangladesh	17 to 23
Mutahid, Afghanistan	26.6
Reef, Palestine	23 to 24
Kaah, Somalia	16 to 24
Al Amal, Yemen	21
Kompanion, Kyrgyzstan	30
Ebdaa, Sudan	30
PASED, Sudan	24
BASIX, India	20 to 30
MicroDahab, Somalia	16
ACCSL, India	25 to 30
Vasham, Indonesia	27
BMT Daarul Qur'an, Indonesia	21 to 24

the transactions, but these factors may be outweighed by the other advantages; generally speaking, the clients of these IMFIs do not appear to be paying a significantly higher price for *Shari'ah* compliance.

Despite the limitations of the available financial products, and the sometimes cosmetic nature of most *murabaha*, which is the dominant product, *Shari'ah*-compliant finance, as it is now offered, does appear to be affordable and widely acceptable, and it can also be profitable for the institutions providing it. The major existing constraint to the growth of Islamic microfinance appears to be the shortage of finance for existing and new IMFIs.

Akhuwat, which is by a wide margin the largest independent institution in the collection, is an exception in two ways: it has grown, very dramatically, in spite of the totally uncommercial nature of its financing; and its only financial product is in no way cosmetic – Akhuwat's *qard hasan* is quite different from anything offered by 'normal' microfinance institutions. Akhuwat has been able to access the finance necessary for its growth, and to finance part of its operating costs, partly because it has received donations from a wide range of supporters, including its own clients. Initially, these funds were from local sources within Pakistan. More recently, Akhuwat has also received funding from an increasing number of foreign sources, and, unlike any of our other cases, Akhuwat has been the recipient of very large interest-free loans from government institutions, particularly from Punjab Province. These loans are nominally repayable, but are effectively grants that Akhuwat can continue to use so long as they are properly employed to alleviate poverty and promote enterprise.

Government grants have often damaged or even destroyed microfinance institutions, sometimes because the loan recipients treat them as handouts, and because governments use them for political rather than development purposes. Dr Amjad Saqib was a senior member of the Government Service before he established Akhuwat, and he has thus far successfully avoided problems of this kind; this source of finance, however, is very much dependent on the organization's personal links to senior authorities, and is in some sense not replicable.

Savings

The major traditional source of finance for retail banking institutions of any kind is their clients' own savings deposits, and most such institutions hold a higher amount of clients' savings than of outstanding loans. Microfinance is usually different. This is partly because the pioneers of microfinance not unreasonably (but mistakenly) believed that poor people could not save and did not need savings facilities, and partly because deposit-taking institutions must rightly be supervised and licensed to ensure that they do not lose or steal their clients' savings. It is also generally less expensive to borrow large sums from international development or other institutions than it is to manage – and pay even a modest return for – the small demand deposits and withdrawals that are needed by poorer people.

This is changing, as more MFIs such as Grameen Bank start to offer demand deposit services to their clients, and some – such as Bandhan in India – have themselves become licensed banks. Bank Rakyat Indonesia, which is not Islamic but is by some measures the world's largest and most profitable MFI, mobilizes some four times as much finance from its clients as it lends to them.

Savings are not, however, an important component of the finance used by the 15 IMFIs described in these case studies. Six of them offer savings services as well as credit, but only Islami Bank, Al Amal, and Daarul Qur'an raise more than 10 per cent of the funds they use for financing their clients from their clients' savings. The Islami Bank's RDS is part of a large, full-service Islamic bank, and its clients have deposits amounting to about a third of the outstanding loans, while Al Amal raises about two-thirds of its loan portfolio from clients. Some IMFIs, such as Ebdaa, have many more savings accounts than loan accounts, but the aggregate balances of the savings are far below their loan portfolios. Ebdaa remunerates its longer-term depositors with a share of the institution's annual profits, on the basis of *mudaraba*, but this is generally impractical for low-value, short-term demand deposits that are frequently paid in and withdrawn in small amounts.

The IMFIs in these case studies are not very different from most MFIs in respect of the nature and volume of the savings services they offer to their clients, but the requirement that the sources of their finance as well as their loans must be *Shari'ah* compliant further constrains their ability to offer a full range of financial services to their clients.

In the future, IMFIs, like conventional MFIs, may develop and promote secure, accessible, and remunerative savings products, and in any case their ability to offer such products will in part be a function of the financial strength conferred by the equity in their balance sheets. The case study institutions have been capitalized from a variety of different sources, and their balance sheets do not appear to be seriously over-leveraged.

Other sources of funds

At least three of the IMFIs – namely MicroDahab, Kompanion, and BASIX – appear to be constrained mainly by a shortage of funds and to be 'investment ready', in that additional funds would enable them to achieve break-even within a short period. This may be an over-positive assessment, based as it is on a rather small amount of information, some of which will be well over two years out of date at the time of publication, but it is to be hoped that these and other IMFIs will in time be able to access funds and grow.

In order to be fully *Shari'ah* compliant, an IMFI must not offer products based on interest, but it must also be funded from sources that are themselves *Shari'ah* compliant. This requirement is something of a problem for Vasham, although Indonesia is a primarily Muslim country, and it may also constrain other institutions' success in obtaining funds. The case studies are focused on the IMFIs' clients and financing methods, and do not dwell on the institutions' efforts to raise finance. It is again important to stress that this is not a representative sample of IFMIs, but it is noteworthy that most – although not all – have been funded mainly by secular 'Western' institutions such as CARE or Mercy Corps. This bias may result from the types of contacts through which the case study institutions in this collection were identified, but there are large amounts of *Shari'ah*-compliant funds in Western as well as Middle Eastern and other financial centres, whose managers and investors are anxious to 'do good' as well as to 'do well'. There is a number of specialist well-funded investment vehicles for microfinance, or 'MIVs', but there are as yet no Islamic MIVs. It is to be hoped that, in a small way, this collection will facilitate more linkages of this kind.

The largest independent institution in the collection of case studies is, of course, Akhuwat, which has reached over a million clients in Pakistan and is continuing to grow. Its total capitalization exceeds US$70 m, and this and its operations have been almost entirely financed by donations and grants from individuals and institutions, including its own clients, and from government. Its management has to work hard to raise the funds for this, as do the managers of any financial institution, including those that depend on funds from commercial or semi-commercial sources. However, it is remarkable that the biggest, and by many standards the most strongly established and in some sense the most 'sustainable' institution in the collection, is one that depends almost entirely on donations and grants, including substantial amounts from government and from its own clients.

Akhuwat is, of course, not reaching every potential client in Pakistan who needs and could benefit from its services, but in 15 years it has achieved national coverage, and it is to be hoped that its example can be emulated in other countries. It is not perfect, but it is continually evolving and improving, and the example of Grameen Bank demonstrates that an effective model that works in one place can be successfully adapted and followed elsewhere.

If Akhuwat is excluded, these case studies show that the forms of Islamic microfinance that presently are most widely practised are less suitable than 'normal' microfinance for very small-scale clients and for non-business uses such as consumption or healthcare, and have higher transaction costs than interest-based loans for both the institutions and their clients. The average size of their credits is also consistent with this, in that it is rather higher than loans from other MFIs operating in the same communities. IMFI credits also appear to have few if any compensating advantages apart from their conformity to *Shari'ah* rules, however those rules may be interpreted in their respective communities.

This is not necessarily a wholly negative conclusion; religious observance by no means always dictates the most financially profitable or convenient choices. A system that enables people to follow the letter of their religion and thus to feel comfortable with what they are doing, and at the same time to benefit from its services, is much better than a system that prevents them from obtaining the services at all, even if it involves some inconvenience.

Regular fixed-interest microfinance is widely used to finance so-called 'consumption' purchases, as well as for enterprise expenses. It is difficult to cover the costs of items of this kind with existing Islamic microfinance methods, particularly when the purchases are unexpected, are of relatively low value, and are bought from informal suppliers. *Qard hasan* is appropriate for such needs, and it also avoids burdening poor people with interest costs in addition to the original debt. It is, of course, 'unsustainable' in a purely financial sense, but the example of Akhuwat demonstrates that it is not only possible but can grow and reach very large numbers of people.

The current turmoil in many Muslim countries in the Middle East is already pushing many middle-income people back into poverty; they may have previously outgrown the need for microfinance, but they now need credit to survive and then to start to rebuild their livelihoods. The case of Al Amal in Yemen shows how this is already happening, but *qard hasan* is the best form of *Shari'ah*-compliant finance for people in such difficult circumstances, and, it can be argued, it is more suitable than fixed-interest loans in that it is free of cost and is in some sense a hybrid between pure charity and regular loans. It is to be hoped that the example of Akhuwat will be widely followed outside Pakistan, particularly in communities affected by conflict, and we hope that this book will play a small role in facilitating this process.

The cases show that there is as yet no accepted 'best practice' in Islamic microfinance; there is still a great deal of experimentation to be done, and the 'ideal' methodology has yet to evolve. *Shari'ah*-compliant product design will inevitably vary from one location to another, because it has to be sustainable for clients and for the institutions, and it must also be approved by local religious authorities, whose views often differ from one place to another.

It may be that future innovations will enable for-profit Islamic microfinance, like regular microfinance, to grow very rapidly quite suddenly, so that it reaches a far more significant proportion of the millions of people who want it and can benefit from it. Or, it may always be something of a niche undertaking, which is acceptable to religious people in some places but never really reaches its apparent potential.

Much (but not all) regular microfinance has become heavily commercialized. It has become closer to regular profit-maximizing consumer finance, and in many cases it has lost its original welfare objectives. Islamic microfinance is still young; if it can maintain its original spirit – of fairness, transparency, and sharing – the future can be bright, whatever methodologies are used. If it loses these ideals, however, it may devolve into nothing more than clever cosmetic exercises that mimic conventional interest-based finance but use different terms. Only time will tell.

References

Ang, K. (2013) 'Filling a niche for Islamic banking', The New York Times, 26 March <www.nytimes.com/2013/03/27/education/filling-a-niche-for-islamic-banking.html> [accessed 16 November 2016].

El-Zoghbi, M. and Tarazi, M. (2013) *Trends in Sharia-compliant Financial Inclusion*, Washington, DC: CGAP (Consultative Group to Assist the Poor).

Harper, M. (2012) 'Microfinance interest rates and client returns', *Journal of Agrarian Change* 12 (4): 564–74.

Kumar, K., McKay, C. and Rotman, S. (2010) 'Microfinance and mobile banking: the story so far', Focus Note 62, Washington, DC: CGAP (Consultative Group to Assist the Poor).

Morduch, J. (1998) 'Does microfinance really help the poor? New evidence from flagship programs in Bangladesh', Stanford CA: Department of Economics and Harvard Institute for International Development, Harvard University, and Hoover Institution, Stanford University.

About the author

Malcolm Harper (malcolm.harper@btinternet.com) was Professor of Enterprise Development at the Cranfield School of Management, UK.

Index

Page numbers in *italics* refer to boxes and tables.